Ferrari

The Passion and the Pain

Ferrari

The Passion and the Pain

JANE NOTTAGE

Foreword by
NIKI LAUDA

CollinsWillow
An Imprint of HarperCollins*Publishers*

Dedication

To my parents, Geoffrey and Margaret Nottage, for their unconditional
love and support and Sophie the Doberman dog, for her complete loyalty
and for giving me hours of exercise.

Acknowledgements

I would like to thank the following for their practical help and moral support:
Ferrari past and present – Luca di Montezemolo, Jean Todt, Antonio Ghini,
Giancarlo Baccini, Stefano Domenicali, Ross Brawn, Paolo Martinelli and the
engine men, John Barnard, Vijay Kothary and all at FDD, Rory Byrne,
Willem Toet, Gustav Brunner, Giorgio Ascanelli, Nigel Stepney and all the
'boys' including Ignazio Lunetta and Luca Baldisserri, the race engineers
and, of course, Michael Schumacher and Eddie Irvine, Heiner Buchinger and
Sonia Irvine. Three people have been exceptional in their support and
commitment and without them this book would not have been written:
Jackie Ireland of Shell, Claudio Berro of Ferrari, and Derick Allsop – friend
and colleague. Other colleagues including Stan Piecha and Ray Matts have
been ready with wine and song at the end of a hard day. Roger Kelly and his
team at the *Mail on Sunday* have also been great. I must thank all at Shell for
their professional attitude and outstanding technical expertise; and
Edward Asprey, Rosalind Milani Gallieni and everyone else at Asprey who have
added glamour and style to the project. Also high in the elegance stakes is
Chantal Cerruti, a beautiful woman and a loyal friend. Maurizio Arrivabene and
his loyal team at Marlboro have also made this book possible. At publishers
CollinsWillow, Michael Doggart, Tom Whiting, David Lennox, design guru
Arthur Brown, and their respective teams, have produced a wonderful book.
There are many other friends whom I should thank: my Lynden Gate buddies,
especially Liz Chisman – wife of the sexy Neil and mother of the beautiful and
talented Abigail – who is like a sister to me; Fiona Wilson, a good friend
and intelligent adviser; Patrick and Heather Mayhew, who provided a safe
harbour; Lizzi Capper; Stefanie Moore, who helped me settle in London;
Alison DeMarco for spiritual guidance; Father Vincent Coopers for attempting
to keep me morally upright; Kate Mcguire for helping me to be happy;
Desmond Kelly for the Prozac; David and Maureen Royston-Lee for their
constant friendship; Ron, Reg and John; Rebecca Spencer-Underhill; and last
but not least Paul Wiget for simply being himself.

Picture credits

All photography by **ERCOLE COLOMBO, Studio Colombo** except:
Action Images: 84; **Alain Benainous**: 22; **Allsport/Mike Hewitt**: 90t, 163;
Allsport/MSI: 17b, **Allsport**: 220, 223b, 224; **Asprey**: 12, 20, 31, 62, 76, 130,
160t&b, 166; **Glenn Campbell**: 39, 57, 67, 122; **Cerruti 1881**: 60, 140, 158;
Flavio Mazzi: 82, 131, 168, 169, 170, 171; **Fotosport/Beppe Vezzelli**: 61;
Gary Gold: 130t, 121, 134; **Shell Photographic Services**: 14,15,16, 23, 28, 51,
87, 127b; **Sporting Pictures UK**: 110b; **Sutton Photographic**: 74, 102, 143

Illustrations by Peter Cooling and Tish Mills

First published in 1997 by CollinsWillow
an imprint of HarperCollins*Publishers*
London

© Jane Nottage 1997

1 3 5 7 9 8 6 4 2

A CIP catalogue record for this book is available
from the British Library

ISBN 0 00 218777 9

Designed and produced by Cooling Brown
Hampton-upon-Thames, Middlesex, UK

Origination by Colourscan, Singapore
and Dot Gradations, Essex, UK
Printed and bound by LEGO SpA, Vicenza, Italy

Contents

Winning a world championship with Ferrari is a special feeling. Winning two is simply unforgettable. Enzo Ferrari, like his cars, came out of a unique mould. He was sometimes difficult and intransigent, but above all he was the driving force behind one of the greatest racing teams of all time, and that is a hell of an achievement. We had some memorable run-ins during my four years at Ferrari, but my respect for this giant of motor racing and what he accomplished eclipses all else. Having started my own company, Lauda Air, I understand the effort required to build up and maintain a successful business.

There are many good memories from my time as a Ferrari driver, but one or two are outstanding, such as the first time I won a Grand Prix with Ferrari. It happened at Jarama in 1974 and after this I understood what it was like to feel the warmth of the passionate *tifosi*, who

Tips from a World Champion
Eddie Irvine takes on board some useful advice from the experienced Niki Lauda.

were overjoyed. Winning my first Formula One World Driver's Championship with Ferrari was one of the highlights of my life. It was the pinnacle that I aspired to throughout my racing career, and when it actually happened everything seemed to go by in a flash: the celebrations, the victory dinner, meeting the fans. But at the end I was left with an intense feeling of happiness which I will never forget.

I was fortunate enough to have Luca di Montezemolo as my team manager when I won that title in 1975. As well as a colleague, Luca became a friend and when he returned to Ferrari in 1992 as Chairman, I became a consultant to help rebuild the fortunes of the team. Luca is a brilliant strategist and visionary. He recognised the need to employ the right people in the right places, and over the last five years he has done that. The result is that the Ferrari Formula One team is finally back in contention for the Formula One World Constructor's Championship. That kind of action takes courage and perseverance, particularly in a company such as Ferrari, which is quintessentially Italian in its approach and its

methods. Politics and intrigue have always played a part in the management, and it isn't easy to cut through that and prepare the company for the future. To that end Luca has done a brilliant job, as have all the members of the team, especially Team Principal Jean Todt and, of course, Michael Schumacher, who is the best racing driver of his generation.

Foreword
by Niki Lauda

Above all, one must never forget that Ferrari is a team made up of different nationalities, and different personalities and each and every one of them plays an important role. A racing team works under constant pressure, so the most junior mechanic is as important as the most senior manager in that he must execute his job efficiently and quickly.

This book is unique in that it offers the reader a glimpse of what life is really like working for one of the most glamorous and enigmatic teams in Grand Prix motor racing; and, for the very first time, the sweat and toil and the passion and the pain of being part of Ferrari can be observed at close quarters.

NIKI LAUDA, *Vienna, 1997*

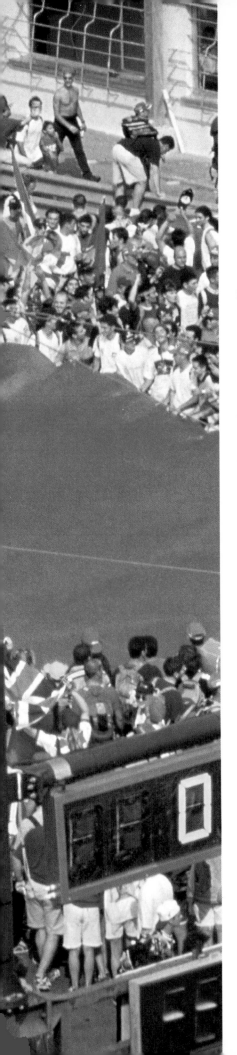

Introduction

THE SOUND IS UNMISTAKABLE. A deep throaty roar leading to a high-pitched whine. It's another day, another country and the millionaire boys are playing with their favourite toys. Round and round they go, darting in and out like multi coloured insects engaged in some ancient ritualistic dance.

Bearing the names of their sponsors like proud warriors they automatically draw attention from the small groups gathered on the slopes overlooking the circuit. National flags wave in the gentle breeze and the onlookers express their delight as their favourite driver passes by. The cars in their distinct livery, each driver locked in his own private race to go ever faster, dance over the tarmac – dark blue, gold, grey, white with a tartan strip and light blue.

The circus continues and then from the distant pits another sound is heard and the crowd stirs in eager anticipation. A guttural battle cry is followed by a roar of power as the V10 engine propels the car down the pit lane and onto the glistening track. A flash of scarlet as the founder member of Formula One motor racing joins the rest. Anticipation changes to raw passion as the fans erupt at the sight and sound of the bright red car driven by the supreme warrior himself.

Michael Schumacher is in the Ferrari. Individually enticing, together they are an unbeatable combination of power and emotion. The brilliant German driver in the car that stirs the heart. Amongst a family of beauties the Ferrari stands head and shoulders over the others. And not just in Formula One.

From the boardrooms of Manhattan to the deserts of Africa, owning a Ferrari is the embodiment of many people's hopes and dreams, something that represents escape, beauty and the good life. It has also transcended the role of being a mere form of transport and become a focus for the emotions of the whole Italian nation. When Ferrari does well the nation dances, when Ferrari does badly the nation cries.

But what is it like to carry the hopes of a nation? To be responsible for the intangible feelings that ebb and flow around the stable of the prancing horse?

Rewind to January 1997. Dateline: 10.30 am, 7 January 1997. Place: a large marquee in the middle of the Ferrari test track at Fiorano, next door to the factory at Maranello in Northern Italy. It is a wet, grey day with a dark, dank mist hanging over everything. A typical winter morning when you turn off the alarm clock and go back to sleep again. Except today there's a party. The launch of the F310B is about to take place. The VIPs, sponsors and journalists take their seats. In front of them is a stage, in the centre of which stands the new car shrouded in red silk. At the rear of the stage is a large motorhome painted in the new dynamic red and with the words Scuderia Ferrari Marlboro flashed across the side in white letters. A lot of people do a double-take. It is the first time that the hallowed name of Ferrari has been linked in this way to the main sponsor. In the 1980s when there was Saudia Williams, John Player Lotus and Marlboro McLaren there was only ever Ferrari. Another chip falls from the block of tradition. But money wins World Championships, and money demands some recompense. It could have been worse. At least the car is still red.

There is a buzz and the place comes alive when the charismatic Luca di Montezemolo, the Ferrari Chairman takes centre stage with the drivers to unveil the new car. Montezemolo is the man who has pulled Ferrari out of the doldrums and put the company in good shape to face the

21st Century. The high performance road cars have never been healthier. The sleek, elegant, comfortable models are highly sought after throughout the world. All that's missing is the Formula One World Championship. The Chairman talks of winning more races than in 1996 (when Michael Schumacher won three races), and he talks of the importance of sponsors and technical partners like Marlboro, Shell, Asprey, Cerruti, Magneti Marelli, Goodyear and of course the advantage of having double World Champion Michael Schumacher on board. It looks slick, glamorous and co-ordinated, but behind the scenes the pressure is on.

Focused on the Future
Ferrari's rise to the pinnacle of Formula One has been aided in no small measure by the world's best driver, Michael Schumacher.

• • •

Dateline: 8 January 1997. Place: Ferrari Head Office, Maranello, Northern Italy. The country's biggest sports newspaper *La Gazzetta dello Sport* has published a stunning full-page poster for its readers. The photograph shows Fiat Chairman Cesare Romiti with Ferrari Chairman Luca di Montezemolo. (Fiat being Ferrari's parent company.) On either side of them are the two drivers, Michael Schumacher and Eddie Irvine. Conspicuous by his absence is Ferrari Team Principal, Jean Todt. He is the man who has revolutionised the Formula One team to bring it into a position where it can make a serious challenge for the World Constructor's Championship. But politics are at play. The outside world must see a united Fiat-Ferrari front, and this means both chairmen and drivers sharing the stage together, on their own.

Claudio Berro has taken over as Press Officer from Giancarlo Baccini who is spreading his wings into pastures new. Berro is Todt's right-hand man, but theoretically the position of Formula One Press Chief comes under Communications, which is headed by Antonio Ghini. Ghini is Montezemolo's right-hand man and like Montezemolo he has a creative mind and a desire to make sure things run smoothly. He arrives in Berro's office to impose structure and make sure everything is under control. It is time to make sure that autonomy doesn't extend to full home rule on the part of the Formula One team.

Meanwhile, upstairs the Design and Development branch of Ferrari is in danger of dissipating before our very eyes. John Barnard is negotiating his divorce settlement from Ferrari for the second time. The two parties simply cannot live together. The new baby prancing horse has been safely delivered and now is the moment to face the fact that there are too many incompatibilities to make the relationship work. Ferrari need to have their Chief Designer based at Maranello. John Barnard has always made it clear that, like certain wines, he doesn't travel well.

The discussions go on, some heated, some calm, until there it is, the unmistakable roar of the V10 engine. Everything stops. Fans gather on the small bridge overlooking the circuit. Montezemolo waits like an anxious parent to know if the new baby is healthy. Jean Todt hopes it will be a competitive car. Claudio Berro handles the press with ease. Ross Brawn and John Barnard are both lost in thought. For Barnard it is his last Ferrari baby. For Brawn it is his first taste of being on the inside. The seconds tick by. Then, movement. A finger on the clutch lever, a light pump of the throttle and the new F310B bursts forth out of the garage with Michael Schumacher at the wheel. He passes through the winter mist and into the sunshine. There is a round of applause as he sets off round the track. He comes in for some minor adjustments. Then he's off again. Round and round. A collective sigh of relief. No major problems to report.

Jane and Jean
Jean Todt finds time to look through proofs of the book with the author.

Plots and counter plots are long forgotten. The pace and reliability of a small red car is what matters. Ferrari might make Machiavelli seem like an innocent but it is the only company to have perpetrated the myth of desire for fifty years; the only Formula One team that attracts a passionate, committed army of supporters throughout the world. We stand on the threshold of a new millennium and we are still transfixed by the power and emotion generated by the need to feel we can be a part of Ferrari, maybe one day drive one of their cars. We need to be a part of the dream even if, for some of us, that dream is as elusive as scaling Mount Everest. If the emotion is strong on the outside, what is it like on the inside? Let's take a journey into the heart of the stable of the prancing horse and find out.

JANE NOTTAGE, *London, 1997*

CHAPTER ONE

The Legend Lives On

'Ferrari *is* motor racing. It is the representation of everything motor racing stands for – speed, glamour, style and excitement'

Bernie Ecclestone
FOCA President

The Creator

The legendary Enzo Ferrari in action as a racing driver in 1924.

Once upon a time there lived a man called Enzo Ferrari. He produced beautiful cars, won many World Championships, built a company that became famous throughout the world, lived in a lovely place called Maranello where the sun always shone and he lived happily ever after. Fairy stories. Wonderful aren't they? They allow people to dream of a better world and believe that everything is always beautiful. The heroes are always good looking and the future is always full of hope and happiness. Not unlike life at Ferrari, or so most people would have us believe. Over the years the legend has been carefully constructed and perpetuated by the people at the stable of the Prancing Horse, to make us believe that Ferrari is the ultimate dream, the legend that delivers your fantasies.

Even the famous emblem, the black prancing horse, is shrouded in mystery. Folklore has it that Enzo Ferrari was enjoying success as an Alfa Romeo driver, when after yet another victorious race a man pushed his way through the crowd that had gathered round the winner, shook Enzo's hand warmly and invited him back to his house so he could make a presentation. This man was the father of famous World War I flying ace, Francesco Baracca, who had shot down 35 adversaries before his life ended in 1918. As his personal badge, Baracca had used a black prancing horse. After his demise, his family was sent the prancing horse symbol on a piece of aeroplane fabric and it was their wish that this famous emblem should be passed onto Enzo Ferrari in recognition of his courage and talent on the race track.

There is no doubt that Enzo Ferrari was a remarkable man. In 1947 he started to produce and sell road cars to enable him to finance his racing career. He was perceptive enough to realise that if he created exclusivity there would be more demand than supply and so he built up a company that today, as we stand on the threshold of the next millennium, is still the marque that most people dream of owning and driving. He also created a Formula One racing team that has become a legend within the rarefied world of motor racing. Ferrari is a name that is synonymous with glamour, style and power.

However, being a genius who built up an empire from nothing didn't necessarily make him a wonderful person. People seem to link the two, but most really successful businessmen are single minded, despotic and completely egocentric. Enzo Ferrari was no different. He often treated staff like mere servants, enjoying his absolute power as leader. He kept racing drivers in their place (bearing in mind the over-inflated egos of some of today's drivers, many would list that as a positive characteristic) and he was hardly a New Man. His wife cannot have had an easy time being married to a legend. He built a house on his test circuit so he could be near to his first love, racing, and know exactly what was going on both with the car and with the team. He fathered an illegitimate child, Piero Lardi, whom he welcomed into the business after his own son died. His wife, naturally, as was the tradition of the times, would have been expected to put up with it all, plus have the dinner ready for him when he wanted it. He was demanding, selfish and authoritarian, but nevertheless a brilliant man, and in spite of or maybe because of his faults, he is always remembered with great affection by people who knew him.

Niki Lauda, the man who won two World Championships with Ferrari remembers Enzo Ferrari as a man of extraordinary influence. 'Enzo Ferrari was demanding, charismatic, strong-willed and he always had it in his mind to win. He believed in the car and there was always a lot of pressure from him to win. As soon as you made a mistake you got shit, but if he made a mistake you couldn't discuss it. You needed to be strong to work with him. If he liked you, then he respected you. You had to find a human relationship with him and I admired him enormously. He was unique.'

Winning two World Championships would make any team special in the eyes of its driver; however Ferrari has something extra that is part of its mystique. It is wrapped up in the history and tradition that is an intangible part of the Ferrari factory at Maranello in Northern Italy. As Lauda says, 'Ferrari has something extra. It's something indefinable and unique and every time I walked through the doors of the factory at Maranello or stepped into the car, I felt the added importance of being that unique thing – a Ferrari driver. There was, is and always will be a special place in my heart that is reserved for Ferrari.'

Jody Scheckter, the last driver to win the World Championship for Ferrari in 1979 is more pragmatic. 'It wasn't my boyhood dream to drive for Ferrari and it still wasn't when I first came to Europe. Ferrari had a bit of a bad name and the team wasn't doing well, but I spoke to them every year until eventually I joined the team in 1979.

'When I first joined everyone warned me that it was a big mess and no-one gave us much chance of making it work. I'm known to be a difficult person and the Italians are excitable. As it was I had a wonderful time and got on with everyone including the Italian media. I like to think I gave them as much bullshit as they gave me. Over there, being part of Ferrari is like being part of the Royal Family. As there are three daily newspapers specialising in sport, news about the team would be on the front and back pages of the newspapers. In England it is only ever on the back pages.

'When I met Enzo Ferrari, having been smuggled into his office, the first question he asked was "How much money do you want?" My overall impression was of a very smart, very tough guy. He ruled by putting the fear of God into people.'

The Director
Time moves on and it is 1967. Having created Ferrari, Enzo Ferrari is leading the company into the history books as one of the most successful and glamorous teams in Formula One racing.

Despite his laid back approach, Scheckter was soon captivated by the whole experience of being a Ferrari driver. 'The magic of driving for Ferrari is that you're driving for the whole of Italy, not just Ferrari. It creates the myth and the magic. I remember once walking into a large restaurant in Modena and everyone stood up and clapped. After I'd retired I doubt if I could have got a table in the same restaurant!'

When Scheckter won the World Driver's Championship, Enzo Ferrari's reaction to it was cool. 'He just said "champion, champion" to me as he walked past. It was his way of keeping the drivers in their place. I didn't mind. I didn't want to be more important than other members of the team.'

Nigel Mansell is the last English driver to drive for Ferrari and feel the passion of the fans, the *tifosi*, at first hand. Nigel the Lionheart, as he is known by his Italian admirers, was an instant success when he won his first race for Ferrari in 1989 in Brazil. 'I think for any driver of any ability to drive for Ferrari is a dream come true. It is still the most historic marque in motor racing. To win first time out for Ferrari and to be the last driver to be hired by Enzo Ferrari himself is something very historic and a great achievement for me and for Ferrari. Driving for Ferrari offers a very special experience. They are true thoroughbred racers, they only want to win and for me the reality was very similar to the dream, However, if you do not win then part of the dream does not come true.'

Early Years

John Surtees driving a Ferrari 3-litre Formula One car during the International Trophy Race on 14 May 1966.

The commitment and warmth of the fans will always bring back good memories. 'I have memories of the famous tifosi and the family atmosphere, but above all I am proud to have driven for Ferrari and to have won for the fans. I think the Italian mentality and my own personal mentality are parallel to one another, and so we understood one another well. I have the most fantastic gift of a World Championship trophy presented by the fans and this holds pride of place in my trophy cabinet. I can sum it up by saying that I think the two years I spent with Ferrari were two very special years in my life.'

Even the Pope is not immune to the evocative delights of Italy's famous car company. He visited the factory in June of 1988, and rode round the Ferrari test track, Fiorano, in an open top Ferrari Mondiale, which was driven by Enzo Ferrari's son Piero. Enzo himself was already ill and not able to attend the visit. It is hard to imagine the Archbishop of Canterbury driving around in an Aston Martin, or being asked to bless Damon Hill's Arrows car. But in Italy life is different.

Even those people who currently work at Ferrari are bewildered by exactly what it is that captures the heart and induces such fervent adoration. Team Coordinator Nigel Stepney is an Englishman who has made a success of his transfer to Ferrari. He has worked for them for five years and says, 'People say the English are passionate about football, but they haven't seen anything until they've been to Italy. When Ferrari wins a race, people go mad. They get in their cars and drive around Maranello and other cities sounding their horns and waving flags. It is just total passion here. It is difficult to understand at first, as it is such an explosion of excitement and joy. The Italians live on highs and lows much more than the English, and at Ferrari we are the target of their hopes and aspirations. It's a bit like *Saturday Night Fever* on a grand scale. If we win it's great, you really feel the warmth and happiness of the people. But if we do badly we have to go into hiding.'

The Priest in Maranello, Erio Belloi was a staunch fan before his untimely death in 1997; when Ferrari won a race he used to ring the church bells. In Australia a few years ago, they were ringing at six in the morning!

• • •

Behind the romantic mystique and glamour of Ferrari lies sheer, raw power. Formula One is a breeding ground for power but Ferrari is the master. Max Mosley, President of FIA (Federation Internationale de l'Automobile, the sport's governing body based in Paris), explains how Ferrari

Divine Intervention
The Pope, John Paul II, visits Maranello in June 1988. Enzo Ferrari's death in August was followed a month later by Ferrari finishing first and second at the Italian Grand Prix at Monza.

Mr Consistency
Jody Scheckter, who won the World Driver's Championship in a Ferrari in 1979.

entered the inner sanctum of Formula One and became the main power broker. 'Politically, Ferrari has always been a major force in FIA. Until the emergence of British racing in the 60s, all decisions were made somewhere between Paris and Turin. It was just a question of which year and where the centre of gravity was. The Concorde Agreement (the Maastricht treaty of Formula One) was drawn up in 1980 and 1981, and it has a provision that when Formula One matters are discussed the vote of the President of the Manufacturer's Commission would be exercised by a representative from the legalist's side. The legalists were one of two factions which formed in the late 70s and early 80s. It was basically Ferrari, Renault and Alfa Romeo, and the other faction was us, together with the FOCA (Formula One Constructors' Association) teams. FOCA had a seat on the World Council, and we found a compromise whereby in addition to Formula One having a seat on the World Council, another person who is President of the Manufacturer's Commission has a seat. He represents the World's Motor Industry, the big manufacturers. When Formula One matters were discussed, the legalists had their representative and historically this has always been Ferrari.'

Mr Fixit

Bernie Ecclestone (right) is the man who has made Formula One visually entertaining and a commercial success. Here he chats to new Ferrari boy Eddie Irvine and Eddie's manager Rod Vickery.

Ferrari, in typical Latin fashion, has always been alert to the most imperceptible political currents, and it was this talent that kept it in the thick of things. As Mosley says, 'In the 70s when FOCA became powerful, we ended up with FOCA on one side and FIA/FISA on the other, with Ferrari as the fulcrum. They'd move a little bit one way and then a little bit the other way, influencing the decisions. Enzo Ferrari was an absolute master of that sort of politics. He wanted to make sure Formula One succeeded, so he nearly always backed Bernie [Ecclestone], as he realised that Bernie was going to make Formula One into something big. However, by moving a bit towards the governing body he could obtain a more favourable position in negotiations, which was a very wise move. Now all the relationships between me, Bernie and Ferrari are very solid.'

So what if, for arguments sake, someone stood up and said 'Well, Williams should be our representative as they have been the most successful team in the last five years,' or 'McLaren because they dominated the 80s'? What would happen?

Mosley smiles before replying with certainty. 'Nothing would happen. It would stay as it is. Ferrari have got one overwhelming advantage and that is they were there on 13 May 1950 (the first Formula One World Championship race) and have continued to be there, and even when they weren't winning they have been a tremendous part of Formula One. Now they are right up at the top again. As Chairman Mao said, "Power comes from the barrel of a gun." Although in the case of Formula One power comes from success. If you're successful and have got tradition, your political position is very strong.'

Mosley also has first hand experience of Enzo Ferrari's schoolboy type humour. 'Twice a year all the teams and everyone would go down to visit Ferrari, and we'd all have lunch together. Enzo Ferrari would always sit Bernie next to him, and when Bernie wasn't looking he'd slip a large piece of parmesan cheese on his plate. According to the old man, parmesan has aphrodisiac qualities, and he'd always say without fail "that will get the little man going". It always made him crack up right to the end of his life.'

A clever man with a keen nose for politics, Mosley freely admits to being completely seduced by Ferrari. 'If someone said to me you can have any job in motorsport, I'd choose to run Ferrari. I quite envy Luca [di Montezemolo, the present president] his job. I know it would be challenging and difficult, but then all the top jobs are. I have no doubt that it would certainly be the most interesting.'

Bernie Ecclestone, the President of the Formula One Constructors' Association (FOCA), is the man who has made Formula One an exciting, visually entertaining sport and a business that is a commercial success. Having known Enzo Ferrari so well, he fondly remembers the old man, and his trepidation at what might happen after his death in 1988.

'I have many happy, personal memories of Ferrari as I had a long friendship with the great Enzo, who was always supportive of all I did. When he died I missed him on a personal level and I also wondered what would happen to Ferrari and if it would continue in the same way. I am delighted to see that the team has followed in the footsteps of tradition and is being run in the same way by the right people, who will ensure that it grows and develops as we enter the second millennium and the 21st Century.'

Ecclestone goes on to explain the importance of Ferrari to Formula One. 'Ferrari *is* motor racing. It is the representation of everything motor racing stands for – speed, glamour, style and excitement. It just gets stronger and stronger and I am sure that the patience and hard work of the team will soon be rewarded with another World Champion.'

Flavio Briatore, the flamboyant, glamorous boss of the Benetton team with whom Michael Schumacher won two World Championships, is also a Ferrari supporter. 'Ferrari is fundamental to Formula One. It is necessary to have a competitive Ferrari for the good of us all. We need excitement and entertainment and good competition between the teams.'

The passion of winning, the pain of losing. Ferrari has known both. Here we are on the threshold of the next millennium, a sophisticated race of super-achievers, living in the world of hard, clinical high technology, but still we can be entranced by tradition and mystique. What is it about the red racers that continues to entice and seduce? Above all, what is it like on the inside, to be a part of the team that is part of Formula One folklore? Let's part the shrouds and take a journey to the heart of the Prancing Horse.

CHAPTER TWO

The Dawn of a New Era

'I needed a new challenge and

Ferrari came along and offered me

a great opportunity.'

Nigel Stepney
Ferrari Team Coordinator

The death of the great Enzo Ferrari in 1988 was the end of an era at Ferrari. He had been the creator and motivating force of the car company for over forty years and now, finally, it was time to take stock and move on towards the 21st Century.

When Chief Designer John Barnard left Ferrari for the first time at the end of 1989, Alain Prost nearly won the World Championship the following year in 1990 before the famous coming together with Ayrton Senna at Suzuka effectively lost Prost the Championship.

The Leader
Brilliant international businessman Luca di Montezemolo sits behind the wheel of a classic Ferrari. He is the man who is leading the Prancing Horse into the 21st Century.

This prompted Ferrari to appoint a new heir to not only take over the running of the company, but lead it into the new millennium. The new messiah was Luca di Montezemolo, one of Italy's brightest international businessmen, who had already achieved success at Ferrari when he was Team Manager at the time when Niki Lauda won two World Championships in 1975 and 1977. Early on in his career, Montezemolo had been earmarked for great things by his mentor, Fiat boss Gianni Agnelli and he had moved through the ranks at Fiat. He had also been head of the organising committee for the football World Cup held in Italy in 1990, before he had been offered the top job at Ferrari in 1992.

As well as being bright and vastly experienced in the realms of international marketing and commerce, Montezemolo was also aware of the tradition and history that is an integral part of Ferrari. He was therefore ideally placed to lead the company. It was to be a quiet and dignified revolution as opposed to an outright battle.

Montezemolo's strategy was to get the best people in the top positions to enable the Formula One team to start winning again after a disappointing 1991 season. One of his first moves was to recapture award-winning designer John Barnard to prepare a competitive car. Barnard had already worked at Ferrari between 1986 and 1989 for Enzo Ferrari, as technical director. He was interested in rejoining the company, but not prepared to move house and home to Italy. Barnard takes up the story: 'Ferrari contacted me towards the end of 1991 to ask if I would be interested in returning to Maranello as technical director, which was the position I was in before. I went to Italy a couple of times and had a couple of meetings, but I said I didn't want to live in Italy or commute during the week.

'Things went quiet after this and then I was contacted by Niki Lauda, who was acting as a consultant for Ferrari, and he said that Ferrari had decided to do something in England and was I interested? I said yes. I also said they had to listen to me, it wasn't straightforward. I already had three years experience of trying to do this and you couldn't just have a technical director who lived and worked in England. That doesn't work. It had to be structured in a different way.

Further discussions took place and it was agreed that I would maintain a fairly self-contained UK-based factory while the day-to-day running of Maranello would be someone else's responsibility. I joined Ferrari on 1 August 1992.'

Barnard is a perfectionist and very aware of how it all could go horribly wrong if things weren't discussed and agreed at the outset. He is also an innovator. Barnard was the designer who introduced carbon-fibre monocoques into motor sport, with the objective of finding a material that would allow a smaller chassis and, therefore, improved ground effect, but which had the same stiffness and was lighter than a larger chassis. He also introduced carbon disc brakes at McLaren who won the World Championship in 1984 with Alain Prost. After joining Ferrari in 1986, he designed and developed the electro hydraulic semi-automatic gearbox, which has since become standard fitting on all Formula One cars, and recently on Ferrari road cars as well.

However, it usually takes time to sort out teething problems on new items of the car before they can be deemed to be reliable and give maximum benefit. Barnard, driven by his desire to push the industry forward and develop new concepts, is prepared to work long and hard to sort out what he believes in and his track record proves that he is a successful innovator. Raging against this is the fact that Ferrari, for all its promises, wants to win and win now.

When Barnard arrived at Maranello in 1992 for his second visit, he was aware of the political currents that ebb and flow around the factory like the Spring tide, but despite this he took up the challenge of getting involved in a team that was on the edge of a new renaissance. Like many clever, successful men he was seduced by the thought of getting it right at one of the most difficult, disparate teams in Formula One, and he had enough self-confidence to think he could pull it off. In theory it should have been a happy union between a large budget and a well respected talent. But for the Ferrari-Barnard association to be truly happy it would need serenity, patience and total commitment on both parts and that wasn't going to be easy.

It started off full of golden promise. Barnard was under the distinct impression that he had made it clear that he would not get involved in the day-to-day management at Maranello. 'I was very straight about not being responsible for monitoring or organising the day to day technical activities at Maranello. It just isn't possible to manage people via telephone and fax. I get heavily involved in my projects. I don't just have meetings and issue memos or dictate what is to be designed by others. I get involved right down to the small details. The idea was that Ferrari Design and Development [FDD, the operational set-up in England] would work on prototypes, not just for the next race but for the next half of the season and for next year. As well as having a fairly self-

The Perfectionist
The good times. John Barnard shares a joke with fellow Englishman Nigel Stepney in the Ferrari garage.

contained unit with some manufacturing, design and aerodynamics, we would also have our own wind tunnel facilities and I organised that at British Aerospace at Filton, near Bristol. The wind tunnel in Italy is too far away. I need it here at my fingertips. Besides, their wind tunnel could only run a ⅓ scale model, although they are now building a new one, and I needed one that would take a ½ scale model. In any case Harvey Postlethwaite, then Technical Director, was in Italy running the technical side of things. That reassured me that Ferrari didn't expect me to get involved with the running of Maranello on a day by day basis. In fact, when I agreed to return they called a meeting and left Harvey and I in a room by ourselves. I think they thought that one of us would emerge with blood dripping from our fingernails, but I just said to Harvey, "Does it bother you if I come along?" and he replied, "It doesn't bother me if it doesn't bother you; let's just take the money and get on with the job."

Harvey Postlethwaite is one of Formula One's great characters. A fluent Italian speaker, lover of the good life and earthy realist, he has seen it all. Like Barnard it was his second visit to the stable of the Prancing Horse. First time round he had stayed eight years. 'The first time was wonderful, when I was working for the old man (Enzo Ferrari). He could be difficult but everyone knew where they stood and he kept it all together by ruling with a rod of iron. The second time was awful. On my first day back in 1992, I realised I had made an awful mistake in being persuaded to return. There was no direction and things changed every five minutes. It was the start of two truly awful years and I couldn't wait to get out. I used to keep a piece of paper with my salary written on it in the top drawer of my desk, and when things got really rough, I would open the drawer, look at the figure and remember the reason I had returned!'

Postlethwaite sums up his feelings by declaring, 'Ferrari is like a film star with halitosis – from afar it looks glamorous and seductive, but get near and it poisons you.' Exit stage left and into the arms of Tyrrell Racing, where Harvey remains today.

In principle, the idea of having a facility in England was great. Move the creative, innovative stuff away from the frenetic day-to-day activity, and allow the imagination to work in peace. As Barnard admits, 'I cannot think in Italy, you never know if you are on foot or horseback. The press are always ready to grab a straw and make a haystack. It's guaranteed that if there are ten journalists present and you say one thing, you will get at least six different stories out of it. The whole idea is for FDD to stand back and take in the overall picture. If I need driver input, like how the car is running and what he likes and doesn't like, I can get that by talking to him. I don't have to be at every race. I receive all the race data on CD and I can replay the telemetry read out after the event.'

However, it wasn't so easy in practice. Barnard had to gather a new team to work at the new offices in Shalford, Guildford that would effectively be the design centre for Ferrari Formula

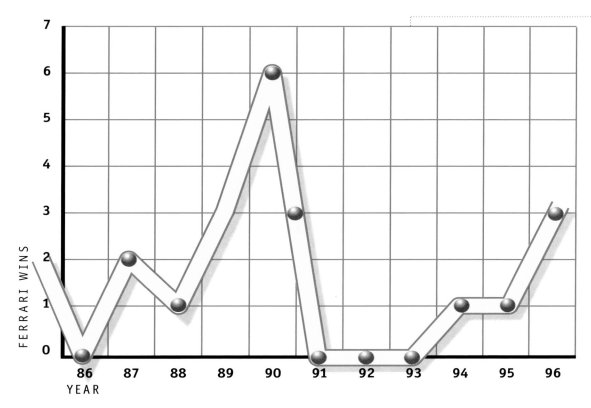

Fortunes on the Rise?
It's been seven years since a Ferrari driver even came close to winning the World Championship; Frenchman Alain Prost, in 1990, finished just seven points behind champion Ayrton Senna. But since 1993, the trend is clearly upwards...

One cars. At the same time he was under pressure to produce a new car for 1993. 'We agreed that I would take an overview and get things up and running. But within days of signing the contract, I was being asked how quickly I could do a new car. I hadn't even got a building to work from! There was an enormous amount to do before we could even make a drawing, never mind anything else. Yet here I was being asked to come to Maranello, fix problems and design a new car. We must win next year, we have to do something, it's important we turn it around now, blah, blah, blah. It was as if all the conversation and the agreement that I would take a more removed position in England, before the signing of the contract, had never happened. It was at that moment that I realised that the bottom line of my return to Ferrari was that they wanted me, John Barnard, signed up to Ferrari, because I had a name that would give everyone the feeling that yes, here we go, we're going to get back up to the top again, and this would also attract drivers like Schumacher. I thought, "Welcome back to Ferrari!" There was nothing left to do except batten down the hatches and get on with the job.'

It is true that if you study the graph published in *La Gazzetta dello Sport*, there appears to be a Ferrari four or five-year cycle. When Barnard joined Ferrari in 1986, their fortunes had been down; when he left in 1989, he left them with a car that nearly won the Championship in 1990. After this, everything was dismantled and the team's fortunes plunged until his arrival in 1992, when things would once again look up. Now, the pressure was on again and within a few weeks he was back on the drawing board designing the car for the 1993 season.

Having secured a slightly cynical but nevertheless brilliant designer and parked him in England to get on and design a new car, Montezemolo continued with his search for the right people. Next on his shopping list was Frenchman Jean Todt. Todt is an exceptionally gifted team manager, having led Peugeot to several World Championship titles in sportscars after a successful career as a rally co-driver. He was enjoying his job at Peugeot but wanted the ultimate challenge of Formula One, and when Peugeot declined to compete at that level, he was ready to try new pastures.

An Englishman Abroad
Team Coordinator Nigel Stepney and his French girlfriend Nathalie enjoy the delights of Italian pasta. According to Stepney, joining Ferrari was 'like being thrown into the lions' den.'

'I wanted to do something new, I needed a new challenge and Ferrari came along and offered me a great opportunity.' The decision to join Ferrari was not taken easily or quickly. The internal politics and the pressure to win make it both rewarding and exhausting. It took seven or eight months for both Montezemolo and Todt to decide that employing a Frenchman at the helm of an Italian team was the right thing to do. In July 1993 Jean Todt moved to Italy and set about re-organising the team. Like Barnard he found the reality slightly more awesome than expected. 'I knew what it would be like but there is a different picture behind the job. Everyone sees the tip of the iceberg, but there are many other problems and issues that nobody sees. This unseen part is what causes the most stress. I knew it was going to be tough and it *is* tough.'

However like Barnard, Todt is made of stern stuff and as his track record in rallying would indicate, he doesn't give up easily. A small, Napoleonic character with a severe countenance but an understanding heart, the job of Team Principal at Ferrari was one challenge Todt was determined to see through to the end and achieve his objectives of bringing structure and organisation to a team which sorely needed it.

Team Coordinator Nigel Stepney was one of the first to feel the benefit of Todt's talents. He recalls how he joined Ferrari and the pre and post Todt periods. 'I joined Ferrari in 1992 and it was the realisation of a dream. I had worked with various English teams from 1978, and everyone warned me against going to work for Ferrari. They said, "It's big, it's political, you won't survive." After that, Ferrari became my number one choice, I love a challenge and it was a personal challenge for me. I thought I'd show a few people what I could do.

'When I worked at Lotus, we were next door to Ferrari at the races, and I used to see the Ferraris and think, I want to work for them. However, ten or fifteen years ago that wasn't possible, as they didn't take on English people or many foreigners. It was essentially an Italian team. It was very closed. Every one of us used to look on from the outside and see this glamorous image.

'When I finally walked through the door in 1992, it was like everyone said it was, it was like being thrown into the lion's den. I came in from FDD, John Barnard's company, as John wanted someone to co-ordinate some of the work that came from FDD. When we were building the new car, I would liaise with John on his concepts and the work he wanted carried out. The first year was very tough, I didn't speak Italian so communication was very difficult. Harvey Postlethwaite was in charge on the technical side and he put me in a non position so I was there but not there. I had no specific job description. In addition, I had to learn about the place. In fact after four years I'm still learning! I went to all the circuits as we had active suspension and I had to sort it out. But I was never really part of it. Once I got through the first year, things got better. The job evolved and I wanted to succeed, so I made it work. I had never lived in another country before and it was interesting. I was beginning to enjoy myself. But what really turned it round for me was the arrival of Jean Todt at Ferrari at Magny Cours (the French Grand Prix) in 1993. I was still there but not there. I had no set role and I wasn't in a position that benefited either me or Ferrari. Todt changed that. When he arrived the whole structure of the place started to change. He picked me up and put me into a position, that of Team Coordinator, which I knew and could grow with. Jean Todt is brilliant at restructuring, and good at giving you support and confidence. If he trusts you and believes in you, he'll give you support and make you feel strong. That was vital at Ferrari.'

Nigel Stepney was not deliberately placed in a 'non-position', it was just that pre Jean Todt, decisions were taken, overturned and reinstated in the space of minutes. It was difficult to plan ahead as the old regime reigned without imposing clear objectives, or a clear overall strategy. Top managers came and went until Montezemolo started to turn it round. However, it was Jean Todt's arrival that really got the show on the road.

As Stepney says, 'Before his arrival, it was very easy to feel insecure at Ferrari. Everyone was constantly trying to make you feel insecure, as they were insecure themselves. You expected the knife in your back at any moment. It was like *Julius Caesar* every day here. The Italians used to bunch together and it was difficult to fit into that structure. But with Todt's arrival a lot of people were able to start work and have definite responsibilities. It was like a breath of fresh air.'

In the new set-up, Stepney's job was to fill the gap between the chief mechanic and the team manager. He would report to Team Manager Giorgio Ascanelli, the man responsible for the chassis and all operations at the track. In reality this meant that Ascanelli would give the specification on preparing the cars and what he required at the circuit. The team would then have to build the cars to that specification and it is Stepney's job to put that plan into action. He has to make sure that everyone does the right job and the team has the right materials to do the job. As Stepney says, 'I have to ensure that we have everything we need to operate as a team at the circuit. If we have problems building or maintaining the car to the specification required, we have to give feedback to the engineers, so they can solve or try to solve the problems.'

Gradually things started to improve as Montezemolo created a strategy that was designed to put Ferrari back at the top, where it belonged. Stepney is proud to be a part of the new era. 'A lot has improved in terms of cleanliness, and attitude to work. I think we are climbing over the hill. I hope I am part of the renaissance of Ferrari, in which we will see Ferrari where it should be. I want to see us win back the respect the team deserves.'

Respect was still at a low ebb in 1995, when a lot of people still criticised the amount the team was spending. Stepney defends Ferrari and explains: 'Everyone thinks we spend more than Williams, but it must be remembered that we produce the entire car, including the engine. Williams and Benetton have Renault behind them. We do have more people but we are still behind in terms of facilities. We are building a new wind tunnel near the factory and when we finally have that set-up we will be almost complete. The whole of the car is now developed around the aerodynamics. Regulations dictate how the car will be, and the number one priority is to have the right wind tunnel, which will give us valuable information from which we can build a good car.'

Simply the Best
Michael Schumacher looking thoughtful as he contemplates his move to the stable of the prancing horse.

It was to be another year before Ferrari took the last step in their renaissance and employed a World Champion as their driver. Gerhard Berger and Jean Alesi were the present Ferrari drivers and were competent and talented, but their constant bickering did not help the team. The arrival of double World Champion Michael Schumacher from Benetton would change all that. When Schumacher won his first World Championship in 1994, he dedicated it to Ayrton Senna, 'the man who should have won it.' Strangely enough, it should have been Senna who joined Ferrari in 1996, not Schumacher. Ferrari Press Officer Giancarlo Baccini says, 'Senna had always wanted to drive for Ferrari. Before he went to Williams he came and talked to us and said he wanted to drive for Ferrari. We told him we weren't ready for him. We just weren't able to provide him with the car and facilities he needed. He was brilliant but also demanding and it would have broken the team to have a champion at that time. We told him to wait for a couple of years and then we would be ready. That would have been the 1996 season. He agreed and we continued to rebuild the team. But destiny decreed otherwise. That is not to say Schumacher was second choice. He is absolutely a world class driver, and who knows if Senna would have joined us or not. The initial discussions with Senna were before Schumacher won his first World Championship and emerged as one of the all-time greats.'

The arrival of the brilliant German driver was almost the final piece of the jigsaw in the rebuilding of the team (Ross Brawn would arrive as Technical Director in December of 1996 and

Rory Byrne as Chief Designer in January 1997). Montezemolo chose the moment carefully before taking on a driver who would demand the best in everything, and was also capable of giving the best. At the launch of the 1996 car, the energetic Montezemolo was full of optimism and determination. 'Just as a football team doesn't expect to win a major title immediately the team restructures, we have the same philosophy of making steady progress towards our target of winning the World Championship. Three years ago we were two seconds off the pace of the best cars, now we are up among the best. By having Schumacher as our Number One driver we are demonstrating to the world that we are prepared to do everything possible to win. Also we feel ready to make the final leap to success. If we didn't feel ready, then we wouldn't have brought the best driver in the world into the team.'

To emphasize the importance of the occasion, Fiat boss Gianni Agnelli blessed the launch party for the 1996 car with his presence and gave his good wishes for a successful 1996 season. Irishman Eddie Irvine was chosen to be Schumacher's team-mate. His name was top of the list of leading sponsor Philip Morris. The company wanted a young, hip image and they thought that Irvine, with his good looks and uninhibited behaviour would fit the bill. Rumour has it that another crucial factor was Irvine's meeting with Ferrari Chairman Luca di Montezemolo at the Argentinian Grand Prix. Irvine, bold as brass, went up to the Chairman and told him that as much as he enjoyed driving his Ferrari, the parts were far too expensive in Ireland. Would it be possible to get a discount?

Irvine denies that this had anything to do with him getting the drive and says, 'I spoke to Jean Todt earlier in the season and he said keep in touch, and so I did. We had a couple of meetings, during which time the press was saying that every driver in the World was coming to Ferrari except me! I think that once Ferrari knew I was leaving Jordan that changed the situation.'

Being number two to a World Champion isn't easy as several of Schumacher's team-mates have found out. However, Irvine was distinctly underwhelmed by the whole Ferrari mystique, which helped keep his feet on the ground. 'I'd been there before and it's just a factory making cars. However, the more you're with them, the more you realise what a big deal it is.' The only thing that Irvine found difficult was the total loss of freedom that comes with being a Ferrari driver. 'I was in the Irish pub in Bologna having a quiet drink, but within five minutes there was a photographer there. I now go to Bologna only when there is something to do, otherwise I am in Dublin where I am left in comparative peace and can relax.'

Schumacher's arrival was less surprising. A double World Champion at only twenty-six years of age, he was emerging as one of the best drivers of his generation and Ferrari were now ready for him. They knew they'd have to pay for the best, and they did to the tune of US$25 million

Playboys
Michael Schumacher and team-mate Eddie Irvine live up to the image of Formula One playboys as they relax before the start of the season.

Red Hot Passion

A sea of Ferrari flags heralds the start of the Schumacher era and reflects the feeling of hope with the arrival of the double World Champion at Ferrari.

dollars. But as John Barnard says, 'When Ferrari signed Schumacher it was like they opened another piggybank. Suddenly money was no object. You need a new machine? Buy it. Expand, employ the people you need and so on. It was a surprise as for the last three years we'd been told to hang tight, cut back, think before spending any extra money. Suddenly that all changed.'

Fortunately, when he met the press for the first time, Schumacher didn't repeat the mistake he made in his first press conference. When asked what his father did, he replied with a straight face, 'He likes screwing.' For once the hacks were rendered speechless, until it was explained that in German a screw is a carpenter, someone who likes playing around with wood. The mistake was not repeated!

● ● ●

Another vital ingredient to the rebuilding of Ferrari was the return of Shell as a Ferrari partner, along with fellow sponsors Philip Morris, Asprey, Magneti Marelli, Telecom Italia, Goodyear and Pioneer.

Shell's return to the fold after a twenty-three-year absence was going to prove decisive in the fight back to victory. Most people thought Shell had returned because they needed to repair the Shell image in Germany in the aftermath of the Brent Spar disaster, but nothing could be further from the truth. Roger Lindsay, now retired from Shell but still in sparkling form, has been at the front of the oil company's involvement with Formula One since the beginning. He describes how the relationship with Ferrari re-ignited.

'I was at Suzuka in 1994, just a few days after the announcement that the new Mercedes-McLaren alliance would not run on Shell but on Mobil. Despite the miserable wet conditions, several teams were anxiously courting the Shell representatives. One team definitely not doing that was Ferrari.

'I was moving along between the portakabins and boxes that pass for pits at Suzuka, when I spotted my old ex-Honda-McLaren friend, Osamu Goto, who was by then at Ferrari. He was standing outside the Ferrari office. "No more F1, then," he said with a wry smile. "Looks like it," I replied. "Any chance here?" I asked looking at the Ferrari door. "I'll ask," said Goto and went inside. He re-appeared shortly and said, "Come back in an hour."

The one hour became two, but finally I went into Jean Todt's office. He gave me his famous look of appraisal and said, "Yes?" I gave him my card and said, "I'm Roger Lindsay from Shell. We supply fuels and lubricants for Formula One cars."

To which he replied, "We have a very good supplier already." I said, "Yes, I know but we are better," feeling a bit cheeky.

He scrutinised the card again and said, "I'll tell my boss and maybe I'll call you."

Well, he did call and Shell and Ferrari were together again for the 1996 season, after a separation of over 20 years.'

The red hot passion of Ferrari combined with the cool, clinical, technical expertise of Shell is a forceful combination. Fuels and lubricants are a vital aspect of improving performance. In-depth research and development at the Shell Research and Technology Centre at Thornton in Cheshire, has led to a far more efficient and powerful engine. The engine was to be an important factor in Ferrari's return to the top. Eventually it will benefit you and I in our road cars. Today's Formula One car is often a research vehicle for tomorrow's road cars, and in this case Ferrari have their own road cars as well as the Formula One cars. It would be a beneficial partnership for all parties.

According to Raoul Pinnell, Head of Global Brands and Communications at Shell, 'Shell and Ferrari share the appetite for always breaking new ground. That's what inspires Ferrari's engineers and Shell scientists. It leads to better cars. And to better fuels and lubricants too.'

Edward Asprey, the tall, distinguished director of Asprey and leader of the Asprey sponsorship of Formula One was sure he and the company had made the right decision to back Ferrari. 'When we looked at various sponsorship options, we found that there were only a limited number which reflected our objective of technical excellence on an international basis. Ferrari stood out as a team that had an international following and also combined glamour, craftsmanship and style. It is unusual to find two companies with the same aspirations and values and it is working very well for us.'

Style is an inherent part of Ferrari, right down to the smallest button on the team uniform, which was designed and is produced by leading fashion house, Cerruti. Nino Cerruti, an avid race fan was delighted to continue his relationship with Jean Todt, who had worked with Cerruti when he was at Peugeot. 'There is only one name that symbolises Italian style, with a car that has spirit and is magnificent inside and out, and that name is Ferrari.

Party Time
Edward Asprey, Director of Asprey joins Prince Albert and Ferrari's Stefano Domenicali at the Cerruti Asprey Party during the Cannes Film Festival.

Completing the dawn of a new era for the Italian car giants, on 15 February 1996 the new Ferrari Formula One car was unveiled and presented to the international media. More than half a million people logged on to the Internet to follow the presentation ceremony. There was much hope and optimism that finally the tide was turning in favour of the stable of the Prancing Horse. The scene was set, the players were in place. The rest was up to the team.

CHAPTER THREE

On a Wing and a Prayer

'I'm not harder on the team

than I am on myself.

If I make a mistake,

I kick myself.'

Michael Schumacher
after the 1996 Argentinian GP

Despite the atmosphere of hope and optimism that surrounded the presentation of the new F1 car on 15 February 1996, there were many crossed fingers as well. The car was late, very late, partly because the development of the previous season's car was still being carried out in England rather than at Maranello. Because of a shortage of staff, FDD had not put that development down early enough to get on with the new car. A major concern for Ferrari was that there was hardly any time to test before the season's first race in Melbourne on 10 March.

John Barnard has been criticised for being removed from the realities of modern Formula One racing. It is an accusation that he is keen to dismiss. 'I only have one problem and that is that everyone expects me to produce something new and take the next step. If I don't do that they just say it is only another Formula One car, he must be finished. I push hard to find something new, but the realities of modern Formula One racing are quite simple. If you want to win and be in the top group, you need more than two hundred people, a sizeable budget and a good engine. There is no way of cutting corners. You have to build up to that point.'

At Fiorano, the Ferrari test track just outside Maranello, a problem emerged involving slight cracks in the gearbox bellhousing which caused an oil leak, and the team decided to go to Estoril

A Star is Born
The new F310 is carefully removed from the Ferrari lorry to be unveiled before an adoring public.

in Portugal to try and rectify the situation. It was the start of many sleepless nights for the Ferrari Team Manager, Claudio Berro. The 39-year-old Berro is the person responsible for shifting men and machines around the world and ensuring that everything arrives on time in one piece. He also has to ensure that the team has acceptable accommodation and transport, and that the team personnel are warm and comfortable whilst they are away from the factory. He also liaises with the motor racing authorities, FIA and FOCA, and attends meetings with the Team Principal, Jean Todt.

It might seem like a job from heaven: constant travel, exotic locations, five-star hotels, the chance to meet, beautiful, rich people and have a good time, plus the glamour of being part of Ferrari. However, on a wet, freezing cold, fog infested morning in the middle of nowhere in Northern Italy, glamour and having a good time were far from Berro's thoughts. His immediate problem was how to transport the race cars, the team and the accompanying equipment to Portugal for the hastily arranged test, and be ready to meet the departure schedule for Australia. The team were due to leave on an Alitalia flight bound for Melbourne at 12.30 pm on Friday 1 March.

It was quickly apparent that the team couldn't travel as it normally does by road; it would have taken five days for a trip to Estoril and back. A quick alternative was needed and needed fast. It required a cool head and plenty of stamina to put it all together. Fortunately, Berro is

The Heavy Brigade
One of the huge Ferrari
transporters departs for another
Grand Prix.

calm by nature and solves problems in a logical and efficient manner. 'I investigated the
possibility of renting an aircraft, and found a Russian Antonov aircraft for the cars and
equipment and a jet for all the technicians. I asked for detailed measurements of the Russian
aircraft as I had to be absolutely sure that everything would fit in. We had six or seven cases of
small spare parts as well as crates of larger spare parts and the racing car. This was the start of
ten sleepless nights for me. The cars were at the test track at Fiorano until the afternoon, then
they were transported to Bologna and the plane took off at 3 am. It landed at 6 am and I was
constantly on the phone to check and double check that everything was going according to plan.
I had an aircraft on standby for two days, for which we had to pay a penalty, but we had to be
sure we could take off at short notice. We had a combination of cars moving between Fiorano
and Estoril, we had the old car/new engine, then the new car and then the old car/new engine
back at Fiorano. We had trucks to transport them from the airport at Lisbon to the track. I also
had to make sure the technicians arrived, and so it was a hectic and complex period. All in all, it
was the most difficult part of the year.'

Difficult is an understatement. It could have been disastrous. Ferrari Chairman Luca di
Montezemolo admitted later that 'we risked not sending two cars to the first race of 1996 at
Melbourne in Australia.' This would have been unthinkable. Ferrari is Formula One, it has
competed in the Formula One Championship since its conception in 1950, and a non-appearance
at Melbourne would have been a hammer blow to the team and its fans.

Against this background of uncertainty, it was with understandable trepidation that the team arrived in Melbourne. Berro, however, was the most relaxed. 'As soon as I boarded the plane I fell asleep and slept for a solid twenty four hours. I stepped off the plane feeling great. Everyone had jet lag, but I didn't. I told them the solution is to avoid sleep before the trip. That wasn't the most popular suggestion of the day!'

Berro saved the day and enabled Jean Todt and his team to get on with the job of fixing the car. Berro had worked closely with Todt at Peugeot, from the time they were rally co-drivers to their individual rises through the ranks which saw Todt as the overall boss and Berro as Director of Sport for Peugeot in Italy. The two men have an almost telepathic understanding which is necessary when working in the hot cauldron of pressure that is Maranello.

As the Italian population slept unaware that Ferrari racing cars were shooting backwards and forwards across the airways, Berro's team were already checking and rechecking arrangements for later in the year. Miodrag Kotur, Pino Gozzo and Massimo Balocchi make up the logistics group. They oversee the movement of the trucks, team personnel, and equipment round the world. Giuseppe Gozzo, Pino to his friends, is the man at the track who has the sometimes difficult if not impossible job of making sure all the travel arrangements run smoothly. When things go wrong he has to put them right. With thirty-five years' experience with Alitalia, including stints as station manager in Libya, The Sudan, Somalia, Egypt, Malta, Tel Aviv and Turin, organising the movements of Ferrari team personnel is relatively problem free. The one thing about Pino is that nothing, but absolutely nothing changes his sunny, helpful nature. He is also dedicated to Ferrari. 'I love my job, it is my biggest love after my wife.'

It is a job where the saying 'it's not what you know, but who you know' comes to the fore. When team personnel want to change their flights and travel arrangements during a period where the aircraft are overbooked, he has to use his wide range of contacts to pull strings and make sure that people get to their destinations on time. He remembers an incident where his knowledge of airport life and the staff proved useful. 'The team needed a replacement engine urgently at Estoril. The weather was bad at Bologna and the flight was cancelled so it looked as if the engine wouldn't make it until the following night. I suddenly remembered that there was an early flight from Turin to Lisbon, so I contacted my friends at Turin airport and they said "Just send the engine, we'll make sure it gets to Lisbon." In fact, the packing case was too big, so the staff worked late into the night to re-pack the case and make it smaller and off it went. That sums up what Ferrari means to the Italians.'

Action Man
Michael Schumacher gets his first taste of the 1996 Ferrari as he starts the defence of his World Championship.

By nature the Italians are creative, passionate people, and unlike the Northern races, more inclined towards lateral thinking. The need to think laterally was never greater than in making sure the team arrived in Japan for the penultimate race in 1995. There was an air-traffic controllers' strike in Italy and the team was booked onto a jumbo jet leaving from London. They had to connect with this flight from Milan. Some aircraft took off from Italy, but no Alitalia flights were being let through. The team was sent to Linate (Milan airport) at mid-day on the Sunday, but nothing happened, and they were still sitting there in the afternoon. Drastic action was needed. The Ferrari managers contacted Alitalia and discovered that the strike was aimed against them. No Alitalia planes were being given clearance to take off, although other planes were being allowed through. Then an idea struck the senior Ferrari management. Why not change the aircraft number? So instead of, for example, being AZ1234, it became SA1234. They submitted their new flight number to air-traffic control and hey presto, they were given a slot time to take off, as those in charge thought it was a charter aircraft. It wasn't until the team was under the control tower and they saw this plane with Alitalia markings on it, that they realised, too late, it was an Alitalia aircraft. As one team member said, 'We were not being dishonest, but we had to resolve a situation that if it had been allowed to continue would have caused us and Italy severe problems. Ferrari isn't just another racing team, it is part of Italy.'

The long distance 'flyaways' (races outside of Europe) are complicated. Three jumbo jets leave Europe, two from England and one from Italy. They each hold about 100,000 kg. Ferrari send between 85 and 90 cases of equipment plus three cars each weighing about 600 kg. The jumbo jets have special racking onto which the cars are wheeled and strapped down. The front nose of each is removed along with the wings, then plywood is placed on the side and underneath to protect the bodywork. The car is then bubble wrapped and a cover goes over it. Ferrari take up between 20,000 and 22,000 kg – a lot of baggage! Everything the team needs from olive oil to nuts and bolts are in the packages.

Once at the track, there have to be enough telephone lines, faxes, kitchen equipment and rented cars to make sure everyone can do their jobs. Unlike in Europe where the huge motorhomes and trucks lumber across countries carrying cars, spare parts, the kitchen and the offices, outside of Europe you have to make do with local supplies and those things you send from home. Berro makes the garages feel like home by ensuring that the partition screens that divide up the different working areas and keep the team's secrets hidden from prying eyes, are 'decorated' with the sponsors branding and the drivers' photographs. However, you still get the impression that the removal men are due any minute. Large crates lie in rows containing the spare parts from drive shafts to screwdrivers. They are all carefully placed in order, even the tiniest screws are kept in a specific drawer in a designated case so that the mechanics can find them in a split second – in this game a second can make a difference between snatching pole position and wallowing lower down the grid. More than any other sport Formula One is about speed, both one and off the track.

• • •

Although the team arrived in Melbourne feeling far from confident, they were in for a pleasant surprise. Things were not quite as bad as they thought. They had feared being right off the pace and a long way down the grid or even worse being unreliable and only lasting a few laps, but they put on a good show, even though there were problems.

Williams, as predicted, outshone everyone, with Villeneuve and Hill on pole position and second respectively. But Ferrari did well: Michael Schumacher qualified fourth and his team-mate Eddie Irvine started third on the grid.

For Chief Engineer Giorgio Ascanelli, the team really was living on a wing and a prayer in Australia. Ascanelli is the man in charge of the team at the race track; he talks to the drivers and their race engineers about the race strategy and set up, but ultimately it is his decision. He is responsible for directing the whole operation and so he has the weight of Italian hopes and fears placed squarely on his shoulders. He is an emotional, volatile character but is also strong and direct which helps him to cope. Ascanelli doesn't mince words or suffer fools gladly. As he says, 'Leading a team of people is more difficult than managing objects. In Formula One speed is essential

Looking to the Future
Giorgio Ascanelli, the man in charge of the Ferrari Team at the track, feels the weight of his responsibility as he contemplates the future.

and there isn't time for diplomacy and politics. The pressure on Ferrari is greater than in other teams as the success of Ferrari has an effect on every aspect of Italian life, including the government and the humour of the people. When the Italian football team won the 1982 World Cup, it gave the Italian people and the economy a real lift.'

Ascanelli has some astute observations about Formula One motor racing and Ferrari. 'Historically, Ferrari has always enjoyed success. One of the reasons is that we were already an industry and in the past we were really only competing against teams with kit cars. Then Bernie Ecclestone took Formula One into the 20th Century. He made it what it is today, and we had to face serious contenders.'

Like most of his colleagues at Ferrari, Ascanelli is a fervent believer in stability. 'It has been difficult for people to come in after Enzo Ferrari and we have struggled to maintain some sort of stability. Williams has become strong through building up a team that can work together.

Making a Difference
The Ferrari pit stop crew are ready for that sub 10 second pit stop – crucial to their drivers' chances.

Their team doesn't change much from year to year. I believe stability is very important. There is an intrinsic amount of information in a person's head and because we are all so busy we just don't have time to pass everything on to a new person.'

Race strategy and set-up is a complex business. The set up of a car is based on many different factors. You can either alter the set up and improve the overall balance of the car aerodynamically, by increasing or decreasing the downforce, or you can play with the anti-roll bars, springs and ride heights to improve mechanical grip. There is a certain amount of overlap between these two things, and the weight, shape and position in the car of the engine and gearbox also affects the balance of the car. The tyres are also vital to balance. Some circuits are hard on tyres, such as the Hungaroring in Hungary, where it is usually hot and the track has lots of corners. This means the tyres get very hot because they have no time to cool down in the straights. Huge downforce is required, as you have to use maximum cooling, and when you do that you sacrifice some aerodynamic performance. After only one lap you can lose up to a second. It can be said that all the teams will suffer the same problem, but if the team is already struggling with balance, then these other aspects such as tyres, can increase the difficulties. Williams has an advantage as it is a stable well balanced car with good mechanical grip, allowing them to run less aerodynamic downforce. In 1996 Ferrari was already struggling with a completely new car.

Race strategy is as much about outfoxing your opponents as taking external elements into consideration. You can use your number two driver to the advantage of your number one, for example, by bringing him in or keeping him out depending if he is leading an adversary, or in traffic. Of course, mechanical considerations come into play. But success comes from experience and a little bit of luck. You can't always account for the weather, sometimes it starts to rain when rain isn't forecast or the track will dry half way during a wet race. You also cannot account for accidents; if the driver has made his pit stop just before the safety car comes out, it is an enormous advantage as he is ready to charge off when the pace car goes in, whereas the other drivers will still have to make their pit stops.

Then there is the question of the driver's style. Schumacher's brilliance can to some degree be explained by his style of driving, which is very unusual in that he tends to drive with a lot of downforce on the front wing as he hates understeer. This counteracts the usual understeer problem, where the car has the tendency to drive straight on through the corners, but can produce the opposite oversteer as the rear becomes twitchy and ready to snap out of line causing the car to spin. Despite this Schumacher drives on the limit all the time. If you follow his braking on the telemetry readout, his lines are the smoothest, and even more surprisingly he uses less fuel than many of his competitors. As John Barnard says, 'Schumacher is naturally very quick.

A lot of drivers have to work at being quick, but it just comes naturally to him, so it allows him to release a lot of mental power on thinking about the race. However, where Schumacher really scores is that he has the ability to impress a calmness on the team even when things aren't going well. It's a "let's not panic" syndrome which is absolutely essential at Ferrari. He was double World Champion at twenty-six and commands an enormous amount of respect for that. If in addition he can keep things calm, it does help.'

Schumacher is of course, not without his weaknesses, and like many people the things that make him brilliant can also work against him. His determined, focused approach is helping Ferrari to concentrate its resources and work out problems, but he doesn't take on new ideas very easily. Barnard laughs as he says, 'If you can explain things logically to him, he'll take it on board, but if it is a hunch, getting him to change is like turning the Queen Mary. It's not easy.'

• • •

In Australia the main problem was unexpected cracking of the titanium gearbox casing. Shell, Ferrari's technical partner, detected traces of titanium when they analysed the lubricant. It was an unpleasant surprise. Barnard says, 'We had been running the engine in a hybrid version of last year's car and we hadn't seen that happening. We think the engine is vibrating badly, and causing the cracking. It is the first time we've used a V10; we ran using a titanium gearbox behind a V12 in 1994, and we didn't have these problems.'

There was also contention over the re-design of the cockpit area. Some teams felt that Williams and Jordan had not kept to the spirit of the new regulations drawn up to give drivers extra protection and were therefore, having an aerodynamic advantage over the rest. Ferrari, like many others had designed a high-sided cockpit.

Overall, the 1996 car was proving to be very difficult in terms of drivability. Irvine's third place in Australia was a bonus, but the team returned to Maranello with a lot of work to do in the ten days before they left for the South American races. The races in Brazil and Argentina were not only long distance but 'back to back' (a week apart), and the old gearbox

Taking a Break
Michael Schumacher with his personal trainer Balbir Singh just before the start of the Argentinian Grand Prix.

had to be fitted in the car. Unfortunately, it isn't as easy as simply replacing the new with the old. As Ascanelli says, 'We knew there was a hell of a lot of work to do between Australia and South America. We had to have a new water system, do electrical work, bodywork, a new starter motor and we had ten days to do it in.'

The team went to South America feeling unhappy and things went from bad to worse. Ascanelli says of Brazil, 'The Sao Paolo circuit is very bumpy and doesn't suit our car. We had to just limit the damage and wait until we could get back in the wind tunnel and do the necessary work to improve the car. The race went worse than I expected. After two days of sunshine, I was writing the race preparation report with ten minutes to go before the pit lane opened, when I looked up and saw it was raining. Disaster! There was no time to alter the fuel level, and our two-stop strategy which was good for the dry, was not good for the wet, where we would have been better with one stop.'

Schumacher demonstrated his class and pulled off the impossible by bringing the car in third. His calm approach was paying dividends and he refused to get caught up in any hysteria. 'I am enjoying driving for Ferrari. It is a challenge and I wanted a challenge. I am paid to work, not be on holiday. The car will be in the wind tunnel for the whole of April and we will be working hard to alleviate the problems. The car was worse than in Melbourne, we seem to be losing power everywhere, but the V10 engine shows good potential.'

A Dog named 'Floh'

Michael Schumacher's hard, austere image is unfair. The real man is warm and compassionate. He actively supports UNESCO and he and his wife, Corinna, are lovers of animals, and will help them whenever they can. His house in Monaco was already home to his West Highland Terrier, Jenny and two Belgian Shepherds, Bonny and Tracey. Now they were to be joined by a new addition. On the Thursday before the Argentinian race, Corinna was sitting in what could loosely be described as the team motorhome (a concrete garage), when she was joined by a flea-ridden but very pretty stray dog. The dog, who recognised a good thing when she saw it, stuck to her like glue and at the end of the day she couldn't leave it behind, with the result that Michael and Corinna returned to the five-

A driver's best friend...

star TransAmerica Hotel with their new canine friend.

While members of the racing press were in the bar swapping stories and relaxing, the double World Champion was kneeling by the bath cleaning the dog with carbolic soap purchased from a local supermarket. The next day, after a visit to the vet to have all the necessary injections, the dog was well on its way to becoming part of the Schumacher household. With tail wagging and looking decidedly less depressed, the newly christened Floh (German for 'flea') was on top of the world. She had won first prize in the canine lottery and in keeping with her new status flew by private jet to Buenos Aires, for the Argentinian Grand Prix, and then from there by First Class to Europe.

A Question of Fuel

Fuel is an issue that raised its head in Brazil in 1995, when Benetton and Williams were accused of using illegal fuel. After an investigation, Schumacher, then driving for Benetton, had his points reinstated, but the team had them deducted. The whole issue of fuel is a strange one. We are told that Formula One fuel is the same as that which we use in our road car, but is it? And if it is, why don't they just all fill up from the local petrol station, instead of hauling gallons of fuel from one side of the world to the other?

Simon Dunning is one of the Shell men at the track. Using sophisticated analysis equipment, Shell help Ferrari to monitor the fuel and lubricants. Dunning explained to me, 'These days the formulation of an F1 fuel is achieved in the same way as for the fuel you buy to fill your Renault Twingo. But in the past, we used to be able to add hydrocarbon materials to the petrol to enhance performance, but the authorities started to clamp down in 1992, and after Senna's death in 1994 they really changed the rules and regulations. FIA consulted the fuel companies and asked us to produce fuel that was basically the same as that used in road cars. The components are the same but the combination might be different. Formula One is like a thoroughbred horse. You may have different trainers but broadly speaking the recipe is the same. The experience and type of your horse affects your decisions, and you adapt the fuel to suit your horse. Unlike a road car, we don't have to make fuel to cope with cold weather conditions, or a lot of start stop situations, and it doesn't have to cope with Sunday drivers doing 20 mph down the motorway. Our major concern is to extract maximum power. A modern Formula One car will do about four miles to the gallon, although fuel consumption is an issue only where consumption makes the difference between two and three pit stops. However, our in-depth research helps improve the fuel that you use in your road car. You've probably noticed that the 'pinking' that used to be heard in your car as you changed gears and power, is very rarely heard in today's modern road car. This is due to the improvement in fuels.

'Shell have an expert in house who can tell them what difference the various fuels make to a racing car, even if it is one that isn't in the same class as the Ferrari Formula One car.

'In Formula One, fuel regulations are very tight. You always have to submit a sample of any new fuel to FIA, and once it is approved you make it up into big enough quantities to usually supply two races. To avoid last year's problems, every time we make up a new batch we submit it for approval.'

So what did happen last year? Were Benetton and Williams really cheating? It appears not, as they submitted a sample of fuel which was approved. The large batch then differed slightly to the sample, but not in any performance enhancing way, so it was all a bit of a storm in a tea cup and as often occurs in motor racing, a compromise was found in which the team was punished, but the

Shell's continued research and development into fuel is a vital part of their ongoing relationship with Ferrari.

driver wasn't as he couldn't have known he had an advantage at the time.

There isn't a lot of room for improvement, but in this game any advantage, however, small can make the difference between winning and losing, so Shell's continued research and development is a vital part of the Shell/Ferrari relationship. None of the teams really wants refuelling, but it does provide excitement and makes the race less predictable. In 1995 with a thirsty V12 engine Ferrari wanted to keep refuelling, but now with a V10 it isn't so critical, even though it is likely to stay. The large television audiences might drift away without it, and people like Max Mosley and Bernie Ecclestone are unlikely to let that happen.

A Presidential Visit
Argentinian President, Carlos
Menem visits the Ferrari pits
before the 1996 race in
Buenos Aires.

The V10 engine was proving to be a good move. As
Barnard says, 'I promoted moving from a V12 to a V10
engine for a long time. When Jean Todt arrived it made
things easier, as he was also a fan of the V10. You have to
pay a heavy penalty for the V12 in terms of the overall
package. The cooling requirements for the V12 are very big,
it is longer, it is heavy and it is fuel thirsty. Offsetting these
negative aspects was the fact that the V12 should have a
higher top-end power than the V10. However, I was always a
bit dubious about this. Now we have the V10 we can see this
is true. After limited development the V10 is proving to have
nearly as good top-end power as the V12. The negative side
of the V10 is the vibration problem, which seems to lead to
the gearbox cracking. We are investigating this further.'

• • •

There were to be no Easter celebrations for the two Ferrari drivers in Argentina. Schumacher
qualified in second place for the race, with Irvine tenth. Irvine brought the car home in fifth
place, to gain two valuable points, but Schumacher was forced to retire when a piece of debris
from another car hit his rear wing.

Even though we were only three races into the new season, the rumours were flying
around as speculation mounted that Ferrari was going to build a new car to take them through
the rest of the season. Jean Todt remained firm and publicly stated, 'We need more time testing
before we can make a decision.' Privately, he was less convinced declaring, 'I'm not happy, I'll
only be happy when we win.'

The atmosphere was muted as the team left South America and headed back to Europe.
They had survived the first three races, but only just. The first European race of the season was
at the Nurburgring and the fans would be out in force. Publicly, Schumacher was remaining calm,
privately it was another matter. As Nigel Stepney says, 'Schumacher doesn't wash his dirty linen
in public as our previous drivers did. He can give shit behind closed doors, but he does it in
private, which is much better as if everyone knows our problems, they know our weaknesses.
There is a much better atmosphere than last year. There will always be pressure on us, but it is
more contained. If we lose a wheel nut in a race, the media will analyse it forever, but if Williams

lose a wheel nut they are not put under a microscope like us. The difference is that now we look at the problem and rectify it with the minimum of fuss. That is a big step forward.'

Schumacher says, 'There's no point in criticising the team in public. I work with the guys and they all try and do their best. If we feel there should be some improvements then we have to discuss it between ourselves. I don't think I'm particularly hard. If I notice a mistake, then I will point it out and try to improve it. I'm not harder on the team than I am on myself. If I make a mistake, I kick myself. You shouldn't make a difference between how you treat others and how you treat yourself.'

Loading Up
A damaged prancing horse is rescued and brought back to the pits for reconstruction surgery.

There was a big prang in Argentina, but it came after the race rather than during it. Claudio Berro explains, 'When I was sitting on the pit wall during practice, I looked at the start lights and registered that they seemed to be hanging lower than normal. Then it went out of my mind until the day after the race. The trucks arrived to take the cars to the airport, loaded them on and drove out of the circuit. There was a horrible crash and it was proved that the lights had been lower than normal, about four metres lower in fact, and the result was they'd hit our cars on the trucks. Eddie Irvine's car had been smashed, the suspension had been damaged and it had been pushed backwards into the spare car which was loaded behind it. About 200 million lire's worth of damage was done. That was all we needed with the work we had to do on the cars anyway.'

Work, work, work. There was a never ending list of modifications needed. When Schumacher was asked to discuss the improvements needed on the car, his reply was to the point. 'This press conference is too short!' There was also another reason to feel nervous. Schumacher had received a death threat in the form of a letter claiming to come from a Kurdish liberation group, sent to two Belgian newspapers. It said that the terrorist organisation would kill German Chancellor Helmut Kohl, Foreign Minister Klaus Kinkel and Michael Schumacher.

The Car (overleaf)
The F310 in action in the 1996 Argentinian Grand Prix.

• • •

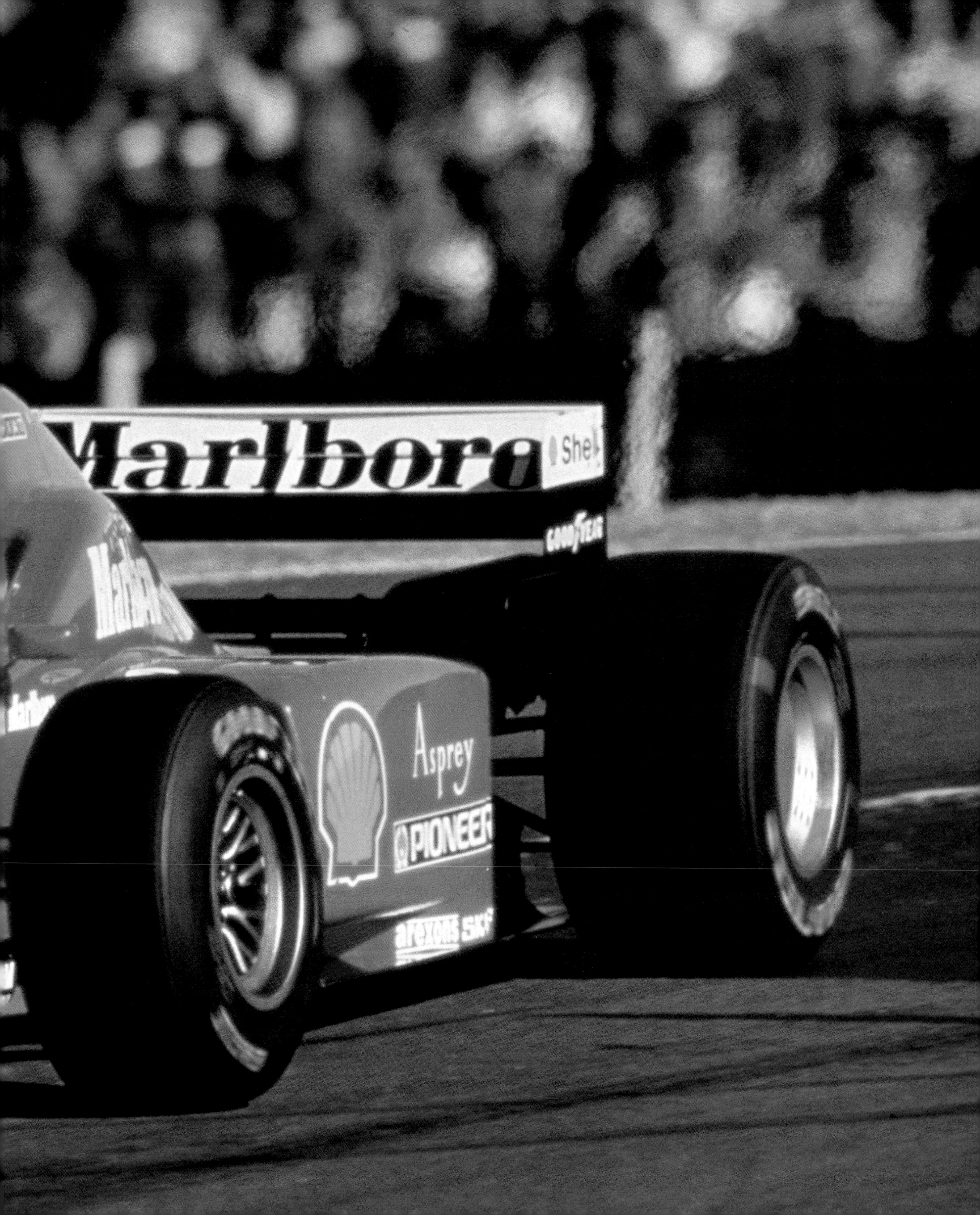
Marlboro
Asprey
PIONEER
arexons

Cooking for an Army

Claudio Degli Esposito in the heat of the kitchen.

In charge of the team motorhome are cooks Bruno Romani and Claudio Degli Espositi. During the race weekend it is hard work to feed the fifty or so team members. The cooks arrive at the circuit at 6.30 or 7.00 in the morning and leave at 11.00 or 11.30 at night. The salami, proscuitto, mortadella, parmesan cheese, pasta, olive oil and balsamic vinegar are all brought from home. The fresh vegetables are brought in locally.

During the year for each Grand Prix the team consumes enough to keep an army on the go, as the following list shows:

10-12 bottles of olive oil.
40 kg of pasta.
10-12 kg of parmesan cheese.
20 kg of proscuitto.
7 kg of salami.
8 kg of mortadella.
150 litres of mineral water –
    ¾ natural and ¼ fizzy.
40 bottles of wine.
45 kg of vegetables.
25 kg of meat.

Although Claudio and Bruno cook for the entire team, Schumacher's personal fitness guru, Indian maestro Balbir Singh supervises his meals. On the first day of free practice at Nurburgring, the Schumacher stomach was slightly out of sorts. Claudio comments, 'Mr Singh prepares Schumacher's lunch at mid-day, he usually has boiled rice and a selection of vegetables, such as onions, broccoli, carrots, and beans. It's a bit of a stir fry with soy sauce added, and a dash of curry powder of course. Schumacher wasn't very well yesterday, so he asked for a special lunch, he had a different combination of vegetables but still had curry powder.' Claudio raised his eyebrows and looked quizzically at me as much to say no wonder he has an upset tummy.

Despite his reservations about the wisdom of using curry powder as a cure for an upset stomach, Claudio admires the Schumacher balance of eating and driving. 'Schumacher is fast on the track and slow at eating – it's the ideal combination for him and the team.'

Stick your head in the kitchen at almost any time day or night and there is something cooking. On the Saturday at Nurburgring, it was fusilli pasta with a spicy tomato, bacon and onion sauce, followed by veal fillet with balsamic vinegar, oven roast potatoes, broccoli and grilled courgettes. Claudio and Bruno ensure that the meal is balanced, with nutritional ingredients essential for a hardworking team. The enticing aroma was floating across to the Ferrari garage, where the mechanics were preparing the car after a satisfying first day of free practice.

Bruno Romani keeps things on the boil.

The beginning of the European season brought some respite for Ferrari. It is easier to work on the car nearer to home and also easier to transport equipment. There are also more VIP visitors and new team members joining the European circuit, such as Shell truck driver, Norman Davenport who drives the fuel and lubricant to and from the track. Driving a large truck to and from a point in Europe doesn't appear to be a complex job, but appearances are deceptive. Norman, who has driven for Shell for 21 years, brings nine 200 litre drums of fuel and nine 25 litre drums of lubricant to each Grand Prix and he is quick to point out, 'There are strict regulations governing the transport of inflammable materials. We can only use certain ferries where we can park on the deck so if a lorry catches fire it can be pushed over the side. We also have limitations on when we can drive around Europe and also when we can board the ferries.

A Refuelling Issue
None of the Formula One teams wanted refuelling in Grands Prix, but it does make races less predictable.

We can't drive around Europe before 10 pm on a Sunday, or use the ferries on a Sunday, that is unless you are French when they seem to be able to use their ferries at anytime!' However, inspite of the restriction, Norman is very happy. 'It's a great job, I get to watch the races, and I'm my own boss, who could ask for more?'

Life isn't quite so simple for Jean King, who is in charge of logistics back at the Shell Research and Technology Centre at Thornton in Cheshire. It's a rarely know fact but the European Grand Prix season coincides almost exactly with pigeon racing in France, which starts in April and finishes in September. As Norman has pointed out, Shell have to use cargo ferries, but if there are more than 42 people on these cargo ferries, they change

status and become passenger ferries. So when the old pigeon fanciers get on board with their wives, kids and pigeons, it completely messes up Shell's ferry programme and the Shell lorries are pushed off.

There are books and books of rules and regulations which stem from the United Nations code of practice which governs the transport of hazardous goods by any mode in the world, and makes Jean King's life difficult to say the least as there are different rules for air, sea and road travel. For each Grand Prix Ferrari needs 1800 litres of race fuel, 200 litres for the generators on the trucks, 160 litres of engine oil, 60 litres of gearbox oil and when testing 300 litres of fuel per car per test day.

A Happy Shell Customer
Carlos Menem, President of Argentina, enjoys a day at the races as a guest of Shell.

Transport Traumas
Loading and unloading the Ferrari transporters is a demanding exercise when you're trying to move tons of equipment in the shortest space of time.

Working on the Move
The latest technological and communication systems in the Marlboro motorhome.

When you have a 'flyaway' the whole lot has to be flown out. The canny Jean King sends all the fuel and lubricants to the various Shell operating companies round the world, which costs less than using the official channels. The whole Grand Prix season costs about £75,000-£80,000 in transport excluding the tests or what gets used at the factory. 6,000 litres of fuel arrive by tanker at the Ferrari factory once a month. The combined testing at Fiorano and bench testing takes 1½ tons of engine oil and three or four times a year 500 litres of hydraulic oil arrives at the factory.

The organisation and customs clearance can be a nightmare. It takes up to two months to organise the paperwork for the Brazilian Grand Prix, with up to a week needed just to arrive, as the planes go via the rest of the world delivering goods before arriving at their final destination.

As Jean King says, 'When the team arrives on Monday or Tuesday, they panic if they don't see the fuel and oil, as they aren't going to get far without it. We had a real tense situation with McLaren in Australia. I had sent the fuel and lubricant off on 1 September for the race in November. Well, the team arrived, there was no fuel or lubricant, so mass panic ensued. I phoned around and discovered that the ship was still in the Pacific Ocean as the captain had decided to wander off and pick something else up. I called Shell Australia to ask whether they could blend some more. They could but it wouldn't have the same properties and so this may have caused a problem with FIA and the strict testing of fuel. I then phoned the Chairman of the shipping line to explain our predicament and he put out a call over the oceans to say "Come in number 32, your time is up" and in it came double quick! We had customs and excise waiting on the quayside and we managed to get it to the circuit in time.

'Things aren't much better in Europe. Our driver, Peter, was stopped and Shell fined in Italy because the local authorities had decided the day before that they wouldn't allow dangerous goods on the road. Each country has a right to change its regulations whenever it wants.'

•   •   •

The new Marlboro motorhome made its debut at the Nurburgring. Shiny, bright red and constantly preened and polished, it is a focal point in the paddock and a home for the official team press conferences, as well as for guests. As befits one of Ferrari's major sponsors, it was very impressive, with state of the art offices on the upper level with smart red and black leather chairs and a complex communication system of faxes, computers, modems, photocopiers and telephones including a small hood-like enclosure containing a telephone. Philip Morris employee and our host, Maurizio Arrivabene and his trusty team of Stefania who runs the office and collates and distributes press releases, Filippo who runs the motorhome and makes sure the guests are well cared for, and cooks cum bodyguards Ivano and Salvatore create a smooth and welcoming atmosphere.

• • •

Schumacher was second fastest on the Friday (even with or maybe because of an out of sorts stomach!) with Irvine wallowing down in fifteenth place. The cars were now fitted with the 1996 gearbox and a few new aerodynamic modifications after testing at Mugello.

A Home from Home
The Marlboro motorhome is a focal point in the paddock and a venue for the official team press conferences.

Irvine's car suffered a misfire, which remained a puzzle until a few laps before the end of the session. He was also suffering from a lack of testing. Most, if not all of the testing has been done by the number one driver, and it hasn't been easy for the Ulsterman to sit back and watch. He has to his credit accepted his lot with his usual dark, dry humour. When asked how he coped with Schumacher's supreme fitness, Irvine remarked, 'I just call him up, ask him how many press-ups he's done, and then ask him to do a few for me.'

Schumacher was, once again, cautious about his prospects for the race. 'I tried many different solutions and although the car is quite good I did not manage to get it perfectly balanced. I will try and improve tomorrow (qualifying) but the position I am in today is pretty much what I had expected. The testing at Mugello was positive but our progress can only be measured in tenths of a second and definitely not in "a few" seconds.'

With the media hanging around waiting for a disaster and the Fiat hierarchy sitting in the background, the man right in the middle of the heat was once again Jean Todt. It was difficult to hazard a guess at what he might be thinking. However, talk to him and behind the diffident air is a sensitive and highly perceptive professional. To allow the team to work with confidence he is happy to delegate responsibility to his managers and allow them to get on with things. But that doesn't mean he is unaware of what is going on. His quick mind picks up and tunes into other people's insecurities as well as their strengths and weaknesses.

At Nurburgring, his thoughts were on the team and his future. 'It is difficult to find good people, and that is why we have been slowly building the team, until now, when we are at the point of having very good people on board. It is then difficult to get people to work together efficiently and difficult to build stability. I like to be aware of and in control of everything.'

The man whose job epitomises the expression 'the buck stops here' is under relentless pressure, but he is unlikely to give it up until he has seen it through to the end and at least one World Championship. You don't build a team, take on the double World Champion as your number one driver and then turn your back on it and hand success on a plate to another man.

The Mugello test had been of vital importance in more than one way. Nigel Stepney takes up the story: 'I am spending more and more time on pit stops as it's an area of great importance. At the moment we can win or lose a race on pit stops. We have to practice on the race car as each car is slightly different and there are twenty people to coordinate in seven seconds. We were slow on pit stops, so after the South American races I analysed all the pit stops to see where we were making mistakes and losing time. Like Williams, Ferrari tends to fluctuate on pit stops, whereas Benetton is very quick. Shell then came to our rescue by shooting an ad all day at Mugello, which required us to do pit stops. It was the best practice we have ever had.'

Ferrari Chairman Luca di Montezemolo visited the team and gave his interim headmaster's report on the progress of his star players to date. 'I am very pleased with Schumacher, he is not only quick and strong, but he has a deep good relationship with the team during the week as well as at weekends. It is the best example of the driver and team working well. Jean Todt is straight and loyal and I am happy with his work.'

Comfort

Ferrari Chairman Luca di Montezemolo, gives his full support to the man taking the strain, Team Principal Jean Todt.

He was also supportive of Eddie Irvine, the man who has to be content to be number two. 'It is not easy to be number two to Schumacher. Eddie doesn't get much testing done but he is nice and co-operative. I'm very pleased with the drivers, now I need some results and I want to achieve our goal of winning two races.'

John Barnard still had Montezemolo's full support, even if the Ferrari Chairman let it be known that he expected close co-operation and results from his investment in the office in England. 'I expect all the elements to be a better package in 1996. Last year the car was easy to drive, it was good in the rain, but this year's car seems to be very nervous. I expected a better chassis. I'm not altogether happy to see Williams in front of us by more than a second. Having said this we are all working together with a good, positive spirit. John [Barnard] is aware of the pressure by now, and we leave him alone to work in peace in England. I am very pleased to have John Barnard but I hope he realises that Italy is not so far from England.'

Back in England, John Barnard was wrestling with his desire for perfection and the lack of time to achieve it. He wanted to continue using titanium for the gearbox casing, but the pressure of time had forced him to relinquish his drive to push Formula One forward into the future, and develop new ideas that in the long run will prove better and more efficient. Like a lot of new concepts the teething problems were not difficult to rectify, but it needed that elusive element, time, and time is one thing you just don't have in Formula One racing. 'The gearbox starts its life as machine plates and some of the types of joint were not good; we made corner welds which were difficult as we couldn't wrap them or overlap them. What we really needed were some more plates with this flange machined on rather than welded on. It was a simple design change but we ran out of time. It's a bit disappointing that we have opted to go for steel plates this time. We know that steel is easier to weld and so it is an easier bet. But I know that we could easily make the titanium part if we could just make the design change on the plate. Now the steel is in the system, we'll have to work through it and then return to titanium.'

Rubber Power
Piles of Goodyear tyres are lined up ready to go into action during the Nurburgring Grand Prix weekend.

At the Nurburgring Schumacher proved that he is worth the $25 million that Ferrari is paying him and after qualifying third, came second behind the Williams of Jacques Villeneuve in the race. It was an unexpected result that delighted the thousands of Schumacher fans who crowded round the podium to celebrate.

Schumacher declared, 'I didn't expect to run so close to Williams. I am pleased for the mechanics and all the crew.' Part of the reason for his determination was a phone call from his brother Ralf, who had come third in his race in Japan and who asked his brother to beat this. He promptly did! Montezemolo was ecstatic and celebrated with the team, although like everyone he tried to play down the next race at Imola. Schumacher was about to race for Ferrari in Italy, for the first time. After this result the *tifosi* were hot for more, and nothing would dampen their spirits as they prepared to make the journey to Imola.

Imola, like Monza, is a little bit different. The *tifosi* follow Ferrari to the ends of the earth, but when Formula One comes to Italy, they really push the boat out. Flags, banners and scarves litter the banks and stands around the race track, and in keeping with Italy's reputation as a Mecca of style, Antonio Ghini, Director of Communications ensures that the Ferrari fan clubs use the right marque, logo and colours. 'For years millions of products were produced and sold unofficially, but now we have developed a close relationship with the fan clubs and we ensure that they have the right products at the races. The image of the exclusive Ferrari marque must be conserved and maintained.'

Such is the passion of the fans that Claudio Berro had to devise an ingenious way of getting Schumacher in and out of the track. 'We had three or four plain clothed policemen to help us, and we could use a police escort if necessary. He used to arrive at Fiorano by car and then we would transport him by helicopter to the circuit. We had a Fiat Ulysses with darkened windows to transport him from the helicopter to the track.'

Eddie Irvine got a round of applause from the media before he had even set foot in Imola. He spoke in Italian at the Fiorano press conference on the Thursday before the race. This was definitely scoring brownie points off team-mate Schumacher. Schumacher was again being cautious and declared, 'Imola is a very bumpy track. Our car has problems over bumps as the aerodynamic system is not perfect. I expect problems to get the car handling right. The chances are we won't be as successful as we were at Nurburgring. We need time to translate the changes we've made in the wind tunnel to the car. The car has potential.' Schumacher also paid tribute to Ferrari Designer, John Barnard. 'I think Barnard is very good. The success we had at Benetton is due to a certain extent to him, as he started the car.' (Barnard worked at Benetton for eighteen months until the end of 1991.) This was another example of how Schumacher protects his colleagues who are in the firing line. His ability to quickly paste over any cracks in team loyalty was going to prove vital in the months to come.

Sea of Support
The Ferrari team is never short of support, with the fans turning up in their thousands to get a glimpse of their heroes on the track.

A year in Formula One is like a lifetime in any other industry. Last year the fans hated Schumacher, this year they are warming to him, if not actually loving him. 'I feel part of Ferrari. It's nice that the fans have changed their mind about me. The fact that 99% of the Italian fans are behind me is a great motivation. It's six months since I joined Ferrari and I expected it to be difficult. I needed time at Benetton to understand the people and it is the same here, although the people here are warmer and it is easier to get closer to the team. People express their emotions more easily.'

There is a great family tradition in Italy and it spreads to every aspect of the Italian lifestyle. In Italy the football teams always spend the night before a match together, to build team spirit. The Ferrari team is the same. The night before the team left for Imola, the drivers and management had dinner with Montezemolo, who impressed calm and optimism on them in equal quantities.

By this stage Jean Todt had decided that the car would not be rebuilt, but that they would work on improving the aerodynamics. He said that there should be improvements by mid-season.

One of the improvements was seen a little before mid-season. The V10 engine had been consistent and good, but there was a new improved version due at Imola which proved to be reliable, although the top speed was still a little way off its competitors.

However, doubts were pushed aside as Schumacher took his first pole position for Ferrari at Imola. He pushed Damon Hill off the number one spot in the closing moments of the session, before spinning to a halt with a broken left rear track rod as he turned into the Tamburello corner. Jean Todt was very happy with the pole position. 'This result has come from hard work and a combination of the improved aerodynamics, a more drivable engine and of course, the power of Michael Schumacher.'

The Rat Pack
Michael Schumacher under seige from the media at the Nurburgring.

Giorgio Ascanelli was worried about the brakes rather than the engine. They had decided not to run the new version of the brakes in the race, due to caution rather than any actual problem. After the second practice Ascanelli, wiping sweat from his furrowed brow said, 'I'm not happy with the way things are going. I'm not worried about the race, but I am worried that the brakes won't last the race.' It was an observation borne out from long experience. Schumacher crossed the line in second place and his car ground to a halt as the brakes gave out.

Imola is hard on brakes, but that wasn't the only reason Schumacher's had failed. Barnard explains, 'When Schumacher came to us I asked him, "Would you like a three-pedal or two-pedal

Speedy Getaway

Exit from the pits for Eddie Irvine during the Grand Prix at Imola, where he finished fourth after a poor start.

car?" He said "I had three at Benetton and I don't see the need for two pedals." I said, "Are you sure?" to which he replied "Yes". Then Eddie Irvine comes along and says "Oh, I've had two pedals at Jordan, it's the way to go." This means you have the brake and throttle on the foot and on the steering wheel there are paddles for operating the gears and clutch. It's a clutch rather like motorbikes have on their handlebars. Anyway, Eddie had been testing somewhere shortly after the first race, jumped out of his car and for some reason the team wanted to pop Schumacher in quickly before the end of the test. The car still had Eddie's two-pedal system in it. They asked Schumacher if he minded using two pedals and he said "No, I don't mind, I'll drive it for a few laps." He gets out a few laps later and says "I want a two-pedal car." So we're all back to two pedals. Now that is great but the problem with two pedals is that you can go on the brake pedal before you come off the throttle. You can position the brake pedal more to the left so you can use your left foot for braking. The problem is that Formula One cars are very sensitive to

Time for a Laugh
Michael Schumacher and team-mate Eddie Irvine find time to share a private joke before the more serious business of racing starts.

change, just lifting off the throttle gives you something like ½G braking force. You probably don't use ½G in a normal car even when stopping sharply. To get a smooth change in a Formula One car you can still be flat on the throttle when you start braking. Once you feel the brakes bind you ease off, it's much smoother but it eats the brakes alive. At circuits like Imola which is a heavy duty braking circuit, the disc is wearing out along with the pad. On a road car the pads are wearing out 10 times earlier than the disc. Schumacher was lucky at Imola, coupled with the fact that he is just an outstanding driver and sensitive to every change in the car. However, he'll need to be aware of going a bit easy on the brakes at heavy braking circuits.'

Eddie Irvine finished fourth and for the first time both drivers were in the points. Things were looking up, although new modifications were still needed, not least with the clutch which was not proving reliable and led to the difficult starts that both drivers were experiencing.

However, Schumacher's success entranced the Italian population. Over ten million people watched the Grand Prix on television in Italy. That was a 55% share of viewing figures and an absolute record for Formula One. There had been nothing like it since eight million people had watched Prost when he drove for Ferrari in the Italian Grand Prix. It showed that people were once again believing in Ferrari.

• • •

After Imola, the mood was buoyant and optimistic as the team set out for Monaco. Monaco is less about motor racing and more about parties. The motorhomes gather round the port area like colourful Lego kits at a childrens' party. The big boats anchor out in the bay and the rich kids go to play in a big way.

Cerruti held a fashion show on the beach in front of the famous Carlton Hotel in Cannes, and Asprey provided some spectacular jewellery for the occasion. Michael and Corinna Schumacher were guests of honour, along with Prince Albert of Monaco, Nino and Chantal Cerruti, Edward and Christina Asprey, Roman Polanski, David Ginola and an assortment of weird and wonderful young actors and actresses.

The high sophistication of the catwalk may seem far removed from the dirt and oil environment of motor racing, but in many ways designing clothes for a Formula One team is more complex than designing for a supermodel. Patrick Banville is the Cerruti designer who has taken up the challenge of making clothes that are not only stylish but easy to wear. 'The Formula One project is an interpretation of the Cerruti style married to Ferrari. It had to be ruled by practicality and comfort, but still be elegant and classic. We drew on the old classics like the 1940s American pilots, for our waterproof leather bomber jackets. All the team wear had to be comfortable, so we chose fabrics like jersey that is easy for comfort. At the same time we didn't want the team looking like they'd come from Mars, so the extra movement was obtained through the subtle use of pleats to increase movement, whilst still maintaining the basic elegant shape. We also had a heavy emphasis on nylon as it often rains!'

Ferrari Team Principal, Jean Todt was a guest as well as being a Cerruti customer. As he says, 'I have dressed in Cerruti clothes for years, it's part of my lifestyle. I like nice, good quality things. Once I've found something I like I don't change, and Cerruti combines elegance with comfort. There is comfort in developing good habits.' It was this philosophy that led to the Cerruti becoming a part of the Ferrari family. Todt was unhappy with the team uniform when he joined Ferrari in 1993. He thought Cerruti would be the most suitable supplier and so he talked to Luca di Montezemolo, who agreed and in 1994 Cerruti became the official stylists for Ferrari wear, and now as the team travel and work they reflect the unmistakable Cerruti style of elegance and comfort. It's a relationship that has expanded to include the new sportswear line available through exclusive outlets, including La Galleria at Maranello.

Nino Cerruti is a perfectionist who oversees everything, and aims to provide clothes for people to wear, rather than for a stick-thin 6ft tall supermodel. The Ferrari team wear is a reflection of modern clothes for the modern man. But like Ferrari, Nino Cerruti is also a romantic and declares, 'Ferrari reflects the heroic glamour found in romantic films, and we have sought to perpetuate the myth and produce a line of merchandise that is exclusive but also captures the magic of the team.'

High Fashion
Top fashion house Cerruti shows off its latest designs on the catwalk.

A few minutes before the models started to parade down the catwalk, Asprey Sponsorship Manager, Rosalind Milani-Gallieni appeared holding a stunning gold leopard broach encrusted with canary yellow and white diamonds, for Chantal Cerruti to wear.

While the movers and shakers were partying the night away, Marlboro put on a special 'Marlboro Experience' for the fans, with the drivers in attendance. Michael Schumacher went along on Saturday afternoon, and Eddie Irvine on Friday and Saturday evenings, to give the fans a chance to see their heroes at close quarters.

Monaco may be a party town, but it was impossible to escape from the racing. Wherever you stand in Monaco, the roar of the Formula One engine can be heard – this is somewhat unnerving when you are standing in the local supermarket buying vegetables. But it is part of the legend that is Monaco. Like Spa or Monza, but for different reasons, it is the one place where drivers want to win more than anywhere else. Ferrari, at least on paper, should have been in with a chance of winning. Schumacher's Race Engineer, Ignazio Lunetta was in an upbeat mood. The race engineer is the man closest to the driver. He cares only about helping his guy to win, even against his team-mate. It is a close and trusting relationship as the race engineer is the man who translates what the driver says into changes on the car. The quiet, unassuming Lunetta had worked with Jean Alesi before Michael Schumacher arrived at Ferrari, and was finding Schumacher a very different cup of tea. 'Schumacher is more in one line, he pushes a lot and he works very hard. Alesi was lazier whereas Schumacher is constantly stimulating work. The biggest problem is to get to know Schumacher. It is very important that I can read his thoughts and get to know exactly how he likes the car in various situations. At the moment I am doing the tests with him as well as the races. He understands things very quickly and works a lot, but he still needs to be guided as he is quite perplexed a lot of the time. However, I have never seen anyone as constantly quick as Schumacher.'

Like his team-mates, Lunetta was quietly confident about Monaco. 'The engine is good, the aerodynamics have improved and the car is easier to drive. One of our biggest problems is the clutch which is difficult to control. A little movement and it over-reacts and creates wheelspin.'

Back in England, John Barnard was also hopeful. 'The main thing I hope for is that Schumacher can qualify on the front somewhere and then he'll have a good chance as it's a very difficult track to pass on.'

Looking Good
Nino Cerruti, head of the famous fashion house discusses the new look Cerruti race wear with Ferrari Team Principal Jean Todt.

Obligingly, Schumacher qualified on pole position. He outpaced Hill by half a second, an incredible feat on the tight Monegasque circuit. However, he shot himself in the foot by waving to the crowd when the qualifying session wasn't quite over and Gerhard Berger, who was still trying to go for a quick lap, crashed into the back of the Ferrari. Schumacher later apologised to Berger for going too slow.

After two dry days of practice, it poured with rain on race day and on the first lap of the race having made a poor start, Schumacher made a mistake at the right hander after the Loews hairpin, getting halfway onto the inside kerb, then pushed the car into the guard-rail. It was all over before it had hardly begun.

Schumacher to his eternal credit took the blame full on the chin. He returned to the team garage and apologised to everyone. Lunetta says, 'He came in looking like a beaten dog. He was devastated and said sorry to everyone. We forgave him, he gives such a lot, and he is only human, he has to make mistakes sometimes.'

Team Principal Jean Todt put it succinctly as he commented, 'Michael accepts errors from others, but not from himself.' Meanwhile Eddie Irvine had qualified seventh but had a disappointing race after being given an illegal push start by the marshals and then having Salo and Hakkinen crash into him and end his race.

End of Monaco. Deep depression. It was quiet on the way home as everyone pondered on what might have been, and wondered when the next good chance would come along.

The Rain in Spain
An overjoyed Michael Schumacher celebrates his historic win in Spain by drowning Jean Todt in champagne.

However, there is nothing as contrary as Formula One and disaster can turn into victory in the space of a couple of weeks and that was about to happen. Next stop was Barcelona and the drive of a lifetime.

To say it rains in Spain is like saying it snows in Switzerland. There is normal rain and then there is Spanish rain which falls in torrents. King Juan Carlos turned up for the race and Schumacher took him for a spin round the track, pointing out the dangers of driving in the wet! From third position on the grid, Schumacher made a poor start due to the temperamental clutch and was briefly down to sixth before overtaking the hapless Hill, who was soon out of the race. He then took on Berger and Alesi. By the twelfth lap Schumacher had left the others behind, was out in front and in a class of his own. He pulled away from the others at a rate of four seconds a lap. It was awesome to see and put Schumacher firmly up there with the all-time greats. The most recent comparison had been Senna's remarkable drive at the European Grand Prix at Donington in 1993. Team-mate Eddie Irvine qualified sixth and spun out of the race after one lap. It was a shame because Ferrari had clearly got the set-up and race strategy perfect and could have had a one-two finish.

Time to Celebrate
Corinna Schumacher joins in with the celebrations after her husband's stunning win in Spain.

Edward Asprey will never forget it, as by chance, nearly the whole Asprey hierarchy were present to watch the race. 'It was a simply staggering drive by Schumacher, we were all stunned by the drama. We had never expected to witness such sheer talent and guts at such close quarters. It was the indisputable proof of Schumacher's greatness. He just left everyone else standing. It was as though the rain didn't exist. We celebrated with a serious bottle of champagne on the way back.'

As Schumacher took the chequered flag, the Ferrari garage became the scene of a kind of rain dance as the team members celebrated their joy. For Ignazio Lunetta, there was the promise of a brand new Vespa from Ferrari Chairman, Luca di Montezemolo to celebrate the victory; for Giorgio Ascanelli the great satisfaction of knowing that the race strategy of two pit stops had worked to perfection.

Montezemolo was overjoyed, Todt relieved and happy. The media started to talk about World Championships. It was a good job no-one could look into the future. Spain was a high which would be remembered fondly as the team's fortunes took a dive in the next two months. There were still problems to sort out; a new higher nose for the Canadian Grand Prix; a clutch that wasn't so difficult to use, and other small modifications to improve the aerodynamics. On their own these were problems that could easily be sorted out, but combined they were about to become overwhelming and put the team under the kind of pressure that, in the past, had blown it apart.

CHAPTER FOUR

The Summer of Discontent

'Every time I wake up I struggle

because we are not winning.

But the important thing is

to keep on trying...'

Giorgio Ascanelli
Ferrari Chief Engineer after the French Grand Prix

Not even in their worst nightmares could any of the Ferrari team have imagined that the next two months would be as disastrous as they turned out to be.

It all started on a fairly positive note, with the debut of the re-designed raised nose in Canada. This won the approval of both drivers. Schumacher said, 'It's worth between a tenth and two-tenths of a second and more comfortable.' Irvine added, 'The car is more consistent between entry and exit of corners with the new nose.'

There were also some aerodynamic modifications carried out at Maranello, which made the car less sensitive. After qualifying things continued to look hopeful. Schumacher qualified third behind the two Williams with Hill on pole position. Irvine qualified a highly credible fifth.

The atmosphere within the team was calm and relaxed. Pino Gozzo rustled up a penne arrabbiata and hamburgers for Giorgio Ascanelli and Gustav Brunner when they arrived late from the airport, and the mechanics were in a good mood. Everyone expected the cars to show progress, although no one was in any doubt that the win in Spain had been down to

Man on the Move
Pino Gozzo, Ferrari's travel organiser, keeps the team moving like clockwork during the Grand Prix weekends.

Schumacher's brilliance rather than the car. As Nigel Stepney says, 'The win in Spain doesn't reflect our true position. That was down to Schumacher. He was brilliant to watch. He overcomes a lot of problems and is in the same league as Senna. Drivers like that are few and far between.'

However, neither Ferrari driver finished the race. Stepney explains, 'We didn't look good on full tanks during the Sunday morning warm up. There was a problem with the brake balance and the starter motor broke on Schumacher's car only thirty seconds before the grid was due to start.'

In fact, Schumacher was forced to start from the back of the grid, and even though he was up to seventh by the time of his pitstop on lap 41, he was struggling with the brake balance. Eddie Irvine lasted a mere two laps before an unidentified flying object hit his car and the push rod broke, forcing him to retire from the race. Stepney comments dryly, 'When Irvine's push rod went, he came into the pits smelling like a barbecue. This was due to the fact that there is a plank of wood underneath the car and this was quietly roasting!'

John Barnard explains the technical reasons for Schumacher's race problems. 'There was a problem early on in the season with starting the engine. The theory was that in the drive-by-wire throttle system, you don't have the hydraulic pressure to operate the throttle until the engine fires. This means that the engine throttle is in a closed position, unless you can physically get in and mechanically open the throttle, which can cause air starvation during the starting procedure. However, to counteract this the engine people at Maranello, as far as I understand, drilled air bypass holes in the throttle mechanism, which should have allowed enough air in to start the engine. We thought we had overcome the engine problem, but we obviously hadn't.

'We had noticed the driveshaft problem during the previous year. We found we were getting a bent driveshaft on Berger's car, but not Alesi's car (he was using the foot clutch). We started to make a bigger driveshaft to cope with it, but at the same time Berger didn't like the hand clutch and so returned to a three-pedal car. I carried on this year with the same size driveshaft as we'd been using last year. I advised them in Italy that we should have an electronic filter on the clutch take up, as by that time both our drivers wanted hand clutches and two pedals. This was done, but then people at Maranello were under the impression that the electronic filter that had been placed in the clutch was illegal, and so they took it out. I was told that they had asked Charlie Whiting (FIA's technical delegate) and he said it was illegal, but I don't know if that actually happened. The bottom line was that we had a difficult clutch which had a sharp and unpredictable take up and the drivers were unable to make smooth starts. With the removal of the electronic filter we then had a very severe engagement which effectively overstressed the driveshafts.

'When you have a car full of fuel, as we did on the grid at Canada, that adds extra stress. Schumacher had to make two racing starts as he couldn't start the car first time. When he came in for his pit stop on lap forty one, he was told to just drop the clutch as it (the clutch) was a problem. That resulted in another racing start and again having refuelled that was a strain. When he got to the end of the pit lane, the driveshaft had had enough and that was that.'

Ascanelli was more succinct. 'Canada was a race to forget,' he said afterwards, the disappointment still etched on his face as he went on to say, 'Canada should have been one of our best circuits, but we had four or five silly problems which quite frankly were all foreseeable. We have to improve our reliability. Schumacher deserves better. However, there are only twenty four hours in a day and we will keep on with the learning curve. I have to say that overall I'm happier with the car and happier in general with the team. We still lack confidence and tend to panic which is what we did when we had the problem with Irvine's car. The most likely explanation for the broken push rod was impact with a foreign object, but we still tended to go into panic. We haven't got it together yet.'

Ascanelli is hard on himself as well as with the rest of the team. When the team is at home at Maranello, he arrives at work at 7.30 am, downs a black coffee and starts to work through the post, answers his e-mail, and then has meetings to discuss the progress of the car. His office at Maranello overlooks the three bays where the mechanics work on the cars, so at any time he can gaze down and see what is going on.

Not Amused
Ferrari's Director of Communications, Antonio Ghini, reflects on the team's problems as they live through the Summer of Discontent.

● ● ●

Star Attraction
The Ferrari F310 is the centre of attention before the start of a race.

The French Grand Prix is held at Magny Cours, just outside a small town called Nevers, an appropriate name for the coming weekend, which didn't have the most auspicious of starts. Giorgio Ascanelli looked as if he had been three rounds with Mike Tyson. He had in fact been a victim of the recent, violent floods that had hit Italy, when he had been washed off a rock and hit his chin and face. His mood matched his physical state. The pressure was on and there hadn't been time to assemble the cars before leaving for the circuit – this was something that would cost the team dearly when Irvine's front turning vanes were found to be illegal after qualifying. It was all very much a case of wait and see, caused in some part by the lateness of the car. Effectively, Ferrari were being forced to try out various important new modifications either at tests just before the races or at the races. It was causing huge reliability problems. As Ascanelli says, 'Problems occur when you are trying to do something different and you push your luck. First you have to fix the 300 kilometre problem, then the 500 and then the 800, then the thousands. Everything is new this year and so we are bound to have teething problems.'

Ascanelli didn't agree that Irvine's push rod failure had just been down to bad luck. 'You can't say whether it was down to luck. We lost the push rod due to the impact of a nut or bolt from another car. We learnt something from this and reinforced the vulnerable part, so the problem hasn't reoccurred in testing, even though we have hit something similar. Having solved this, it will take something for the same thing to happen again. That is a normal development in motor racing. You always have to make parts to dimensions that you know will withstand the strongest stress that they can come under. You cannot have the luxury of over-reinforcing the car, otherwise it will become like a tank, and that is not a racing car.'

The good news was that John Barnard and his team had already started to design the 1997 car, and that would mean valuable extra testing time. It was difficult to be specific about what was wrong with the 1996 car, but lessons had been learnt. As John Barnard says, 'We did something with the aerodynamics that, when the car was in the wind tunnel, indicated it improved efficiency. We had a double floor area underneath the forward part of the side pod. The aerodynamics maps, which measure how sensitive the car is, appeared to be very similar to the 1995 car which was driveable and comfortable. But on the track it gave the symptoms of being much more sensitive. The floor gave us aerodynamic problems which I am not going to go into, as it is useful information that we found out the hard way. By the time you discover this type of problem during the season, you are already behind. Naturally you try and fix the problem, which means forward development is difficult. Add to that the pressure of being a part of Ferrari and if you don't stay cool things can get out of hand.'

Eddie Irvine, as is his wont, managed to produce a few lighter moments. The Friday Five at Five press conference, when the gathered media are unleashed on five nominated team members, was a little less 'dry' than normal. The big discussion was whether nose plasters, as seen on rugby and football players, improved breathing. It was suggested that they could be useful in motor racing. Olivier Panis, winner of the Monaco Grand Prix, confessed to having tried them and found they did improve his breathing if not his speed, at which point Irvine turned towards him and said with understatement, 'No, it just makes you look like a dick.'

Things turned serious when qualifying for the French GP got underway on the Saturday. It was an electrifying session with Schumacher claiming pole position after Hill, with only a few minutes left, tried to claim for himself. He was faster than Schumacher over the first two sectors of the track, but lost time over the last third. The German domination of Europe was complete when the German football team reached the finals of Euro 96. Schumacher joked, 'We have quite a few injuries, I may have to step in.' His parting shot was that the new clutch (German, of course) on the car was proving to be reliable and efficient.

Irvine lost his sense of humour when the front turning vanes on his car were proved to be illegal after a complaint from a rival team member to Charlie Whiting, who investigated the complaint and upheld it. Schumacher's car was passed. Two questions flashed across my mind. How do you spot a 15mm difference in a racing car in the space of a few seconds? And how did it happen?

Although this turning vane was a Maranello development, John Barnard had his own theory on the first question. 'I suspect that there was a picture somewhere in a magazine which had a front shot of the car. There are always set pieces on a racing car which act as reference points. You know the width across the front wheels, the size of the front tyres and so on, so you can very quickly scale up the other parts of the car. If you look at enough Formula One cars you tend to know where everything finishes. If something looks high you tend to get a rule out and start measuring it and you scale it and then you say, "I think that front turning vane is illegal." The next stop is to go to Charlie Whiting and ask him to check it. If it is outside the legal limit, you're in trouble and that is what happened.'

Man to Man
Luca di Montezemolo discusses with Michael Schumacher the ins and outs of driving a Ferrari Formula One car.

Ascanelli was his usual blunt self concerning the second question. 'The fact is that before going to France, the car was never put together at Maranello, it was put together in France and it was never checked. It shouldn't have happened, there were many mistakes from many points of view and you pay for it on the circuit. In twelve years of motor racing, I've faced many legality problems and this wasn't the worst, but it still shouldn't have happened.'

On race day, there was the unusual event of having a Ferrari on pole position and a Ferrari last on the grid, due to Irvine's disqualification for the illegal turning vane. That wasn't to last long. On the warm up lap, Schumacher's engine blew up in a puff of smoke and his race was over before it had even begun.

He didn't even have time to pull over before the Italian media picked up their poisoned pens and went to town. It was a black day for the Italian racing giants. Schumacher climbed out of the car with a thunderous expression on his face. He later admitted, 'When I got out of the car, I was so angry I could have hit someone.'

Kings and Princes

The Duke of Kent and his daughter Lady Helen Windsor are shown the ins and outs of the Ferrari F310 by World Champion Michael Schumacher.

To make matters worse for Ferrari, Irvine dropped out after five laps with gearbox problems. *La Gazzetta dello Sport* called the French Grand Prix a funeral procession, rather than a race. True to form the media soon started to call for heads to roll, and at the top of their list was Jean Todt. However, unlike in the past Ferrari was determined to keep its problems in house and not make public sacrifices. Ferrari Chairman Luca di Montezemolo was hot on the phone to Todt as soon as the Ferraris were out of the race. He was bitterly disappointed, but reconfirmed his faith in Todt and the team. They would sort out their problems by working hard and sticking together.

The one consolation for Schumacher was that he made it home in time to watch the German football team win Euro 96. The man I felt most sorry for was Shell's 'Stormin' Norman, who having lugged about 2,000 litres of fuel and over 200 litres of lubricant to the track, was last seen hauling it all back on the lorry.

Back at Maranello, the inquest started. It was found that the engine problem was caused by incorrectly machined piston heads. Of course, it wasn't to be found only on that engine and the mechanics had to work day and night to check all the other engines. There is an inspection department at Maranello which makes spot checks on all items. It would be impossible to check every single part and would require at least 40 people working full time. This would cost a fortune and would be impractical. The pressures in Formula One mean that things can and

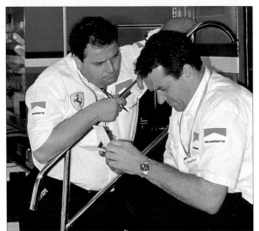

Problem Solving

Giorgio Ascanelli and Nigel Stepney try and work out what is going wrong after another disaster at Silverstone.

do go wrong. The problem was that things were going wrong in a fairly catastrophic manner.

Ascanelli was as pragmatic as ever. 'Every time I wake up I struggle because we are not winning. But the important thing is to keep on trying. I believe that if we concentrate on doing the best job and don't worry about the pressure, sooner or later we will win. Personally, I'd like to achieve it sooner!'

• • •

The pressure was on. The legendary Fiat boss Gianni Agnelli was due to visit the team as was Montezemolo. There was no room for mistakes. Being placed under this kind of pressure would be enough to make even the most experienced mechanic nervous. After all, Agnelli is one of the most influential men in Italy, far more important than the transitory prime ministers who come and go at regular intervals. And Montezemolo is his man and their chief. It is in this type of situation that Schumacher comes into his own. His focused, teutonic nature allows no interruptions during Grand Prix weekend. He refuses to do any interviews outside of the official FIA interviews which take place on the Friday before the race, after qualifying and after the race. He undertakes only minimal sponsorship activities such as the Marlboro Experience in Monaco, or brief appearances for Shell and Asprey to meet their guests. His attitude is that he is paid to race and win, and his energy must be concentrated on this task.

To this end he does not allow disturbances in the garage, and that includes the presence of bosses. If he thinks Agnelli or Montezemolo are making people nervous he will ask them to leave. He did so with Luciano Benetton at Benetton and he will repeat the exercise at Ferrari. Exuding the determination and confidence of a double World Champion, no one questions him. As John Barnard has said, 'Schumacher's ability to impose calm on the team has been vital.' Never more so than at Silverstone.

The team stayed at The Saracen's Head Hotel in Towcester, which has been team headquarters for a number of years. The only problem is that it overlooks the road. Schumacher was not impressed. He arrived at the reception desk to complain about the noise. The receptionists were equally unimpressed by the double and current World Champion. They had regular guests who had already booked in. A stand off situation was reached which was only relieved when the Italians (as ever) found a compromise and moved another couple of people around to allow Schumacher to have a quiet room in which he could sleep.

It was at Silverstone that Edward Asprey realised what it meant to be part of the most glamorous, adored team in Formula One. 'I was walking through the gates to the paddock, when a young boy came up and thrust his autograph book at me, along with a picture of Ferrari for me to sign. I was taken aback and said "But I'm not part of the actual team." He just said, "But you're part of Ferrari", and I realised what it meant to be part of the mystique, power and image that is Ferrari.'

At 10.50 am on the Friday morning Montezemolo walked into the Ferrari garage and greeted everyone. At 11.10 am, ten minutes into the practice session, Claudio Berro and Giorgio Ascanelli took their places on the pit wall. There was still no sign of Gianni Agnelli, who was having trouble getting through security! Bernie Ecclestone and co. introduced a new system for the 1996 season, which involved everyone with pit and paddock passes going through a machine

The Organiser
Team Manager Claudio Berro (later to become Chief Press Officer) finds time to smile as he listens into the commentary on the team radio between practice sessions during a Grand Prix weekend.

turnstyle, into which they would swipe special cards, like credit cards, which recorded their arrival and departure. It was designed, with valid reasons, to stop people from handing passes through the fence once they had got into the paddock. But it was having an off day.

Eventually Agnelli was allowed through and he walked onto the pit wall at 11.20 am with his VIP party. Todt remained in place studying the monitor in front of him. The tension in the air was almost tangible.

With practice over, Agnelli delivered his verdict. 'We are at the Williams home, so it is normal they are faster. They have the best car and start as favourites. We place our hopes in the last part of the season and next year. The World Championship is impossible. We hope to win two or three races. We are doing everything to keep Schumacher and we believe he will stay with us for a long time.'

Agnelli is rather like an agnostic Pope, in that he has absolute power. This is demonstrated by his ability to manipulate and achieve his will through quiet manoeuvres, rather than the usual Latin way of noisy overt demonstrations of police escorts and loud exclamations. A presence such as his is rare to see. Even the normally, contentious media are respectful and quiet, and uncritical. After his few, succinct words, he duly faded into the mists, leaving Montezemolo to take over. Montezemolo ate with the team on Friday evening and stayed until after the qualifying session on Saturday. He was also determined to impose calm and rational order on the team. Despite the problems everyone was looking to the future and Schumacher is a key element. 'We are extremely pleased with Michael Schumacher and it is important to know that he is pleased with Ferrari. I've told Todt to start to talk to him. I like the idea of having Schumacher for three years.' In the end Schumacher signed on a four-year contract up to and including 1999.

At Silverstone Schumacher qualified third behind the two Williams. But there was more than a second gap between Williams and Ferrari. Schumacher explained that he had tested various new parts at Monza, a new gearbox, a new suspension, and worked on improving the aerodynamics, all of which had promising results. However, as Ross Brawn was later to remark, 'change for change's sake is not good for team progress.' The most important thing is to make a change because you are absolutely one hundred per cent sure it is an improvement.

Jean Todt was less than happy. Under pressure from the media he exclaimed, 'I feel like I'm under trial in a court.' It wasn't an exaggeration. The media love scapegoats and Todt and

A Guiding Hand
Michael Schumacher's manager, Wili Weber, offers consolation by reminding Michael of his bank balance.

A Personnel Job

The youngest senior manager at Ferrari is 31-year-old Stefano Domenicali. Young, bright and enthusiastic he is in charge of personnel, as well as the Mugello race track. Bearing in mind the pressure on Ferrari from the outside world, it is a difficult and demanding job. It is made more complex by the fact that Ferrari, unlike the other Formula One teams is not a stand-alone operation; it produces high-performance road cars, and this means that the two areas must be in harmony from the point of view of structure and organisation. As Domenicali says, 'The fundamental thing is that our strategy for our Sports Department fits into the overall strategy of Ferrari. It is vital we have one united image.'

In previous years when the going has got tough, the in-fighting has taken over and heads have rolled. After Montezemolo took over, he was determined to introduce clear strategy and modern management methods into the company. In line with achieving this objective, young, up and coming businessmen like Domenicali have been employed to inject international,

Personnel Officer and Director of the Mugello test track, Stefano Domenicali keeps tabs on the team.

methodical business techniques into Ferrari. Domenicali may be young, but he has the maturity to withstand the tempests caused by problems and place a steady hand on the tiller, so that explosive situations between personnel are avoided. He is also building for the future. 'We are one of the youngest teams in Formula One. In the short term

difficulties arise due to lack of experience, but we have huge potential. We are investing long-term and we must look to the future in a logical and calm manner.'

It is difficult to be serene when the world is falling apart around your ears, but Domenicali has kept his finger on the pulse to avoid personnel problems. 'My job is to manage and talk to people. Every person needs to be managed differently. Understanding people and their various needs is very interesting and stimulating work, and I need to identify potential problems before they arise. Ferrari is different to how it was ten years ago. Now we have many different nationalities who all have a different way of doing things. Some people have difficult, complex characters and I have to act as a negotiator and smooth things over. To achieve this I try and enter into each person's psyche and understand what motivates them. Then you have to decide whether to resolve situations in a soft or hard way. The best way is to sit down and talk, but sometimes we have to remind people of their responsibilities.'

In Action
Grip and turn as the Ferrari F310 takes a tight corner.

The Boss of Bosses
Fiat boss Gianni Agnelli checks
on Eddie Irvine.

Barnard were in the front line, although both men remained supportive of each other and refused to attribute any blame for the team's misfortunes on one person. Todt declared, 'We are part of a team, it's our fault as a team, not one person's fault.'

After saying that the French Grand Prix was the blackest day of his life, Todt could not have imagined that things would get worse. They did.

Schumacher lasted three laps before suffering mechanical failure from a dry brake fitting. Irvine lasted only another two laps before he was forced to retire with a broken differential bearing. Schumacher was bemused rather than angry. 'We did a race distance in the last two tests, running reliably on Friday and Saturday. And then we do just three laps today. There is just no logic to it at all.'

There were cries of sabotage and foul play. However, the truth was somewhat different. A combination of the pain of evolution as the team struggled to bring consistency to a car that was not only late, but completely new, and the dregs of problems that had begun in the past and not been completely resolved by the old guard was to blame.

The pain of change is always intense. Ascanelli has already pointed out the difficulties of integrating new personnel into a team, which relies on experience as well as technical prowess. Before Montezemolo came along, the team was like a chameleon with an ever changing colour, as new faces came and went at regular intervals. As soon as there was a problem, the personnel changed, which didn't provide a solid base from which to build a stable team. And as the personnel went the problems remained. They just passed from one generation to the next, until for some inexplicable reason they all came to the fore in a few tense summer weeks in 1996.

The technical debriefing meeting at Maranello the day after the Silverstone race was tense and lasted over three hours. Montezemolo needed to get to the bottom of the problems and one of his innovations was to make all the technicians responsible for their own jobs, and send a weekly report to Jean Todt giving details of what they had done and what they intended to do. John Barnard was at the meeting and had come to his own conclusions.

'Irvine's differential bearing failure was a modification that hadn't been done, as it wasn't expected that this type of differential would be used again. We discussed ways to solve the problem as there was a titanium-steel bearing on the differential support which needed changing.

A Problem of Stress

Easing the physical burdens of stress at Ferrari are the two team doctors, Fredrick Fernando and Alessandro Biffi. Both of them work at the Sports Science Institute of the Italian National Olympic Committee based in Rome. Fred and Alessandro follow the team at the Grands Prix to ensure that if necessary there is a physician ready and available. They also run a yearly screening programme for all team members in Maranello. Once a month the team physicians are present in Maranello, and if necessary other specialists are called in.

The mechanics have to withstand a lot of stress, including travelling, irregular and often long hours and the pressure of performing at a consistently high level in very short periods of time (such as pit stops). Despite this Fred was surprised at what he discovered. 'The mechanics at Maranello are in extremely good shape. Some can actually be compared to top-level endurance athletes.'

They also have the advantage of enjoying a Mediterranean diet, although diet was the last thing on the minds of the team members as they made the trip to England after the disaster of France. The eyes of the world were upon them and not many team members had much of an appetite.

Long working hours can be tiring (left) and it's up to the Ferrari doctors, Fred and Alessandro (above) to monitor the team's health.

It wasn't done and so when the original differential turned up in a race, it caused a problem.

'Schumacher's hydraulic fitting was not tightened properly at Silverstone. There is no answer to this. It must have come loose in some way. It was something that had been run many times before and had never given us any problems. You simply have no answer to things like that.

'In France, Irvine's car had the wrong valve fitted. Due to the vibration problem there had been a problem with the gearbox moog valves. There was another valve which was of a special variety with specially strengthened parts inside to make it resistant to vibration. Apparently this wasn't fitted, instead the standard valve was fitted. The control went on the gearbox and it was history.'

After Silverstone everyone was very down. The general feeling was: how far down can we go? And the general response was we can't go any further. Well, of course you can, you can fall out of the next race. The big thing after Silverstone was the total incomprehension about the

The Communicator
Ferrari Chief Press Officer, Giancarlo Baccini puts together yet another press release in his office in the Marlboro motorhome.

loose hydraulic fitting on Schumacher's car. Everyone who worked on it from the guy at the factory who put it together to the gearbox mechanics at the track, insisted it had been tight. What can you do? It remains a mystery.

The problems with the gearboxes were now reaching a crescendo and Barnard was fast coming to his own conclusions. 'It seems that our problems had their roots in the era of the change from linear to metric measurements. Before the metric system was adopted, we used to buy our nuts, bolts and washers from the United States. They are very well organised in the States. There are books of selections of nuts, bolts, washers etc. which all adhere to NAS (National Aerospace Standard).

They are all designed from the highest grade of material available and easily accessible. As things went metric the British teams sorted themselves out with similar spec stuff, and everyone goes to the same places for high quality bolts, nuts etc. But this hasn't happened at Ferrari.

'Gradually, we had more problems with gearboxes cracking and studs cracking and so a lengthy investigation has been going on and it has revealed that the nuts have not been tightened correctly by using the prescribed torque settings. One of the reasons for this was that if you used the correct torque setting it squashed the washer out, as the washer was cheap and soft. The question is why use cheap washers? This is something that obviously predates this new era, and probably occurred because no-one said you can't go round the corner to the local hardware store and buy cheap washers. I don't know. Who knows? It is so basic that it is something you really don't question. We only discovered this when David Teletti, the stress guy at Maranello started an overall investigation when we had a lot of stud failures. We now use the correct aircraft quality washers. It was just a basic mistake that had been overlooked for years. You can't blame the present guys at Maranello. It is just so basic that it must have started years ago.'

The pressure from the media was becoming intolerable. Everyone was writing about what they thought was happening and very few about what was really happening. The man who had to act as the buffer between Ferrari and the outside world was Ferrari Press Chief, Giancarlo Baccini. Baccini was an Italian Champion swimmer in the 1960s, before he obtained a degree in political science and then went to work as a journalist. Calm and highly intelligent, he had worked for Montezemolo as Press Officer at Italia 90, the World Cup Organising Committee for the World Cup held in Italy in 1990. When the World Cup ended, Baccini had returned to his newspaper *Il Messaggero* and Montezemolo had gone to run part of the large international publishing group, Rizzoli. When Montezemolo had taken over the reins at Ferrari in 1991, Baccini had hoped there would be a possibility of joining him. Motor racing was a passion and he wanted to work again with the charismatic Montezemolo.

Baccini has a friend who is an astrologer and she predicted a new job, a change of city and she saw the number 27, although she didn't understand what it meant. Historically, Ferrari have raced with the number 27, Gilles Villeneuve's number, and Montezemolo called Baccini on the 27th. He changed job and moved cities from Rome to Modena. Ferrari was his destiny.

Once he was a part of Ferrari, Baccini found that the reality was different from the legend. 'Ferrari was like most work environments, and strangely enough it had certain similarities to the newspaper world. It makes a product and puts that product on the marketplace in competition with other similar products. We are both always working to deadlines. In 1991 when I joined the company, Ferrari was very different to what it is now. There was a tendency to be complacent and just sit and say we are Ferrari. When Montezemolo came in, he wanted to make Ferrari the best because it is the best and not just trade on its name. He wanted to maintain the legend and create a modern company, which he has succeeded in doing.'

Baccini admits that he knew Ferrari would be under constant pressure from the media. 'I always believed what I read about Ferrari, but some journalists write what they want to write without verifying the information. This false information has never created a reaction from inside Ferrari. It was much more serene than I imagined and I discovered that there were more politics in newspapers than at Ferrari. People create stories around legends and many people had created this myth of skulduggery at Ferrari that wasn't true. It is my job to make sure that people are informed correctly and to try and prevent false things being written. This isn't easy with three national sports papers which have to fill their pages, but we have become much more open and much more proactive, and this has helped us to have a more open channel with the press. This has been a difficult period, but the most important thing is that the team has remained united.'

CHAPTER FIVE

'What the hell is going on?'

'I'm still curious

to know how much you can get

Schumacher to change his style

as I'm not convinced his

style is necessarily the best

way to have your car.'

John Barnard
Ferrari Chief Designer 1992-97

The world held its breath at Hockenheim for the 1996 German Grand Prix, Schumacher's home race. Boris Becker turned up to lend his support to his fellow co-national, and Schumacher finished the race, even if it was a poor fourth. Irvine disappeared with a broken gearbox – yet another one. Montezemolo was relieved rather than pleased that at least Schumacher had finished the race. 'We wanted to finish the race and we did. Before the end of the season we count on winning at least one more race.' In the circumstances it was a brave statement. He is used to stress, but the intense pressure of the problems was beginning to get to even him.

The next race in Hungary produced more gearbox problems for Irvine which resulted in an increase in the temperature of the oil in the gearbox so the team radioed him to stop. Schumacher had electronic problems which affected the accelerator and meant he had to switch the engine on and off on the steering wheel to go through the slow corners. Eventually it refused to fire up again and he too had to retire. It was another race to forget...

Irvine was frustrated but not as much as Barnard who was fuming back in England. 'I fully admit that this year's car is not as we wanted; it is not as good as I expected due to problems with the aerodynamics. I'm not covering any of that up, but we have worked to put that right. We have worked around the front wing and made a new diffuser. When I did the gearbox layout, I had in mind to do a new rear suspension and we did that. FDD did the suspension, Maranello did the diffuser. However, I informed the gearbox people at the beginning of the year that I didn't think there was enough oil flow and I thought we had a gearbox cooling problem.

A Sporting Gesture
Tennis ace Boris Becker offers his best wishes to compatriot Michael Schumacher at Hockenheim.

'This went on and on until eventually they found the pressure release valve was on the wrong setting, and had been for about three years. At least we have discovered the problem, and it wasn't down to bad checking, but probably the wrong specification was requested at the beginning. What I find frustrating is that you bang your head against a brick wall, saying check this, check that and nothing happens until the gearbox has blown up in three races and eventually someone has to go and look at it and find out what is wrong. Then when you ask why it wasn't investigated, they say it is because the car is late. No one's going to go back to Schumacher and say the pressure release valve in the gearbox is at the wrong setting. No one's going to go back and say the teeth on the oil pump drive gear were incorrectly made and had an interference fit on the teeth rather than a clearance fit. The simple thing is to blame me back in England.'

So why don't you sit down with Schumacher and tell him? 'If I sit down and tell him now, it sounds like sour grapes.'

Barnard's original agreement with Montezemolo was that he would be left alone to work in England, and so Barnard couldn't be expected to run Maranello when that had never been part of his deal. It was becoming increasingly obvious that a day to day hands on technical director was needed and needed fast. Montezemolo recognised this as a weakness and Todt was already on the case.

It can hardly be fun for the current World Champion to have to suffer the indignities of having a car that sometimes seems reluctant to get off the starting grid, let alone finish a race. Yet in times of trouble Schumacher has handled the situation with a maturity that is rare in a man who is only twenty seven. There have been many instances when things could easily have got out of hand but Schumacher has always kept the lid on the pressure cooker. When the press

Tackling the Problem
Ferrari Chief Designer, John Barnard in deep discussion with the man in charge of operations at the track, Giorgio Ascanelli.

screamed for Todt's head, he coolly announced, 'Todt is the best thing for Ferrari, to get rid of him would be the worst thing Ferrari could do.' He has defended, protected and as Nigel Stepney said 'given shit behind closed doors.'

Many things have been said about Schumacher's supreme talent, but what effect does it have on the team and the car? Is there a case for saying that sometimes his brilliance isn't the best solution for a car that needs sorting out? His ability to be consistently quick is never in doubt. But when you have the ability to drive through problems are you obtaining a quick fix and ignoring the more long term problems of actually achieving a car that is well balanced and great for the future?

John Barnard is ideally placed to comment on Schumacher. As well as being one of the top designers in Formula One, he is also a race fan and this sometimes produces conflict. 'I have already said Schumacher is very quick, and that is an enormous gift. When the back of the car is right on a knife edge round a corner, he is able to drive it without that margin of safety that most drivers want in a car. It is literally ready to pop out and come round and most drivers stay a foot on the right side of that line, but he's on the line. He's continually on the line. Other drivers spend three quarters of their time concentrating on going quick, the really good racing drivers use ten per cent of effort going quick, and the rest of the time they think about what's going on in the race and what the other drivers are doing. They have that reserve left and it is the reserve of the true champion. In addition he has enormous confidence, enormous ability and great speed of reaction. He is also extremely dedicated. He comes from the Senna school of complete dedication which you don't see very often, because it requires a certain type of mental application, and I honestly don't think ninety nine per cent of drivers have that ability to apply that kind of mental dedication to themselves. His dedication shows in his level of physical fitness; he is supremely fit because he makes sure he is. He is very Germanic in his approach, everything has to be proven before his very eyes. That does make him a bit wooden headed, as he is reluctant to try anything new. But he is the guy who is risking his life so who can blame him?

'From a race fan's point of view that is exciting to watch. However, from a designer's point of view, there is another side. Schumacher is guiding the set-up of the car virtually alone and he tends to drive the car from the front. He drives off the front wheels, with the back loose. When Berger got into what had been Schumacher's Benetton he couldn't drive it. Schumacher has the ability to drive on the throttle with a lot more aero on the front, much more grip from the front relative to the rear than most other drivers can handle and consequently he is much harder on the front brakes. This is something I've already mentioned, but he gets on the brake pedal while still on the throttle, which means the brakes are doing twenty per cent more work than on a car where the guy lifts off and then goes on the brake. This doesn't help the life of the brakes with

A Question of Trust

Michael Schumacher with his Race Engineer, Ignazio Lunetta, the man who looks after his driver's interests at the race track and ensures he gets the car the way he wants it.

the result that you have to run more cooling on the brakes and bigger brakes to handle it. You can't really tell the drivers to stop driving like this as they are quicker, and when you say "look, try and not be as hard on the brakes", they'll just say "I'm quicker." It's really tricky. But when you go from power to a heavy braking situation it causes a big change in the car, particularly Formula One cars which are aerodynamically sensitive, and that was one of our problems this year. The car was aerodynamically sensitive when we didn't expect it to be. When you go full power/full braking you have changes in the car. When you brake heavily in your road car the nose dips and the car tilts. You get that type of effect in a Formula one car.

'It's true that everyone wants the car to go as fast as possible, that's the bottom line and that's what we're here for. However, I know that if you could get the car with more aero on the back, working more from the back than from the front, without this inherent understeer, then fundamentally you would have a better car. It will be more balanced and it will race better, and that is what you're trying to achieve as a designer. That will give you a car that is easier on fuel and easier on brakes and it all becomes better by small degrees, and small degrees is what you're looking at. The first ten cars on the grid are often only separated by a second. If you leave the set-up to Schumacher then no one questions you. It is the ultimate arse covering exercise. When it doesn't go right, the simple answer is for people to say "the car's a piece of shit." Well it's been a piece of shit for years according to some people. The 1995 car, which was a good car, was a piece of shit, according to Berger and Alesi. They spent all year going round saying the car's no good. Then Schumacher and Irvine came along and both got in the same car with minimal adjustments. Hey presto, and it's turned from a piece of shit into a good car. They both got out saying, "What's wrong with this? It's bloody great." Irvine came from Jordan and said, "This car turns in at low speed, it's got a front end, it's amazing." Schumacher comes along and says, "Bloody hell, even the engine's pretty good. If I had this I could win the World Championship." That is what he said. Isn't it strange what drivers say when they haven't got an axe to grind?

'I have to say I'm still curious to know how much you can get Schumacher to change his style as I'm not convinced his style is necessarily the best way to have your car. He is unquestionably a great, very fast driver who overcomes problems by just driving through them, but ultimately talking with my designer's hat on, I'm not sure if this is the best way in the long term.'

Michael Schumacher has a different opinion. 'After Benetton I came into a team which had a car with a lot of understeer. It had been set-up by other drivers who preferred it that way, but I don't. To say I like oversteer is bullshit. I like a neutral car. To have a neutral car you can't have a lot of oversteer or understeer, so you find the right compromise. I will not accept having a total understeer car on the entry and in mid-corner, just to have a neutral car at the exit. I'd rather

The Heat is On

Michael Schumacher responds to the questions of a restless press corps as things go from bad to worse at Ferrari during 1996.

have a bit of oversteer in, a bit of understeer mid-corner and a bit of oversteer at the exit. That is the compromise to get as fast as possible through the corner.

'Yes, I drive around problems, but I still know my way out of problems. It's not like I drive round them, so I can't see them anymore. Then it's up to the team to come up with solutions to fix the problem, but neither last year nor up to now [testing the car at Silverstone in May 1997] have we been able to completely fix the problem that's built in. You'd have to change the whole car. The designer obviously hasn't found the way I like the car. I think that's fair to say and that's what we have to change. Obviously, I'm a driver and I have my own style. You have to try and find a car that I can do the things I'm used to doing with it. Like winning.'

Schumacher also hotly denies that he leads the set up of the car. 'It has never been the case that I direct the team. It is up to other people. I can only influence in the way I'm supposed to influence things, and that is by describing the car's behaviour and what is right and what is wrong. It's up to the engineers to find solutions.'

So how did Benetton get it right? Barnard thinks it is probably because Benetton is an English team without the heavy pressures that a team like Ferrari has to suffer. He says, 'They are able to get on with their jobs in a much more straightforward way and they tend to work in a different way with the driver. What surprised me was that when Schumacher came to Ferrari he didn't really know the set up on his Benetton car. He had a good idea, but didn't know the kind of springs, wheel rates and aero balance that had been used at Benetton. It seems as if over the years he had told them what the car was like, and they'd simply gone away, thought about it, sorted it out and then said "we've changed the set up, try that." It is an approach you can have when you've worked with the driver for a long time and there is complete trust between the team and driver. It takes time to build this trust and at Ferrari we all had to start again. You can't blame the driver if he wants to get more involved at the start; he is driving the car, and he doesn't want to head into the first corner and find the thing wants to swop ends as soon as he touches the brakes. If that happens, he's going to come back and say, "What the hell are you doing? Tell me what you are doing?" You have to approach it in a steady, measured way which is where we start to fall down as you can't approach things in a steady measured way at Ferrari. But the ideal way to stop the driver steering too much of the set up is to have his trust so he will let you get on with it.

'We have tried different things during testing. Our guys have been to Barcelona and they have taken the calm, measured approach of saying "Look, we would like to try this kind of set up, will you try it?" and Schumacher has agreed as he isn't looking for a lap time and the pressure's off. You go and test and lo and behold for the first lap or two, Schumacher can be quick with anything. He may be a tenth of a second slower on the first lap, but what you get afterwards is a much more stable lap time because you're not destroying the tyres, you're not hurting things, you're supporting the front tyres, giving them more life because of the new set up. You can maintain your lap time much easier which is a better race car. However, if you're testing at a Grand Prix where perhaps you only do a couple of laps at a time, he goes for the things that gives him the one lap screamer. You cannot approach it any other way or the press will be yelling about poor lap times. That kind of pressure is something you always have to put up with at Ferrari. On the Friday before a Grand Prix, Williams will probably be looking at race set up and not going for the quickest times, whereas we go for the best time. What usually happens with us is that we go testing and get a good set up from the tests, and then because you cannot test the

Pat Symonds on Schumacher and Senna

Pat Symonds was Michael Schumacher's race engineer at Benetton. 'I worked with Ayrton Senna in 1984, which was his first season in Formula One, and I worked with Michael in 1992 which was his first season in Formula One. They were both devoted to work and totally absorbed in what was happening to the car. Ayrton was more involved in the specifics of the technicalities, like what spring rates to use. Michael was more interested in data.

'In Ayrton's days there wasn't as much data available. Even so both men share the same high mental capacity to drive flat out and remember exactly what

happened. Michael would describe everything and then leave you to figure out the solution. He was more trusting. Ayrton would suggest what we could do. You needed to do a lot more with the driver in the 1980s.

'Both drivers have a similar style. They both gain a lot of time going into a corner and find it easier to gain power out of the corner, rather than in the middle. That is difficult as you are on the edge of your performance going into the corner, and this similarity is not present in all drivers. You're braking hard, turning in at the last minute and finding the edge into the corner which is difficult. Ayrton with his turbo car would use the throttle in such a way to keep the boost and maintain a good

throttle response. Michael would keep enough throttle to enable the car to balance itself out and be smooth through the corners.

Away from the track I'd say that maybe Ayrton was a bit too serious, he only lived for racing. He could have relaxed a bit. Michael is more balanced in his approach to life. He is very dedicated, but he also has other things in his life, such as his wife.

'However, both drivers had the motivation to succeed, and it was a real pleasure to work with them as they always gave their best, and that increased the enthusiasm of the whole team. It had a snowball effect. The more you gave, the more they gave.'

week before a Grand Prix, you go to the circuit and the weather conditions have changed. It's the first time you get 20 or so cars testing on the track so things change and before you know it that lovely set up you had in testing now has big oversteer or understeer, so there is a mad panic. Panic with Ferrari is a red flag to a bull and up comes the bull snorting and charging, and there is the usual reaction: front wing on, stiffen up the front, got to get him on pole, and he's on pole and there's your race down the chute [at least that was the case in 1996]. You are now back to where you didn't want to be. It is a nightmare and I don't know what the answer is. It is probably to bring Ferrari to England and build the engines in Italy. You need the kind of team around you that doesn't panic and doesn't get the type of pressure that is piled on in Italy.'

Pat Symonds, who was Michael Schumacher's Race Engineer at Benetton and is now their Technical Director, confirmed John Barnard's theory that at Benetton he had basically decided on the set up after Michael's input from the race track. 'When we first ran at the tests, Michael was a bit cautious. But at the first race at Kyalami in 1991, we had a specific problem on one corner and I could see the problem from the data. Although it wasn't obvious, I made a change. From the outside the change seemed strange, but this was the turning point in my relationship with Michael. He trusted me after this. We had a very good working relationship, we just clicked. Outside the work environment he was a very pleasant guy. We are both very calm characters and I think that helped. We didn't trouble him with the technicalities. We didn't discuss whether the springs should be 15% stiffer, or whether we should alter the dampers. It was a marriage of his description of the situation with my ideas. He didn't have to tell me what to do, there was a high level of trust. I don't think we've seen the best of him yet, and I hope we work together again one day. He is a true champion.'

● ● ●

As the team left for Spa, it seemed as if success was as elusive as ever. Apart from the win in Spain, which as we've said was mainly due to Schumacher's brilliance rather than an improvement in the car, there were very few indications that the team was on the right track in the developments and changes they had made. However, the team dynamics had changed; it was more together and more focused. Jean Todt had succeeded where others had failed and imposed structure and organisation. Giorgio Ascanelli had kept his battalion of men working in one direction and the hard work carried out over many days and nights was about to pay off. Success and the tangible proof that the pain of the summer experience had been turned into positive progress were just around the corner.

CHAPTER SIX

The Road to Victory

'Spa was the best win

of the season. It was like a

breath of fresh air after

all the problems'

Jean Todt
Ferrari Team Principal

There was an air of depression hanging over Maranello, home of the Ferrari team. The season was nearly two-thirds over and there was just the superb win in Spain to show for it – a win that had been down to Schumacher's outstanding talent rather than any improvement with the car. Next up was Spa, one of the great circuits and a favourite with the drivers. Difficult and demanding with the awesome Eau Rouge corner to conquer, there is nothing quite like the sight of the sweeping, misty track to excite the senses of a Formula One driver. Nineteen ninety-six was no different. Spa holds mainly good memories for Schumacher. He made his Formula One debut here for Jordan in 1991 and won the race in 1992. In 1994 he won the Belgium Grand Prix again, only to be disqualified.

After an awful summer, Ferrari was in desperate need of victory. Jean Todt had suffered intolerable pressure both externally from the press and internally as the man at the top holding the ultimate responsibility. The saying 'it's tough at the top' is never truer than at Ferrari, where there is a constant change in attitude and feelings towards people. These changes may be so slight as to be hardly perceptible, but you ignore them at your peril, for combined they constitute the political current of who is in and who is out. This naturally affects work. Like most international high profile companies, Ferrari is geared up to play politics, a situation encouraged by Enzo Ferrari who was a past master at the machiavellian game of power play.

At Ferrari power is dictated by the men at the top. Theoretically, Todt reports to Montezemolo, Ascanelli reports to Todt, Stepney reports to Ascanelli and so it goes on. In reality

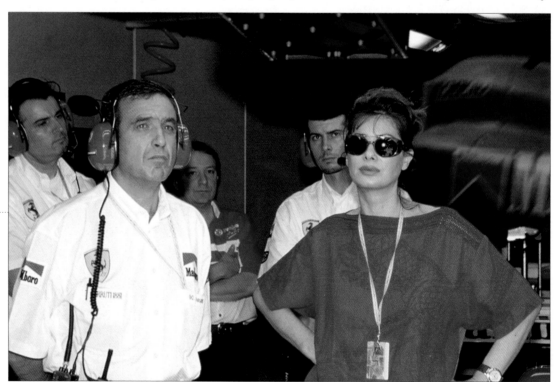

A Touch of Glamour
Alongside Giancarlo Baccini in the pits, beautiful television presenter Edwige Fenech offers support to her favourite team and her favourite man, Ferrari Chairman Luca di Montezemolo who is her husband.

this is often shot to pieces, usually by Montezemolo's enthusiasm to discover what is going on. Blessed with a natural ability to speak to anyone however grand or simple, he'll pick up the phone and talk to the mechanic concerned. The mechanic goes into blind panic and often promises something which isn't feasible. This puts Jean Todt under pressure to deliver. As at Italia 90, where I worked with him, Montezemolo operates an 'open door' policy in which he will listen and give responsibility to bright, ambitious people. This is an intelligent way of giving good people the chance to shine. However it can lead to employees taking advantage of this to try and improve their own positions by promising to do better than the last person. To complicate things even further there is the mother company Fiat, headed by the omnipotent Gianni Agnelli, who has been mainly responsible for Italy's resurgence in the world economy stakes. Agnelli, a highly perceptive and intelligent man, may have retired but he is still capable of making mischief, which he occasionally does with comments about Schumacher such as, 'He deserves to have more money because he drives such a car.'

The Race Team Set-up

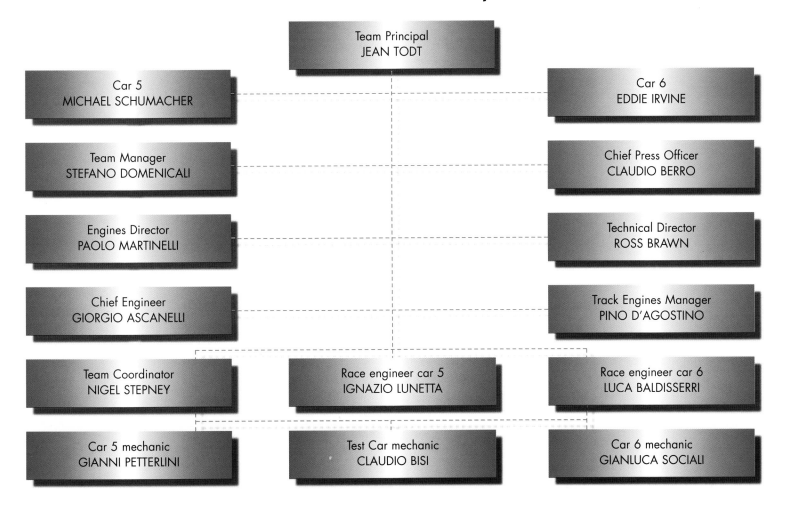

Team Principal
JEAN TODT

Car 5
MICHAEL SCHUMACHER

Car 6
EDDIE IRVINE

Team Manager
STEFANO DOMENICALI

Chief Press Officer
CLAUDIO BERRO

Engines Director
PAOLO MARTINELLI

Technical Director
ROSS BRAWN

Chief Engineer
GIORGIO ASCANELLI

Track Engines Manager
PINO D'AGOSTINO

Team Coordinator
NIGEL STEPNEY

Race engineer car 5
IGNAZIO LUNETTA

Race engineer car 6
LUCA BALDISSERRI

Car 5 mechanic
GIANNI PETTERLINI

Test Car mechanic
CLAUDIO BISI

Car 6 mechanic
GIANLUCA SOCIALI

These comments sometimes get to Montezemolo. It's strange because if you put him in any situation, from a one-to-one meeting to a press conference attended by the world's media, he will command respect and hold the attention of everyone present. However, like most brilliant men he has an Achilles heel and this is his insecurity.

A perfectionist by nature, Montezemolo is concerned about what people think of him, what the opinion-makers write in the press and whether he is doing his job to the best of his ability. Gianni Agnelli, who is also his mentor, rules in a severe, paternalistic way. He encourages but he also has the ability to make grown men quiver, and his words will eat away at Montezemolo. Instead of laughing them off and getting back to work, Montezemolo will sit and worry. Make no mistake, there is no other man who could lead and represent Ferrari like Montezemolo does. His abundance of natural charisma and charm wins friends and placates enemies. But old habits die hard and, encouraged by the ghosts of previous chairmen, there is within the company the presence of a kind of thinly-veiled neurosis that can suddenly manifest itself in strange ways, and which is omnipresent like one of those eternal winter mists.

Against all this background of change and the growing pains of leading a new era, it has to be said that Jean Todt has performed miracles. It must have been a shock to discover that not everything at Ferrari was as it had been described or promised. Other men have attempted to bring order to the chaos before throwing their hands up in horror and blaming everyone from the Chairman to the factory cat for their lack of success. Todt is different. A man of few words and even fewer pretensions, he has the organisational talent of an Englishman, the taciturn nature of the French and the imagination of the Italians. His one failing, if you can call it that, is his suspicious, mistrustful approach to the outside world, which can be detrimental in that it conveys the view that there is something to hide when there is nothing to hide. Nevertheless his determined approach was leading Ferrari out of the dark cold days of failure towards a brighter future.

●　●　●

Spa was a watershed. Todt arrived in Belgium with his energy levels low and prepared to once more go into the breach and fight to the end. It was to be a weekend he would remember for a long time. Despite the poor results, he had kept team morale up and ensured that it was a united, proud outfit that arrived in Belgium to compete in the 13th round of the 1996 Formula One World Championship.

The team worked well; Schumacher qualified third and looked good for a podium finish, although the same was said at Monaco and France. But this time the tide was turning. In the

Maranello: Home to Ferrari

Maranello is a small Northern Italian town near Luciano's Pavarotti's hometown of Modena, and not far from Bologna, one of Italy's gastronomic centres. It is famous for ceramic factories, Balsamic wine and above all Ferrari. The Ferrari factory straddles the main road and is as much a part of the Italian way of life as eating and praying. In fact much of Ferrari's history and tradition is centred on two restaurants, Il Cavallino and Il Montana. Enzo Ferrari had his own room at Il Cavallino, where he could entertain in privacy, a tradition that is handed down to every Chairman and is now the privilege of Luca di Montezemolo, and Il Montana was host to the drivers when they came to town. The walls are littered with signed photographs and pieces of paper from the sons of Ferrari, those drivers and personnel who became part of the legend, like Gilles Villeneuve and Niki Lauda.

Wherever you are in Maranello, it is impossible to escape from the influence of Ferrari. No-one is untouched by Ferrari and Maranello has become like an extended family of the high-profile car company. When the Prancing Horse is unwell, the whole town is quiet and subdued, but when it is first past the winning post, the crescendo of noisy celebration is deafening.

Part of this passion can be explained by the powerful presence of Enzo Ferrari. A strong, hard, and driven man with an overwhelming desire to win against all odds he left an impression on everyone who met him. Priest Don Erio tries to

Press and television cameras descend on Maranello, the physical and spiritual home of Ferrari.

explain the enigma: 'Engineer Ferrari [people are always called by their professions in Italy] was a friend. He remembered the poor in his Will and had great respect for religion. When he came to see me we would speak about religion, and even though he spoke for 90% of the time, and I spoke for 10%, it was always a pleasure to see him. He had enormous respect for the Pope and was delighted when he visited Maranello in 1988. Old Enzo was already too ill to see him, and he died soon afterwards, but when Ferrari raced at Monza less than a month after his death and came in first and second, I think that was a sign that his spirit lived on. I feel the emotion of Ferrari as it stays close to the people.'

Don Erio goes on to talk about his delight at Schumacher's arrival. 'I was one of the first to say that it would be good to have Schumacher. He's a very good driver, very precise and controls everything.'

If you cross over the main square in Maranello and head south you will come across the Hotel Domus nestling into the corner of the next square. The owner is Leonardo Silvano, who went to school with Dino Ferrari. Again the memories are as strong as if they were made only yesterday. The Ferrari memorabilia takes pride of place in a glass cabinet in the entrance near the reception desk, and along with the Hotel Executive, the Hotel Domus provides accommodation for visitors and workers.

Men at Work

The Ferrari mechanics busy in the team garage, where there is never enough time or peace to think.

race itself, Schumacher slipped into second place behind Villeneuve, after Damon Hill had made a poor start. Having made a timely pit stop when the pace car came out after Jos Verstappen crashed, Schumacher overtook Villeneuve a few laps later and destiny decreed that the World Champion went on to win the race, his second as a Ferrari driver. Jean Todt's smiling face said it all. The relief was enormous. Later he admitted, 'Spa was the best win of the season. It was like a breath of fresh air after all the problems.' I asked him if it was the turning point of the season and he quickly replied, 'It wasn't the turning point, it was the most important point. Spa was my favourite win.'

After the race, an inspection of Schumacher's car revealed that the gearbox casing was cracked. Although highly delighted by the win, John Barnard was once more anxious about the treatment of his 'baby'. Having been an only child and used to keeping his playthings in perfect working order, he was finding it difficult to digest the return of his favourite toy, broken and whipped out of all recognition. 'The car was hitting the ground so hard at both ends that it completely cracked the gearbox cases. It had been running quite happily up to Spa, and then it came back all cracked and broken in all sorts of places that would never normally have problems. The bearings on the starter shafts were broken, and they don't do anything except when you start the car. When I was watching on television I noticed that our car was the only one sparking heavily off the ground. It was the set-up again.'

Victory
The pit board says it all at Spa. Schumacher leads over Villeneuve and Alesi on lap 27. Logistics man, Miodrag Kotur, is also in charge of the pit board.

A top designer cannot be neutral about his creation, and it was swiftly becoming apparent that it was not only the gearbox casing that was breaking but the entire relationship between Barnard and Ferrari, poisoned by acrimonious disputes between Ferrari Design and Development in England and the technical team at Maranello in Italy. Barnard was convinced that things were not as they should be. He thought that certain people at Maranello were determined to use FDD and also Jean Todt as scapegoats. It was too easy to say the gearbox broke again, without bothering to go into detailed explanations as to why.

Giorgio Ascanelli, the man in charge of set-up, had other ideas about the cracked gearbox. 'We believe the cracking on the gearbox was due to the type of circuit that Spa is. It is the only circuit that has Eau Rouge, which is a six-speed flat chicane taken at 260 km/h. It is taken downhill and then coming uphill you have such a huge amount of compression that you tend to hit the ground more there than at any other place and this causes some difficulties. There is also a nasty bump at Blanchimont, which is the left hander three corners from home; you hit that at

Past and Present
Whether the cars are old or new they always exude style and elegance. Here old and new sit side by side in the museum at Maranello.

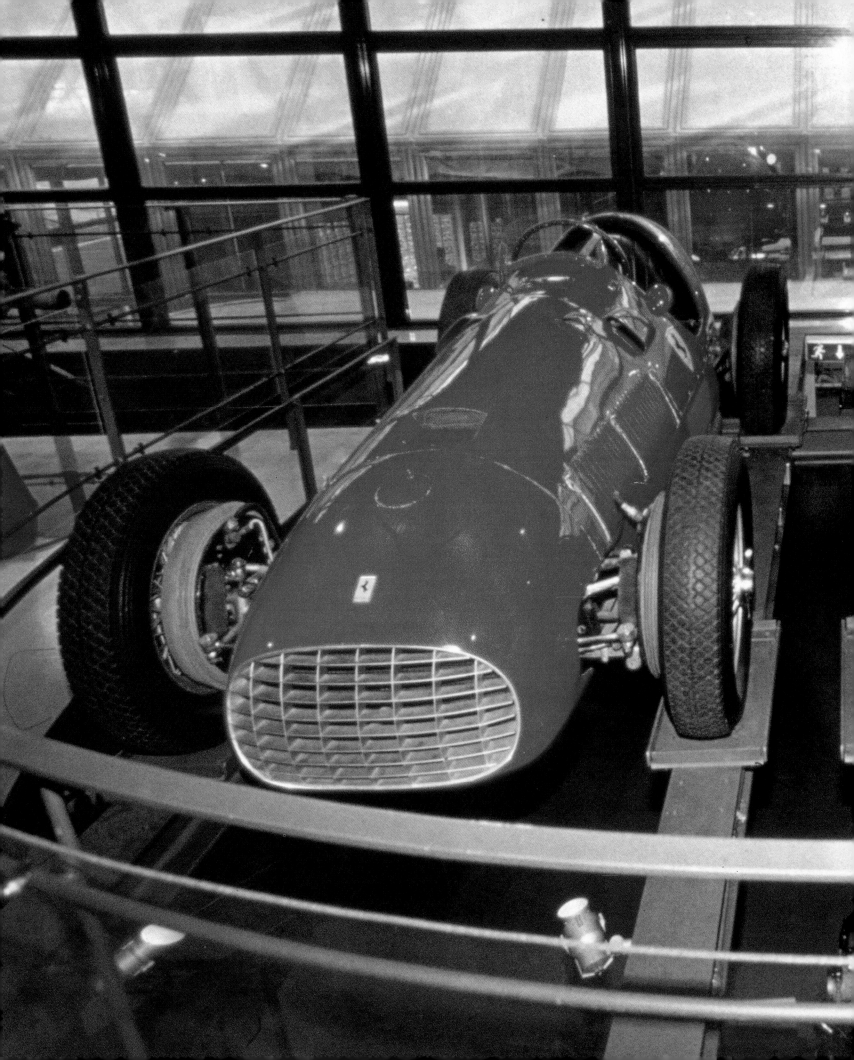

310 km/h when the car is at minimum height and that is the main reason for the cracks. In reality we have had problems with the titanium casing cracking in Melbourne, and so have had to test with the old gearbox until the middle of June, and our pattern of reliability with the new gearbox has never been constant.'

To compound the problems, on a visit to Maranello on 6 August 1997, Montezemolo informed Barnard that he wanted to bring the aerodynamic development back to Maranello and he wanted the FDD team to go to Maranello. It was the only way forward.

As well as affecting next year's car, this announcement effectively made Barnard's contract null and void. However, from Ferrari's point of view they were finding it increasingly difficult to design a car from long-distance via phone and fax, and although it was clear that they, and especially Jean Todt, had great respect for Barnard and his team at FDD, they also needed to have the main design centre at Maranello. It would be Barnard's decision. Ferrari would be happy to have him and his team in Italy, if not they would have to look elsewhere.

After Spa the team was on a high again, although the next race was Monza where the pressure on Ferrari to win is unbearable. It had been eight years since Ferrari had a victory at Monza, shortly after the death of Enzo Ferrari. Now after Spa the fans demanded the ultimate, a Ferrari victory at their home race.

Against this background of expectation, the new car for 1997 was taking shape and Michael Schumacher travelled to FDD in England for a fitting. He flew by

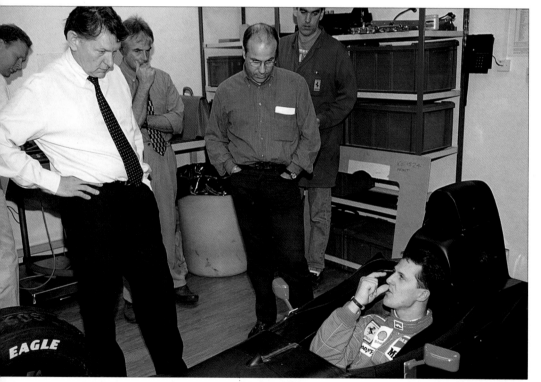

The Refit

John Barnard, Michael Schumacher and Ignazio Lunetta at work on a mock up of the new car for 1997.

private jet to Heathrow, as the local airfield was out of bounds due to the Farnborough Air Show. After a quick trip round the M25 and onto the A3, he arrived at 11 am with the trusty Ignazio Lunetta, his race engineer, by his side.

John Barnard and his assistant Mike Coughlan were there to greet Schumacher, who was then taken into a special room where there was a mock-up of the cockpit, built to the projected dimensions. There it stood in the middle of the room, like a young supermodel parading on the catwalk. And like a supermodel it had a super price. Just to make the mock-up costs about £50,000 – for that price you could buy a smart road car that has the added advantage of having an engine.

It is in situations like this when you realise the value of having a facility like Ferrari Design and Development at hand. No screaming fans or constant interruptions, but quiet concentration on getting the job done. Set in the leafy suburbs of Surrey at Shalford, just outside Guildford, it occupies part of a modern set of buildings on a mini industrial estate. About 41 people work at FDD, which is divided into eight departments: Composites, Machining, Fabrication, Design and Stress, Aerodynamics, R & D, Electronics and Administration. It was set up to design and produce prototype parts for next year's car, and offer a certain amount of production capacity for the racing programme. There is not enough capacity for the whole car and the factory at Maranello does some of the detailed work, for example the design of the gearbox.

The main objective of FDD is to be at the cutting edge of technological development through the innovative use of existing materials, and new materials such as carbon and titanium. There is a big emphasis on quality control which plays an important role. The experienced manufacturing team is also vital, as all the members of the team are conversant with the way John Barnard makes things. Working with new materials requires special skills. The majority of the production work involves the suspension, the carbon spacer (bellhousing), the rear pylon which is in carbon and connects the gearbox to the rear wing and other items. FDD will produce 14-15 car sets of all components. There are four uprights in each car and so about 56 will be produced throughout the year. However, if the design changes then everything made in the old design is scrapped, and the new pieces are made. Where applicable the products have to withstand an impact test according to FIA regulations.

Vijay Kothary keeps the finances under control and also acts as a kind of agony aunt, smoothing the ruffled feathers of the staff and listening to problems and keeping people's minds concentrated on the job in hand, as well as acting as the main liaison man between England and Italy.

As Schumacher walked in, the fabrication department was out in force with Andy Potts, Brian Pepper, Simon Ellison, Dave Chuter and Graeme Eliason all ready to make adjustments. A huge piece of paper is fixed to the wall opposite the car with a curved line drawn on it which represents Schumacher's line of vision in a race. Schumacher eased himself into the car and wiggled about. He commented that he had restricted vision and so the sides were shaped, although they can't be shaped too much as you would loose torsion and stiffness. Schumacher was as focused on this as he is with everything. He wanted the cockpit lower which would mean lowering the whole car by about 10 mm, and the steering wheel was too

Behind the Scenes at FDD
Testing technician Alaister Billing operates the single-wheel test rig on the right rear suspension of the car.

Exactly to Scale
Creating an exact scale model of a Ferrari car is a delicate and time consuming task.

high. The problem is that by lowering the steering wheel you would jeopardise the rule that says the driver must be able to get out of the car in five seconds. The whole day went ahead in fits and starts, things were lowered, raised, swapped, changed, his helmet was compared to Berger's and the clearance on the air flow inlet was checked. Barnard peered at intermittent intervals into the car and listened to Schumacher intently, whilst also maintaining his own overall view of the situation. Both men were intent on getting it right and both had the same objective of achieving as near perfection as possible.

Bits were sheared off the side of the steering wheel, before Schumacher pointed out that the dummy gear paddles on the steering wheel were upside down at one point! As the clock struck 1 pm, Schumacher leapt out of the car and asked where lunch was. His body is as tuned to routine as his mind. After lunch it was back to a hard slog, with the arrival of Andy Willard, who works on the design of the car with John Barnard. There was even time to joke. When Schumacher asked for an even lower cockpit, Barnard quipped that his neck was too long, and it would be easier if he had his eyes higher, like a frog, to which some wit suggested that being French, that must have been Alain Prost's key to success.

At 3 pm the steering wheel was removed in order to check Schumacher's field of vision from the cockpit. At 3.15 pm the moulding ceremony began. It's a bit like something out of a science fiction movie; the car is covered in plastic and a thin rubber cover is placed over the seat area. Then all the creases are carefully eradicated before a creamy brown liquid which is actually polyurethane foam, is poured behind this thin rubber sheeting to make a seat mould, while Schumacher sits in the seat.

At 5 pm the moulding was still being adjusted, as if you put in too little liquid then you can't get an accurate moulding, too much and the driver gets covered with a rising block of foam and risks being drowned!

Designer at Work

John Barnard still feels most at home at the drawing board in his office in Shalford. An award-winning designer, some of his designs are displayed in The Metropolitan Museum of Art in New York.

Schumacher climbed out of the car to phone his pilot and delay take off. Calm and friendly, he signed endless postcards, posters, hats and scarves before disappearing into the night with the comment that Monza could be 'heaven or hell' depending on Ferrari's performance. Schumacher takes a lot of stick for being arrogant, but he is just professional and focused. When he does a job he gives it 100%. Once he is taking a break he turns into Schumacher, the normal bloke and is very relaxed, very approachable and interested in what is going on around him. His life is pressured and busy and like a Royal visit every minute has to be accounted for, but there are times when he relaxes, such as the weekend when he and Corinna take the phone off the hook, snuggle up on the sofa together and watch movies and relax with the dogs. There has to be life after racing.

Back in the office John Barnard was struggling to deal with an FIA fax and keep the design and development of the car on schedule. 'FIA sent around a fax the other day that completely wiped out the side pod work we'd been doing. This is one of the big items we have to do. It takes time and is done by Andy Willard, and we call it the surfacing of the chassis on the computer. This is quite a complicated thing to do on a CAD. We had surfaces ready to go to Maranello for the beginning of production, when bang! this fax landed on my desk, and it literally put the whole thing on its head. They sent round a new interpretation of an existing regulation, which wasn't just an interpretation, it was a new regulation. The result of this was that I had to send a letter to Todt, copied to Montezemolo to say that this fax had completely destroyed our schedule. I then had to spend the day looking at what they were saying and putting a counter argument down on paper, that would get us closer to an interpretation we use today. So far it has cost us a week. Until we get these surfaces done, and I have to get involved personally, as it is what the car looks like and effects how it will be built, we can't move on.

'Charlie Whiting, FIA's technical director, was sent a fax by someone with a sketch of a diffuser with a kind of venetian blind contraption underneath, which is completely illegal. If nothing else, it is against the spirit of the regulation. But instead of turning round and saying forget it, Charlie had gone back to the regulations and said, "I consider continuous to mean blah blah, it must be possible to draw an uninterrupted straight line between any two points." This is completely new so I phoned Charlie and said, "Do you realise that this completely changes our car? This knocks us and a lot of other people on the head completely." He said he hadn't realised it was that catastrophic and so I pointed out that it takes away turning vanes and so we'd all have to go back into the wind tunnel and start again, because that would mean a different shaped monocoque.

'Charlie is an old hand and very experienced so I was surprised by his reaction. In the end he did what should have been done in the first place and sent a letter to the designer of the venetian blind, saying FIA considered the details in the drawing to be completely against the spirit of the regulations and also outside its original intention. It won't be resolved until the meeting of the Technical Committee on Tuesday. It just makes life a little more interesting!

'In fact, due to the problems with the Concorde Agreement, we now have a strange situation with the Technical Committee. The Technical Committee consisted of me, Patrick Head (Williams), Ross Brawn (Benetton), Harvey Postlethwaite (Tyrrell), Martin Whitmarsh (McLaren) and a Minardi representative. Now overnight there's a new group as due to the politics (Williams, McLaren and Tyrrell haven't signed the new agreement), there's only me, Ross and Charlie left.

Inspection
Giovanni Casu carefully inspects and cleans the undertray of the F310.

Forza Ferrari
It is vital that Ferrari are at the sharp end in Formula One, as history has shown that when Ferrari is successful, so is the sport.

We now have new teams present who have no idea what we have been discussing and what we are working towards. It all goes up in the air and as the technical regulations form the basis of the sport, I think it is important to have consistency.'

Technical problems and the finer points of design were forgotten at Monza a few days later. Sometimes in life, there are moments that if they could be captured on canvas would be described as the perfect painting. This was one of them. Northern Italy was bathed in early autumn sunshine. Gone was the scorching heat of the summer and in its place the kind of soothing heat that gently caresses the body and the soul. Combined with this was the exquisite food, wine and welcome that only the Italians know how to produce. It had all the pre-requisites of a memorable weekend.

The mood amongst the team was upbeat. Italian music was played in the garage as the mechanics went about their usual Thursday business, unpacking, putting the car together, starting the engine and practising pit stops. The fans were on fire. After Spa, their hot desire for a Ferrari win at Monza was almost tangible. They filled the stands and the trackside enclosures.

Ascanelli said 'There are seven cars that can win the race, the two Williams, the two McLarens, the two Benettons and Michael. If Hill goes out we have a good chance and this means we have made progress. At the beginning of the year we weren't in a position to compete with Williams or take advantage if they fell out of the race. Now we are nearer to Williams and our objective is to be up in front on a consistent basis.'

Monza Magic

The Moet & Chandon flows as Michael rejoices in his incredible victory at Monza, which made it two in a row and earnt him a brand new Ferrari – the just launched Ferrari Maranello.

The Boss and the Boys
Jean Todt, Pino Gozzo, the
Marlboro boys and the mechanics
celebrate the emotion of victory
at Monza.

Nigel Stepney had a hunch that this was going to be a good one. 'We knew we were in
with a chance after we had a good morning warm up.' When Alesi came into the pits, Ferrari kept
Schumacher out for another vital two laps before calling him in. During these two laps he gained
two seconds as well as two laps. Schumacher then had a great pit stop due to the personnel
changes made after Shell's Mugello ad shoot had highlighted areas for improvement. As Stepney
says, 'Every second counts and races are now won and lost on pit stops. We had problems and I
proposed some personnel changes. I wanted to come off the front control position and onto
refuelling, then I proposed to take the guy off the front jack and into the front control position,
with another guy on the front jack. Giorgio was dead against, but Todt didn't have a problem
with it. In fact a lot of people were against it, but now it has worked they're all for it! In the end
it was Todt's decision as he is the boss.'

It certainly did work. Schumacher had a brilliant pit stop and came out ahead of Alesi to
take the lead. The big question now was: could he maintain it? Ferrari doctor Alessandro Biffi's
face was completely drained of colour as he sat immobile watching the monitor and clutching the
arms of his chair. With him were friends Daniele De Lisi and Pippo De Francesco, who were also
suffering the tension. A few laps from the end nobody could watch the race, but in the end
destiny played a part and Schumacher took the chequered flag and went down in history as
winning his first Italian Grand Prix as a Ferrari driver.

The explosion of relief and joy in the Ferrari garage was catching. Ferrari's oldest fan, 88-
year-old Silvio Ferri danced with delight and Ferrari's youngest fan, six-week-old Callum, son of
Shell's International Sponsorship Manager, Jackie Ireland cooed contentedly in his carrycot,

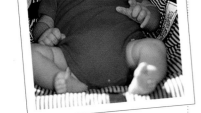

The Old and the Young
88-year-old Silvio Ferri, a lifelong Ferrari fan and 6-week-old Callum, the son of Jackie Ireland, Shell's International Sponsorship Manager, enjoy the fruits of victory at Monza.

unaware that he was part of history. Silvio Ferri has been to 210 Grands Prix since the Formula One Championship started in 1950. He is the only person who doesn't need a pass, even Kings and Queens need one, but he is given dispensation as one of motor racing's staunchest supporters. He remembers the old days of Graham Hill and Jackie Stewart, but he has a special place in his heart for Nigel Mansell. 'The best driver, always happy and content, very strong and very much a family man.'

For Jean Todt, Giorgio Ascanelli, Nigel Stepney, Ignazio Lunetta and all the team it was a moment to saviour and enjoy. Ascanelli appeared soaked in champagne, wearing a Rothmans team shirt, which he had gained in a football pitch 'swap' and grinning from ear to ear. The normally cool Schumacher could not contain himself. For him it was double delight, a win at Monza and the announcement that his wife, Corinna, was pregnant with their first child.

The crowd, charged high with emotion, poured onto the track in front of the podium and unfurled a gigantic banner with the prancing horse in the middle. Schumacher admitted feeling the kind of warmth and emotion he had never felt before. 'It is the best day of my life, Corinna is pregnant and I have won at Monza. I've never seen so many people and felt so much emotion. I have goose bumps all over me. It is wonderful, everyone in the team deserves it.'

Second place, Jean Alesi was gracious in defeat. He had been so near to winning in his time as a Ferrari driver, and he understood what it meant. Victory at Monza was something he wanted more than anything but he said, 'It is wonderful to be on the podium with Michael and see the fans waving flags and screaming. I am really pleased Ferrari won.'

The fans crowded round the entrance to the paddock and all thoughts of leaving were abandoned. Todt and Schumacher went off to the Rothmans motorhome, climbed on the roof and let off fireworks into the night, with the compliments of the vivacious Karl Heinz Zimmerman of Rothmans.

Finally, the time came to leave and I hitched a lift with Jean Todt and Miodrag Kotur, who drove us back to Maranello. When we stopped at the service station for water, the attendants crowded round wanting to celebrate and already looking to the future. 'When will we win the World Championship?' was the burning question. Todt just smiled and promised nothing. Today was the moment to enjoy victory; there was time tomorrow to think of work again.

The only disappointed man was Eddie Irvine who had been running a strong second before going out of the race. As Schumacher crossed the winning line, a disconsolate mechanic from Irvine's car was quietly smoking a cigarette and leaning on the back of the motorhome. The ecstasy of victory, the pain of defeat. There was a sea of happy faces in red overalls, and a sea of disappointed faces in the same coloured overalls. Schumacher did have words of consolation for his team-mate. 'He has great success with women, so he can't have success at everything!'.

The mood was ebullient but steeped in reality. When I visited the team at headquarters just after the Monza victory, there was the feeling that justice had been done and progress made, but it was not a time to get overexcited and start dreaming of World Championships. There was still a lot of work to be done. Nigel Stepney left for England to visit FDD to study the new refuelling mechanism on the new car, and personnel manager Stefano Domenicali also left for England to discuss personnel matters with Vijay at FDD.

Before he left Stepney gave his views on the state of the team. 'Well, here we are, no one's been shot, and we've come through some tough times together and I think that is indicative that the situation is more stable in terms of management. We've got a few wounds, but we have all stuck together in the battle. A few years ago, there would have been a big hands-up session, followed by big changes and, bang!, we would have been back to zero. Now, we are more like an English team and able to work through the problems together. This was a great win, but Spa was probably more special, as we'd had nothing good for the previous four races before that. Although we can't win the World Driver's Championship, we are still in with a chance of finishing second in the Constructor's Championship and that has to be our goal now.'

Monza was a great victory but Stepney like Ascanelli is very aware that not everything is running smoothly just yet. 'We are still very careful on every aspect of safety and security. You always have to keep on top of it, but at the moment we are paying particular attention to everything as we are on the limit.'

Giorgio Ascanelli was similarly relieved that the team had made the huge psychological jump of being mature enough to live through the bad times and come out wiser the other end. 'During the problems we had in the summer, we had to keep our spirits up and stick together. I am very happy with everyone because we remained calm. A few years ago something terminal would have happened to some people and this didn't happen. Those same people who would have been fired, were left alone to resolve the problems quietly and calmly. This is positive for everyone as it helps build team spirit and loyalty, and give people the space to sort things out without forever looking over their shoulders. The boys are together out there even when the going gets tough. Having said this I'm not saying we've fixed all the problems, but we have fixed a lot of them. We still have problems with the clutch and that is annoying us as good starts are vital. Look at Monza, we nearly compromised the victory due to Alesi's magnificent start and our poor one. But things are moving forward. We have avoided some of the old problems, we didn't break a push rod in Spa, we haven't broken a wheel bearing in Monza, all of which were old

Ferrari Glory
Michael Schumacher's victory in Monza was Ferrari's first home win since 1988.

Irish Ire

Eddie Irvine's car is pushed to the side of the track after he exits the race at Monza through driver error, leaving his team-mate Michael Schumacher to bring glory to the team.

traditions of ours! We did manage to lose some bodywork in Monza on the Saturday, but apart from that we are in pretty good shape.'

Ascanelli may be the boss at the track, but he doesn't encourage star status. 'The mechanic who sets the rear tyre pressure is as important as the guy who decides race strategy. Everything is important at different levels. We work as a team and that is truer now than it has ever been.'

Despite the magnificent win at Monza and his relief, Ascanelli was also strangely subdued. I asked him why he wasn't optimistic. 'Because you are never in a condition to ease off the pressure. Enzo Ferrari used to tell me that it takes a lifetime to build up fame, a good reputation and respect, and you can lose it all in a minute. No matter how good it looks, and it looks as though we are finally coming out of the tunnel, we can be back in it again in five minutes if we make a mistake.'

And that is the essence of Ferrari. Nothing is ever good enough, tomorrow is always just around the corner and if you mess things up then victory is quickly forgotten. Life in Italy goes ahead through a series of compromises and Ascanelli explains it to perfection when he says, 'I am a married man and I am happy being a married man. I have a great wife, but she is not the person I like to be with all the time. And I'm sure it's the same for her. It's a fact you have to accept. The life of a single man is easier than that of a married man, but when you get married you have certain advantages. We at Ferrari are "married" to FDD in England and that brings us certain advantages, such as having a group of people who are free to work on new things. Marriage to anybody or anything is like that. I am sure Nigel [Stepney] is not always happy with me and I'm not always happy with him, but we're stuck with each other and so we find a way of working together.'

Spa and Monza were both hard races, and one of the most satisfying aspects of the victories was that the new V10 engine had performed well in its first year, with very few reliability problems. Apart from France, it had worked well and had already made several evolutionary steps to producing more power and improved drivability, whilst maintaining reliability. Forty-two year old Paolo Martinelli is head of the engine department. A quiet, self-effacing, almost shy man, he has been working at Ferrari for eighteen years and worked his way up to the top, through the road car side and then onto Formula One. Like most of his colleagues time is tight and the pressure is always on. He gets up at 7 am and after an English type breakfast, which is unusual in Italy, he takes his eldest daughter Serena to school. Then its into the office and the start of a demanding day.

Martinelli has been quietly impressed with the V10's first year. 'We started off quite well and then made a significant improvement in terms of performance, power and drivability from Imola onwards. We managed to have a better combustion and air distribution using a little more

The *tifosi*
There is nothing quite like the pride and passion of the *tifosi* – the Ferrari fans are part of the culture of Formula One.

air, so we had much better efficiency. We had our first pole position at Imola and four in total, which was impressive for the first year. Schumacher is a big contributor to our success. He is very mature and never complains. He describes in detail any defect or request, modification or improvement. His input is very precise. He can describe each corner, the critical area of the revs and then together we work out what is best.

Stripped Bare
The mechanics strip and prepare the car for the race at Monza.

'Shell have also been vital to our progress. As well as providing an excellent service in terms of research and development, and the analysis service, they have also picked up other areas where potential problems could have occurred, by identifying metals in the lubricant after practice and after the race. This helps us to identify areas of the engine that are wearing and is vital in our search for perfection.'

The basic idea in any car is to get maximum power and efficiency in the engine with minimum wear and tear and maximum fuel efficiency. The core point is the input of air and fuel into the engine through the valves. The process of opening the valves occurs through the cams on the cam shaft. These rotate and open and close the valves. Up at Shell's Research Establishment at Thornton, Simon Dunning overseas the Formula One programme, and one of the more fundamental areas of research is the valve train. At the moment the cam effectively hits the valve and opens it up, in goes the air and fuel before the valve closes again, combustion takes place and energy is created which drives the engine. Now the next stage, which will vastly improve the road cars is to have an indirect method of valve operation in the form of a finger-like contraption that will sit on the cam and actually open the valve. This will have the advantages of being lighter and allow the valve to open more quickly and, therefore, 'breathe' better. This is a real technological breakthrough and Shell's John Bell, who is internationally recognised as a leading 'valve train' expert, and Ferrari's Christoph Mary, spend hours hidden away in their respective offices, discussing and developing this piece of technology.

Nose out of Joint
The cracked nose cone waiting to be repaired during the race weekend at Estoril in Portugal.

• • •

On the way back to Surrey in the car John Barnard speaks to Jean Todt and tells him that FDD are still on target for an early January launch. Barnard also wants a meeting with Todt to discuss his future. Barnard's contract runs out in July 1997 and with the length of time required to build a car, the situation needs to be clarified. He arranges to send a proposal to Todt and then meet him in Italy to discuss things further. The moment of final reckoning is drawing closer.

The last two races go well. There is a heart stopping fight for second place in the Constructors' Championship. In Portugal Schumacher snatches third place from Jean Alesi and Eddie Irvine hangs onto fifth place from Alesi's Benetton team-mate Gerhard Berger. This puts Benetton in second place ahead of Ferrari by just one point. Like the drivers' title, the Constructors' Championship goes down to the wire at the last race. In Japan, Stepney is feeling the pressure. 'The most important thing is that both of our cars finish the race and then we will beat Benetton to second place.' That was the theory but as Stepney admits, 'The last two laps were hell. Berger was quick but he made a couple of mistakes and took Irvine out. Alesi went out which gave us some breathing space. Finally, Michael clinched it for us as he came second. For me this was one of the most important moments of the year, as it consolidated everything we had done. Coming second in the Constructor's Championship is a great achievement as it means the team is progressing and we are working along the right lines.'

The year was over and now was the time to take stock and look to next season. The 1997 car was on schedule and due to be unveiled at the beginning of the year. That would give the team a valuable two months for testing before the first race in Australia.

Despite the caution there was a buzz about Ferrari that hadn't been there for many years. There was an underlying feeling of optimism. When the next prancing horse came out of its stable, there was a fair chance it could be first past the winning post, or at least give the competition a good run for its money.

The Perks of the Job
Eddie Irvine takes his pick of the stunning pack of Marlboro hostesses.

CHAPTER SEVEN

The Winter Break

'If I do anything I hear it back totally different, with piles of top-spin on it. From raking the garden, it changes to me having a fight with my neighbour.'

Eddie Irvine
Ferrari's No 2 driver on being in the spotlight

Away from it All
Michael Schumacher takes to
the ski slopes at the end of
the season.

Teamwork
Good teamwork is one of the most
important factors in Grand Prix
motor racing. Ferrari has
now built a strong, stable base
for the future.

As the winter winds descended on England, John Barnard flew to Italy to try and sort out his future. It wasn't just his future but that of his 40 employees that concerned him and he needed to know what was going on. On Wednesday 13 November, Chief Designer Barnard, his right-hand man and the man in charge of finances Vijay Kothary and Andy Smith, in charge of materials, boarded BA 592 bound for Italy. Barnard is highly superstitious and if it had been Friday 13th he would have refused to travel. However, this morning he had a strangely cavalier attitude about the whole thing. The mood was set when he made for Row 13 of the aircraft, sat down and declared, 'Sod it, I'm going for broke.'

The group arrived in Bologna to discover a kind of Indian Summer, it was 23 degrees and far too hot for winter coats. On arrival at the factory they made for Barnard's office, which used to be Paolo Martinelli's. Over the years, Barnard's office has moved from one place to the next, almost like a ghostly presence in an old house. At the moment it's at the end of a long corridor near the vending machine. On entering the room, the British contingent quickly took up positions round the meeting table, spreading out plans and documents and getting the telephone back in use.

John Barnard was involved in a Direction Meeting with Todt and the heads of departments, whilst Vijay was discussing budgets and Andy the materials side of things. Afterwards, the feeling was upbeat. Even the normally cynical Barnard was quietly pleased with the way things had gone and felt there was still a basis for a relationship between FDD and Ferrari, Italy. He had made it clear that he would not move to Italy, and so this had affected the nature of the relationship, but FDD could still be useful to Ferrari.

However, the fact that the relationship between Barnard and Ferrari had not broken down to the point of involving solicitors, was due largely to the diplomatic talents of Jean Todt. One of Todt's most important characteristics is his ability to make his workers feel secure and protected. Todt and Schumacher have formed a particularly warm relationship and Schumacher acknowledges the importance of Todt and understands his public and private faces. 'I have a very special relationship with Jean Todt. I've found he seems different to outsiders than to how he actually is in reality. But most people think the same about me. They think I'm a strange person and they can't get close to me as I don't let them. Well, I can't let everyone get close to me and its difficult to sort out on a race weekend who is nice and who isn't, so I just concentrate on my job and shut out the rest. But I can say that Jean Todt is one of the nicest people I've met in Formula One. He looks after me like a father. There are very few people in business like him, it gives you faith in the human race. I have a very open and straightforward relationship with him.'

The Wind Tunnel

John Barnard has a wind tunnel facility at British Aerospace in Filton, Bristol which he uses regularly when the car is at the development stage. British Aerospace doesn't have much in common with the high octane glamour of Formula One. But it is in this unlikely environment that next year's dreams are being formed and in the middle of the huge business complex is a half-size model of the 1997 Ferrari Formula One car.

The objective of the wind tunnel is to give Barnard and his team time to study the aerodynamic responses of the car and act accordingly. Usually they target an area for development and work on it. The holy grail for an aerodynamicist is maximum efficiency, i.e. maximum downforce with minimum drag. Barnard explains, 'We may make half a dozen different front wings and then go into the wind tunnel and do some flow visualization. We'll look at

something and say, okay, let's move that turning vane 10 mm in because we see a vortex developing there, and we either want to move the vortex or stop it altogether. Either way we play with the model until we've achieved it. We work on the whole car until we arrive at the point when we can say we've substantially reduced sensitivity, we've maintained or improved efficiency, now what do we have to do to produce that? We may have to build a new nose, different front wing end plates, different front wing flaps, different turning vanes and then out comes the car with the modifications. Everyone is in the wind tunnel all the time, so the modifications are happening constantly. The only difference is that the smaller teams have

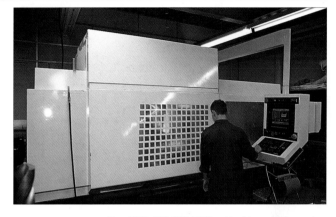

The £350,000 CNC Milling Machine which creates components for the car from data input from the designers at FDD.

a smaller budget and so can't spend as much time in the wind tunnel as the bigger teams.'

The wind tunnel is built of wood with a special rolling road (the moving belt which is part of the wind tunnel and simulates the car moving over the road surface) where the car stands. Basically, wind eddies move over the car at various speeds and angles. The car stands in the middle of the wind tunnel while technicians and software experts get to work.

Austin Rose is the man who writes the software and controls the way the model moves. The process can be sped up or slowed down, and the results are fed into the computer and studied at length. Graeme Eliason, the fabricator and Bryan Wallis the model maker, emerge from the room and the doors are shut for the simulation to begin. Monza, Spa and other Grands Prix can be re-created in this simulated environment.

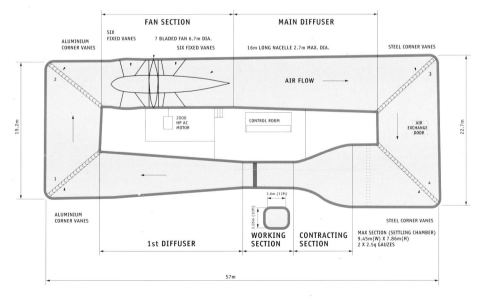

The Factory at Fiorano

The winter months at Ferrari are spent getting the house in order and preparing for next season. The test team goes testing to try out new parts for the car, both major and minor, while the race team builds up show cars out of this year's cars which are prepared for the main motor shows at Bologna and Geneva. The pit equipment is given an overhaul along with the transporters and other equipment, and the team takes a holiday. As Nigel Stepney says, 'The work is less frenetic now, each year brings a calmer pace and progress so we don't have to keep starting from scratch. We are working more like a structured team. Four years ago we were always starting from scratch, it was like swimming against the current all the time. You had to take new people on board and show them what to do. Now we have enough people with experience. The fact that we have different nationalities doesn't matter, what is important is that we work together and Ferrari wins. We may have to change one or two people if we think we need it, but the most important thing is to get the right mix of people for the team to work well. That doesn't necessarily mean the best individuals. It's like a football team, the eleven best football players in the world don't necessarily make the best team. You need to pull together. We can't have the twenty people involved in the pit stops all pulling in different directions, each one trying to be the star of the show. We need people who can work together and have respect for each other.'

Some of the cars are sold to sponsors. Asprey has purchased the winning car from Barcelona and Monza – there was a different chassis used in Spa. The chassis are rotated with the one with the highest mileage going to the test team and a new one brought into the race team for Schumacher. The T-car has a fresh chassis and that was the one used in Spa.

If you walk around the Formula One factory next to the test track at Fiorano, one thing that strikes you is the cleanliness; everything is spotless, even the huge engine assembly room, where after each race the engines are taken apart and studied. It could double up as an operating theatre. In the middle of November, Maurizio Ravazzini was deeply involved in rebuilding part of the engine of Nigel Mansell's old Ferrari, which is now owned by Frank Williams. Ferrari repairing a car for Williams had a strange irony to it.

Unlike some of the functional, clinical factories of other Formula One teams, the Ferrari factory is different. Walk through the side door into the main plant area and you are surrounded by history. Neat signs hang from the doors of various offices and workshops. *Montaggio di motore, officina.* You can almost feel the presence of the Commendatore, Enzo Ferrari and imagine him strolling round the factory checking on his men and his cars – a word of encouragement here, some advice there and a few, sharp words when necessary to remind his staff who was boss.

Everything has its place and must be checked and rechecked during a Grand Prix weekend.

Walk round the corner and up the stairs to what is now Giorgio Ascanelli's office and you have a bird's eye view of the factory floor and the three bays where the mechanics work on the cars. By opening the large window Ascanelli can appear, like Mussolini on his balcony, and dictate the state of play. In this office lay the trails of the footprints of drivers like Tazio Nuvolari, Giuseppe Farina, Froilan Gonzalez, Alberto Ascari, Juan Manuel Fangio, and more recently Niki Lauda and Nigel Mansell.

Wander further along the corridor upstairs and the building takes on the appearance of any late 20th Century office, a large open-plan drawing office furnished with the latest computer equipment and offices at the side for the chiefs, like Paolo Martinelli and one for the soon to be head chief, Ross Brawn. But move further on and you return to the past. As we have already noted the spiritual centre is located in the engine rooms, the central one of which is the engine test room.

About 350 people work on the Formula One side alone, some 50 of those travelling regularly to the Grands Prix. One is constantly reminded that Ferrari is more than just a Formula One team. Walk across the road from the factory and look back. See how the building dominates the area. It's so large that people cycle round inside the building. Ferrari is one of the few companies to have its own Foundry. But the magical moment is when you walk round the corner from the mechanical parts section and gaze on rows of new cars, each waiting to be hand finished.

Each car has a note attached to it specifying its country of destination, the type of car, the colour of the bodywork and the internal colours. They look rather like entrants in a Miss World contest, each one highly painted and as pretty as the last one. Here is the dream centre, the big boys' playroom, the place where only the chosen few, clients and VIPs to be precise, are allowed to wander.

Being part of this exclusive club is an impossible dream for most people, a reality only for the rich few. Peter Everingham is the Secretary of the Ferrari Owner's Club and he tries to explain the passion and mystique of Ferrari. 'The main difference between Ferrari and other marques is the fact that all Ferraris are bred from a race heritage. This affects all aspects of the road car, the noise, the engine, the performance, the shape. It's like driving a small racing car carefully on public roads. Ferrari owners are often not quite as they are expected to be. Unlike some clubs there is no 'us and them' feel about it. The majority of Ferrari owners consider themselves fortunate to own a Ferrari and want to share this good fortune. They're not bothered if someone comes up and asks to sit in the passenger seat for a track run. If there's room they can hop in. We genuinely love the car and enjoy driving it, this comes above any consideration of status or cost.'

The late Gilles Villeneuve's car in the museum at Maranello.

Michael Schumacher is not a hugely complex character. Blessed with a supreme natural gift, he has few pretensions about life. Put him in the countryside with a dog and a packet of Bonio and he is in his element. As the season ended, he took off to his house near Geneva and sought to return to being Michael Schumacher, the man, rather than Michael Schumacher, Superstar. Surrounded by his heavily pregnant wife, Corinna and his four dogs, Jenny, the West Highland Terrier, Floh, the Brazilian street dog, and the two Belgian Shepherds, Bonny and Tracey, he was finally able to relax for a few short days.

Schumacher would undoubtedly like to have more spare time, but time is short and is never wasted. As the Ferrari team were busy preparing show cars for exhibitions and the motor shows and re-grouping for next season, Schumacher was improving his fitness. He is one of the fittest, if not the fittest driver in Formula One, but for a perfectionist that is not enough. He wanted to be in peak condition to meet the demands of the 1997 Grand Prix season. To this end, he went to Portugal for four weeks for special training with the German Olympic team. He felt he needed to adjust his personal training programme and there is no better way than facing the demands of an Olympic training session. He also went to Norway for several weeks to ski with friends and also to work on his fitness programme. Sponsors appearances were kept to a minimum to allow him to dedicate his time to lifting his overall fitness level.

As Schumacher was passing through the barriers of fitness, his team-mate Eddie Irvine was following his own relaxation and fitness programme. He finally got into the car for some testing in the middle of December. He then had three days holiday, before flying to Portugal to meet some friends for three days. He went back home for Christmas and was back on the track on 3 January.

Having Michael Schumacher as a team-mate is not easy as Brundle, Patrese and Herbert all found out. Irvine's natural 'devil-may-care-attitude', coupled with his outspoken manner, indicated that relations between the two would be fraught, but to his eternal credit, Irvine has emerged a winner off the track, if not on it. Despite a dreadful season, due in part to an almost complete lack of testing, he has, unlike some of Schumacher's previous team-mates, refrained from whinging. 'The guy [Schumacher] is brilliant. He is just unbelievable. I can see that he could have a negative effect on his co-driver. You see his times and you think, "Fuck, I've got to push really hard to do that time", when in a sense you don't. You have to sit back and let it happen and then you'll get close to him. He's a genius so if you try and match his time you get freaked out and it all goes wrong.'

Sister Sonia is an important part of 'Team Irvine', as are his delightful parents, Edmund

Dog Power

Eddie Irvine tries his hand at riding a sledge powered by huskies during the Marlboro ski week at Campiglio in the Italian Alps.

Senior and Kathleen. A qualified physiotherapist, Sonia travels with her brother as his physio, but more than that she is also his organiser. 'Sonia is a great organiser,' says Irvine. 'I need her as much to organise me as my physio.' Sonia is enjoying the job which is demanding and involves everything from keeping Eddie's muscles loose to making sure he is attends his sponsors' functions on time and at the right place. But it is also an extension of their big sister/little brother relationship. Unlike Michael Schumacher who has been known to keep his physio/personal trainer Balbir Singh up past midnight when he wants a massage, Eddie is an early bird. As Sonia says, 'Although his room is still a mess, like it was when we lived at home, he loves his

bed. He's in it by ten o'clock which means I can also have an early night, or join the rest of the team for a nightcap, depending on whether I'm tired or not.' A slim, attractive blonde with a very open, pleasant personality, Sonia is ultra fit herself and does regular one-hour runs before working out in the gym for a further couple of hours.

The Family
Eddie Irvine, sister Sonia, dad Edmund and mum Kathleen gather for a family conference.

One of the reasons for Irvine's early nights could be his almost pathological hatred of the trappings of fame. Having a famous face is one thing he hates, and although he is no newcomer to Formula One racing, he has discovered that being a Ferrari driver is different to being behind the wheel of a Jordan car. 'I really don't like people gawping at me. I like to get up, throw on some clothes and a pair of trainers, and wander down to breakfast in the hotel. Now people stare at me. They may be saying "look at that messy bastard", but if I wasn't famous, they wouldn't be staring in the first place. It's much worse being a Ferrari driver than it was when I was at Jordan. If I do anything I hear it back totally different, with piles of top-spin on it. From raking the garden, it changes to me having a fight with my neighbour.'

● ● ●

As the year came to a close, Jean Todt was in a reflective mood. It had been a hard season, his head had been on the line more than once, but there had been good moments like Spain, Spa and Monza. But were they enough to make up for the pain? 'I've no time to be happy, I have to work,' says Todt. 'There are still quite a lot of things that we have to improve. I think we have achieved about seventy per cent of my objectives, but that means we still have thirty per cent to achieve. We have the drivers we want, but that's not enough or we would have won all the races last year.'

Getting Fit
Eddie Irvine on the road to physical fitness...and not looking terribly keen!

Asked what part of his job is the most interesting, his reply was quick and to the point. 'The part of my job that is most interesting is to win races.' Hmm, I suppose three interesting moments a year doesn't exactly add up to job satisfaction. 'This job is like a puzzle, you have to be sure all parts of the puzzle are working well. If only one part isn't, then the whole thing doesn't work. It depends on everyone working in the same direction and slowly we are making that happen even if it is not perfect yet.'

Three wins had been the objective for 1996, and that had been achieved but Todt was not happy. 'Officially, we achieved our objectives, but deep down I think we could have done better. We had a lot of problems, but at the end of the day it all worked quite well.'

The end of the year is a time to dream and let the imagination run a little wild after the pent-up pressures of racing. Jean Todt is happy when he is back in France with his family including his son Nicholas. Those precious moments spent with family and friends are what recharges his batteries. At Maranello, 'in the middle of nowhere' as he puts it, there is no escape. 'I work a fifteen hour day, everyone thinks it's fantastic as I'm travelling all the time, but I don't actually get to see anywhere. He managed to take off to the Ivory Coast for a holiday and do what he enjoys when he is away from the pressures of Formula One motor racing, lie on a beach and sleep.

What would make you really happy? Todt smiles and says without a second thought 'To retire.'

He is keeping his own counsel as to the exact date, but it won't be too far into the future. 'I'll change before the year 2000, it could be the 31 December 1999, but it will come. When I have to turn the page, I turn it when the time is right, not a week, a day or an hour beforehand. I left Peugeot on 30 June 1993, and I was in my office until 11 pm. The next day I was at Ferrari. When I retire I'll do nothing for a while. I may do something but it won't be full time.'

When he leaves the office, the cool professional becomes a man driven by his heart. At the end of 1996 he announced that he had fallen in love with Natalie, a young woman whom he had met through Flavio Briatore. 'My heart is behind my private life, but in my professional life it is different, you don't belong to yourself, you have to think of others and the right way to go. At the moment I am driving along the motorway of life at 250 km/h in a Ferrari, and I have no time to look around. I want to have time to look around.'

A round of Christmas parties completed the 1996 season. Shell had a party in London on the 18 December 1996 high up in the Shell Centre overlooking the River Thames near Waterloo. The ever enthusiastic and well informed Roger Lindsay was already upbeat about 1997. 'I'll eat my hat if Schumacher doesn't win the World Championship,' he declared.

The Shell Christmas present to clients and friends was a large Teddy Bear complete with a Shell baseball cap and a Ferrari T-shirt. When 400 of these arrived at Ferrari Communications addressed to Francesco Orlando on the 19 December 1996, there was practically a fight between the senior managers as to who should have the biggest number. Meanwhile on the same day in Geneva, there was a rather quieter get-together between all the sponsors to decide on brand positioning on the new car.

On the 21 December there were two parties. Ferrari Headquarters held their party at lunchtime in Italy, whilst Ferrari UK held theirs in the evening in England. Some employees, such as John Barnard and Jean Todt, attended both by shuttling from one venue to the other in a private jet. The mood was generally upbeat and at the Ferrari UK party, Jean Todt promised the FDD employees that talks were going on to resolve the contractual situation between Ferrari and FDD. The reality of it was that Barnard wouldn't remain as Chief Designer as Todt wanted everything under one roof, but there was a general feeling that specialist parts and innovative projects for the future could still remain with FDD.

However, as the New Year dawned it would soon become apparent that nothing stays the same for long, particularly in the high octane world of Formula One motor racing.

Strategy and Tactics
Jean Todt discusses the pit wall tactics with his right-hand man, Miodrag Kotur.

One Man and his Dog
Director of Communications Antonio Ghini, relaxes with his best friend, his English Bull Terrier, Bacchus.

CHAPTER EIGHT

New Beginnings

'I don't want to be treated as special because I'm not. I just drive a racing car round in circles a bit faster than anyone else.'

Michael Schumacher
Ferrari's driving force on his position within the team

Countdown
The launch of the new F310B for the 1997 season signalled the start of the countdown to the first race at Melbourne in Australia.

It's the 7 January 1997. Jean Todt, John Barnard and engine man Paolo Martinelli line up on the stage like three prisoners facing the firing squad. In this case it was the world's press. The ever capable, unflappable Bob Constanduros was the host, co-ordinating questions and live television links.

On the stage stood the new car, the F310B, shrouded in red silk, awaiting the moment when she would be unveiled to the world. Behind the stage stood the new team bus, painted in rich tomato red and with Scuderia Ferrari Marlboro written on the side in white lettering.

Marlboro had said they would be putting more into Ferrari since parting with McLaren. Here was the tangible evidence of the power of the dollar, in fact the power of US$60 million if the rumours were right.

Jean Todt started the proceedings and was clearly pleased to have the car earlier than last year. 'It's very important to have the car six weeks before the first race, so we can do the tests we want to do before the start of the 1997 season.'

Last year's problems coming so near to the first race had been almost disastrous, and he didn't want a repeat performance. Todt is not a naturally ebullient man and so he exuded quiet confidence rather than outright optimism. Michael Schumacher was also playing it down. He was keen to point out that '1997 will be a direction year in which we aim to build for the future. Our aim is to improve over last year in terms of reliability and success.'

Luca di Montezemolo, the energetic Ferrari Chairman, took to the centre stage for the unveiling and to a reverent silence the shrouds were removed to reveal a car that was somewhat similar to a Williams or a Benetton. It was a high-nose, conventional car that most importantly, was ready a full two months before the season began.

New Boy
Newly appointed Technical Director Ross Brawn still happy and relaxed at his first Ferrari press conference.

Montezemolo was also playing things down. He wanted 'to win more than last year, but we must keep our feet on the ground.' However, there was an optimism that hadn't been apparent at the 1996 launch when the car had been late and the anxiety level high as the team had an untried and untested car only two weeks before they were due to leave for the first Grand Prix. Now the team was more united, and clearer as to which direction to go in. Schumacher had been with them a year, and his influence was already strong. It was no surprise when ex-Benetton technical director, Ross Brawn, switched allegiance to the Prancing Horse. Technical coordination was something that Ferrari needed badly, particularly after some of the problems of last year.

Brawn had spent four-and-a-half years with Schumacher at Benetton. It was a highly successful partnership, culminating in two World championships in 1994 and 1995. Although he wasn't in the front firing line on the stage, Brawn was in the background and was besieged by the media once the official presentation was over and the scramble for interviews began. He is, however, by nature a very calm and collected character. A veritable gentle giant in a sea of hysteria.

The presentation of the new car was a baptism of fire for him; the main question was how would his arrival affect John Barnard's position? Although officially John Barnard was Chief Designer, which meant that Ross as Technical Director was not a threat, the truth of the matter was that negotiations were pretty far advanced for Barnard to purchase FDD and run it as his own company. He would still maintain contact with Ferrari and make specialist parts, but the design and development would return to Maranello. It was difficult to keep the lid on the pan and deflect questions, but it was just about achieved by Jean Todt's declaration that talks between Ferrari and Barnard had just started.

• • •

On the 8 January Barnard and Todt met at Maranello with the lawyers to try and make progress, although it was to be another month before an agreement was actually reached. It was agreed that FDD would become B3 technologies; Barnard would eventually join Arrows, as would quite a few of his employees, but the core of the company would remain at Shalford. More streamlined, with 30 employees, Barnard's new organisation would still have the capacity to produce high-quality, innovative components to continue his desire to be at the cutting edge of technology. In due course they would look to expand their core business into other areas of the high technology business.

Meanwhile, Schumacher's seat in the new car was still not right and it took two late nights to get it right. FDD's head of composites,

Technical details of the F310B

Chassis
Carbon fibre and honeycomb composite structure
Length . . . . 4.358 m
Width . . . . 1.995 m
Height . . . . 0.968 m
Wheelbase . . . . 2.935 m
Front track . . . . 1.690 m
Rear track . . . . 1.605 m
Weight with water, lubricant and driver . . . . 600 kg
Wheels (front and rear) . . . . 13 inch

Engine
3000 Ferrari (046/1B and 046/2)
Number of cylinders . . . . 10 in 75/V
Number of valves 40
Total displacement 2,998.1
Power output . . . . 650 bhp
Magneti Marelli digital electronic injection
Magneti Marelli static electronic ignition
Drive . . . . Rear
Ferrari transverse gearbox. Limited slip viscous differential semi-automatic sequential electronically controlled gearbox
Number of gears . . . . 7 + reverse
Ventilated carbon disc brakes

Suspension
Independent, push-rod activated torsion springs front and rear

My Man Friday
Eddie Irvine discusses the set up
of the car with his race engineer,
Luca Baldisserri.

Peter Brown, materialised in the reception of The Hotel Executive one morning and was taken to the factory to sort it out. He later joined Ferrari from FDD.

Despite the caution expressed by everyone at the presentation of the new car (apart from Fiat boss Cesare Romiti who gently took Ferrari Chairman Luca di Montezemolo to task for being so cautious in his predictions for 1997), behind the scenes the story was a little different. Heiner Buchinger, Schumacher's press guru and one of the people closest to the German driver, was convinced that his boy would be World Champion for the third time at the end of the 1997 season. Buchinger is an unflappable character with a keen sense of humour. However, he was deadly serious in his insistence that by the end of the 1997 season Ferrari would have a World Champion for the first time in eighteen years, since Jody Scheckter won the title in 1979.

Schumacher has been in the public eye for over six years since bursting into Formula One, but there is no let up in the media's hunger for more and more information. Buchinger can get thirty or more calls a day from the press, all requests for one-to-one interviews, which are only allowed at test sessions. At the races, Schumacher only attends the official press conferences. Although he's building a new house in Stuttgart, Buchinger rarely gets to see it: Last year he spent 210 days away from home, this year will be the same. It might seem like a glamorous life, jet-set travel, five-star hotels, open access to Schumacher, but it has its down side.

Schumacher, at only twenty-eight, already has his own private Challenger aircraft, but like his team-mate Eddie Irvine he craves normality and a respite from the heavy mantles of fame. 'It's a bit easier living in Switzerland, but not as private as it used to be, and not as I would like to have it. I have certain dreams and one of them is to be known as a normal person and be treated like a normal human being who can walk around the street like anyone else. I don't want to be treated as special because I'm not. I just drive a racing car round in circles a bit faster than anyone else.'

An ordinary man with an extraordinary talent. As the rest of us were camped out in The Hotel Executive and The Hotel Domus, wonderboy was settling into Enzo Ferrari's old house which is inside Fiorano, right next to the track. The Old man used to like to be near the cars and the engineers, so he knew everything that went on. For Schumacher it is a haven of peace and gives him the opportunity to live like a normal person. On the outside it is a pretty standard two-storey house, complete with shutters, but walk inside and a sense of wonder takes over. On the ground floor near the entrance is a room with over 25 Prancing Horses displayed round it in varying sizes and made from various materials. Walk up the stone steps and into the room on your left and you walk back in time and into the history books. The walls on all four sides are covered with black and white photographs of the glory days. Here you recognise the superstars: Fangio, Gonzalez, Hawthorne, and Surtees. Every spare inch of wall is covered with a memory. Even the clinical Schumacher feels the history. 'There is a different feeling to Enzo Ferrari's house, it has a very special atmosphere. I feel at home there in my little apartment (a room and bathroom), where I have a television. If the car has a problem I can go back to the house and do what I do at home. Also my family can come and visit me.'

Ferrari has always attracted a large following, but since Schumacher's arrival the level of interest has increased further. The owner of Il Montana restaurant, Maurizio Paolucci, explains it like this: 'Since Schumacher arrived, it's been like a pilgrimage here. Ferrari is very important, it's the heartbeat of Maranello.' Despite attempts by the Ferrari hierarchy to play things cool, the ordinary people on the street were beginning to smell another World Championship, and nothing was going to put them off the scent.

On the morning of the 8 January, out of the cold mists of winter, the familiar sound of the V10 engine could be heard throughout Maranello. The locals appeared on the bridge that overlooks the circuit but is not part of the private grounds. The engineers and workers gathered and so did the Chairman. This was the moment when reality would take over from the previous days' hype. It was also Ross Brawn's induction into Formula One's most historic team. The

Hide and Seek
Michael Schumacher's press officer, the supremely efficient Heiner Buchinger, plays coy with the press.

New Designs
Rory Byrne, newly appointed Chief Designer at Ferrari studies the monitors during testing.

volatile Ascanelli was directing the action. Tense and emotional, he was intent on getting it right and making sure everyone knew their responsibilities. As the commands from Ascanelli grew louder, Barnard smiled to himself and looked over at Ross Brawn. It was his baby now. Meanwhile, the car continued to lap the track, until after 31 laps there was a united sigh of relief. No major problems, basically it was sound. Schumacher jumped out and declared: 'It feels better than last year, it feels more balanced and I think we can make progress.'

On the 9 January there was a snow blizzard. No more testing and John Barnard was out of Maranello like a shot. Overcome by a chronic attack of xenophobia, he just wanted to go home, back to the tranquillity of Surrey where he could think in peace without this madness going on round him. As the dark, low outlines of the Ferrari factories disappeared in a cloud of snowflakes, he and Vijay hurtled along the lanes dispensing showers of snow. Little did he realise that this would be his last view of Ferrari. He would not return again, at least not as a part of the team.

A week later Jean Todt called Barnard to say that Ferrari had appointed ex-Benetton man, Rory Byrne as Chief Designer. It was the end of the Shalford era. Barnard says, 'Jean asked me back in September if I would move to Italy and I said no.

Testing the Suspension
An important area of work at FDD involves the suspension of the car. Here the single-wheel test rig measures the dynamic responses of the suspension and wheel by superimposing loads similar to those experienced out on the race tracks.

From this point it was obvious that we were going to go our separate ways. It was just a case of agreeing on a price for FDD. Jean went out with his shopping basket and started the search for a Technical Director/Chief Designer, and he got Ross Brawn. Even though Ross is a technical director he got most of the accolade for Benetton's success, and I think Jean thought he'd got both a technical director and a designer. But having established that Byrne was the designer he went out again and got him and the team was complete.'

It appeared that money was no barrier to the team, a fact which Barnard has already confirmed. 'Before Schumacher's arrival, we were always being told to cut back on costs, cut personnel, even cut the tests. But when Schumacher joined, it was like Ferrari had opened another piggybank, suddenly it was get whatever you need.'

The source of the money is a well kept secret, but it is likely that a good percentage came from new partners, Shell, the mother company Fiat and new sponsors Asprey. However, the serious finances in 1997 seemed to come from Philip Morris who had ceased supporting McLaren and were now concentrating on Ferrari. In return for funding a large percentage of the budget, the team became Scuderia Ferrari Marlboro, and the deep red was changed to a more electrifying tomato red. People in the know put the total budget for 1997 in the region of £90 million with almost fifty per cent going on engine design, development and production. According to a Ferrari insider, 'At the beginning of last season we were on engine block 40, by halfway through the season we were on 130. That is a hell of a lot of engines to get through and accounts for the substantial cost of development. However, when you are designing a new engine you have to spend a lot of money, and bearing in mind the reliability of the V10 it was money well spent. No other team has put a new engine on the market and had it perform so well so consistently.'

The end of the Barnard era had left its mark. Ferrari has the latest gearbox technology, as well as uprights, bearing and hubs that are well and truly proven and as good as anything you'll find today. The basic manufacturing process is in place. Now the new boys could pick it up and rather than have to build a new car from scratch, they could concentrate on getting the shape of the car right. Even the innovative parts were well in place like the titanium uprights which Ferrari had been using since 1994 and which no other team uses at present. Barnard works to a simple philosophy and that is to make life simple for the mechanic. The torsion bar springs which he developed in 1989 are lightweight springs which are quick to change, much quicker than a conventional coil spring. For a normal set-up under normal conditions, Barnard's springs can be changed in 4 minutes rather than the standard 10 minutes of other teams. The machine torsion bars are such that when you change the spring rate of the torsion bar, it automatically compensates the ride height changes. He was also the first person to create the quick-lock nose box catch, which enables the mechanics to change the nose box in seconds.

Regarding the politics at Ferrari, Barnard is of the opinion that the biggest problem is and remains the press. 'Go to a test and they make a big thing out of the fact you haven't run fastest. It's always time, time, time, even when you are testing some new part where time isn't the most important aspect. The pressure from the press is enormous and very negative to actually achieving anything. Regarding the day to day politics at Ferrari, it is all about covering your arse and I think it was too easy for the two companies (Italy and FDD) to blame each other every time something went wrong.'

Back Seat Driving
Corinna Schumacher offers some advice to her husband.

Nevertheless, Barnard has respect for Todt who he thinks 'is a decent man. I liked him...he has a very difficult job.' However, that doesn't mean there will be a third Barnard term. 'Nineteen ninety-seven was my last car for Ferrari. There will not be another.'

The sad thing is that Barnard should have been around to see the fruits of his work. One feels that if both sides could have compromised then he would still be with Ferrari, and together

Melbourne Madness
Eddie Irvine's Ferrari clashes with Villeneuve and Herbert at the start of the 1997 Australian Grand Prix. All three drivers were forced to retire from the race.

with the team as it is and with Ross Brawn they would have the best chance of winning the World Championship. Barnard had no need to move to Italy with Brawn in place. He just needed to keep in more regular contact and move certain parts of the empire abroad.

It had undoubtedly been a fraught five years. Barnard was disappointed not to see things through to the natural conclusion, a World Championship. 'Yes, that would have been nice, but to be honest I'm not entirely convinced Ferrari can do it now. I hope they do and I wish them well. Ferrari back at the top is good for everyone in motor racing.' I asked him what were his best memories? He paused and a devilish grin came over his face. 'My best memories? Well, that's a difficult one. It's a bit like spending five years in prison and being asked what the best moments were.' Exit John Barnard.

Or nearly. Barnard headed out to the first test in Barcelona. The car looked good but there were several engine blow-ups. Paradoxically, it was almost the result of being too good in 1996. Having got 95% right at the first go, it is very difficult to fine tune the last 5%. Engine Chief Paolo Martinelli was not unduly worried. 'We know the problem and we know how to fix it, so we will soon have reliability again.'

Meanwhile Ferrari had agreed a deal to supply engines to Sauber. With the engines went Japanese engine wizard Goto and, some suspected, the best of the step-one engine. One team member when asked about the Ferrari engine for 1997 commented that it was 'slightly less

Too Close for Comfort
Schumacher's Ferrari sends Barichello's Stewart into a spin in Buenos Aires, leaving the German driver fuming at the side of the track.

powerful, slightly less reliable and slightly heavier than the one we've sold to Sauber.'

Off the track, Schumacher became a father for the first time when his daughter Gina Maria was born on 20 February 1997. He describes it as the best moment of his life. 'The most outstanding impression of my life was holding her in my arms for the first time, especially after all the difficulties I had in getting to the birth on time. I was testing at Mugello, it was late at night and the airports were closing. I didn't want to miss it, but I was a bit frightened about what would happen in terms of whether I would feel ill or suffer in some way. I didn't want to let Corinna down. However, it made me the happiest man in the world. Having seen it [the birth], I never want to miss it again however many more times it happens!' The Schumachers are planning one more child before taking a rest for a while. As Schumacher says, 'It's hard on Corinna as I'm travelling most of the time. If I'm not racing, I'm testing. Having a baby certainly changes your life. When we are both at home we are there twenty-four hours for the baby, unless Grandma takes over and gives us a break. We love it but it changes your life.'

The Team
The Ferrari team pose with their drivers and car before the 1997 Argentinian Grand Prix.

• • •

Back on the track the first real test for Ferrari was the opening race of the 1997 season in Australia. Schumacher and Irvine qualified 3rd and 5th respectively for the race in Melbourne. It was no big surprise that the Williams duo were on pole and 2nd place. In the race itself, Irvine went out on the first lap. He was overtaking on the first corner and took out Villeneuve, himself and Johnny Herbert. The others criticised Irvine. Irvine defends himself: 'Villeneuve had left the door open, he had braked too early. I got down the inside of him, so it was my corner. You don't win races, well I suppose sometimes you do, by sitting back. But sometimes you have to get stuck in.'

Schumacher picked up a valuable six points and Irvine more than made up for his hastiness in Australia by having a blinding race in Argentina. As he says, 'I made a great start in Argentina and went from 7th to 3rd. Was I hasty then? You have to take a chance and go for it, that's what racing is all about.' He also clocked up his best Ferrari result, ending up second. It was an example of getting it right. Ross Brawn had got his feet under the table by Argentina and also felt it was a good race. 'We had a good race with Eddie. There was quite a lot of teamwork involved in terms of strategy, decisions on the tyres [they went for soft rubber] and so forth.

I was much more involved with that than in the first race. However much testing or time you spend at the factory, going to the races is a different situation. Until you've done it, you can't judge where you want to be and where you want to go.'

For once Schumacher was not having a good time in Argentina. Having made a poor start he touched Barichello's Stewart which sent the German into a spin. Unlike two weeks earlier in Brazil, the race was not restarted, and the ex-World champion was left fuming at the side of the track. The only good thing, apart from team-mate Irvine's second place, was that his brother Ralf, driving a Jordan, finished a highly creditable third and earned a podium place in only his third Grand Prix.

In between Australia and Argentina, Brazil, as ever for the Ferraris, had proved to be a nightmare and both drivers complained of lack of grip. Schumacher hung on for a fifth place and two points, while Irvine was experiencing his own hellish race. Forced to take the spare car, which is set up for Schumacher, he soon discovered that Schumacher's seat belts were not to his design and had to make a stop for them to be adjusted to stop the agony in his private parts! Nonetheless, he finished a gallant if unimpressive sixteenth.

Film Star
Eddie Irvine looks mean and moody in his second career as a Cerruti model.

The lack of grip had been due to the wrong tyres, but this was a complex decision as Giorgio Ascanelli explains. 'On the Saturday morning we chose to go for hard tyres, as that seemed to be the right way to go, and in fact we were the only ones who did the same times in the morning as the afternoon. But the race was run on 22 degrees of asphalt and everyone who chose the softer tyres went well. It's very difficult as now we have to make a decision on which tyres to use for qualifying and the race, before qualifying starts on the Saturday, so we can only base our decision on the weather forecast. In Brazil on race day we had an overcast sky with a warm track. This is very rare. It didn't happen during the fifteen days before the race, or for the fifteen days after. It happened on the day of the race and it wasn't seen on the forecast.' The other teams were obviously reading another weather forecast!

Between the Brazilian and Argentinian Grands Prix, the team had taken a holiday in Punta del Este in Uruguay. It was five days of relaxation and peace. Being the closed season in Uruguay, there were few people around and it was a good time to build team loyalty and team spirit. As I have said, the Italians put a lot of emphasis on 'being together'. The football teams always spend at least one night, maybe more before a vital match or if the results are bad, in a hotel or at the team training camp. It is the chance to get to know one another and iron out any differences and face the opposition in a united way.

The flyaway races are complex due to the distance away from the factory. If problems occur it is difficult for the team to sort them out properly until they can return to Europe and get into the wind tunnel and do more testing. Still it wasn't a disastrous start to the new season. The only near disaster was after the Argentinian Grand Prix. Like last year when the lights had hit the cars as they were being driven away from the circuit on the back of trucks, there was one heart-stopping moment for Ferrari. This time it involved the flight. On the way home, a window in the cockpit of the Alitalia plane cracked and the plane had to do a rapid drop in height to ensure the whole window didn't blow. There was some panic amongst the rank and file, but calm was maintained and a safe landing achieved. The general feeling was that maybe next year the team should avoid Argentina altogether!

After Argentina came the first real tough test – Imola. The fans are notoriously demanding and with the first race in Europe at home, it wasn't going to be easy. The man in the hot seat was Ross Brawn, who was getting to know what it was like working for Ferrari. In the business he

Into the Garage
Michael Schumacher's car is carefully guided into the garage by one of his mechanics.

is known as a big man with a big heart, who issues commands with a smile even when under the greatest pressure. However, when required he can be tough and hard, and no-one escapes if their work is not up to standard or they are not putting the required effort into the job.

'There's a lot of pressure at Ferrari, people expect a lot,' says Brawn. 'Sometimes people expect things because its Ferrari, but in reality you have to earn everything you get. Nothing comes free.'

Brawn was pleasantly surprised by his initial findings at Ferrari. Despite the laid back image of the Italians, he found the people enthusiastic and hardworking. The first few months were spent on a company audit. 'The assessment of what we have and how we can improve it is an on-going situation. It's like spinning plates on top of sticks. You get them all going, then some start to wobble and you have to go and get them going again. That's what it's like.'

The general interim report was that manufacturing was very good, and Ferrari has a very good race team. But the weak point was having to put together a design team from scratch. Ross was also having to work with a car that he hadn't had any input in from the start and that was causing a few hold-ups. 'There are some things I'd like to do with the car that I can't do at the moment as it's been designed and conceived in a certain way. It's going to take a few more months before we see the benefit of those things. My opinion is that we need some extra improvements on the mechanical side of the car and the aerodynamics. There's a certain approach I'd like to investigate as to how we run the car in terms of its setting, but at the moment I can't. I think it was this constraint that caused our performance difficulties in Brazil. We couldn't set the car up as I and certain other team members consider to be appropriate for Brazil.'

There was a test programme of mechanical changes in force and also a weight saving programme. Weight is another vital element in Formula One. The cars are weighed with the drivers and have to adhere to a minimum weight, but the idea is to get as near that minimum weight as possible, and that doesn't mean starving the driver! Ferrari were testing lighter wheels before Imola as well as other weight saving items.

The heat was on, but Brawn was looking forward to it rather than scared of it. 'It's good that it's the first European race as we can get on with it now. Obviously, there's a lot of atmosphere as it's Italy. I'm looking forward to achieving some success for these people. You only have to look at Monza last year to see how special it is and I'd like to experience that first hand. The only pressure is friends asking for passes!'

Brawn was slowly and carefully carving out a life for him and his family in his new country. He has started Italian lessons and his wife Jean commutes backwards and forwards from England as his youngest daughter is facing exams and can't be relocated. All the family, Ross, Jean and his two daughters went on a skiing holiday to Madonna di Campiglio, and the culinary delights have been well liked. 'I like pasta so it's the right place to live. However, the standard of food out here has spoilt us. My wife and daughters recently returned to a favourite Italian restaurant which we used to visit at home in England. It was a big mistake. Our standards had changed and it wasn't the same.'

● ● ●

On the first day of practice at Imola, Irvine and Schumacher were the fastest, but as we have seen, Friday times mean very little. Some teams are on race set-up, some aren't, some are on full tanks and on different tyres. It drives the press mad as they never have a reference point to draw stories from. To try and compensate for this the FIA have introduced another press conference which is held on the Thursday afternoon, in addition to the one held on Friday afternoon.

The important day is Saturday and that told a different story with Schumacher qualifying in third place and Irvine ninth. Schumacher, for once, was positively euphoric declaring, 'The gap to the Williams is not as big as in the previous races. Tomorrow I think we can get on the podium and if we get our race strategy right, then I could finish higher than my starting position.'

The fans wanted a win. Camped out on the Rivazza hill, a mass of red flags and banners, they expected the impossible. Being a target of their passions is not always a pleasure. Thirty-

Flag Mania

A new season and a new sense of purpose for the Ferrari fans. Nineteen ninety-seven promised to be a more successful season thanks to a more competitive car and a united team.

four year old Serb Miodrag Kotur, part of the Ferrari logistics team, knows what that's like. 'Last year after our success at Monza, the fans wanted to touch anyone that was part of the Ferrari team. Well, I can tell you it's a frightening experience when ten thousand people want to touch you. It must be like being a rock star, without the minders.'

As well as being in charge of pit boards, Miodrag is directly responsible for taking care of team uniform. He likens it to being in charge of an army, where every button, bootlace and belt has to be in place. It's a demanding job that rarely allows him much time at home in Paris with his wife. It also has its amusing moments, such as last year at Silverstone. Silverstone didn't offer a lot of amusement to either of the Ferrari drivers. To cap it all, after the first practice session, the main sponsors Marlboro were waiting with faces like thunder, demanding to know why their logos were upside down on Schumacher's overalls. Miodrag recalls, 'We didn't check Schumacher's driving suit and the Marlboro badges were on upside down.' He spent the rest of the afternoon with his sewing kit, unstitching the badges and replacing them right way round.

Since then Schumacher has been immaculately turned out. For every race the ex-World Champion has the following gear at his disposal: 2 helmets, 4 transparent visors, 4 shaded visors, 4 dark visors, 20 tear off strips for the visor with 20 Ferrari strips for the visors, 3 racing suits, 3 pairs of gloves, 3 pairs of socks, 2 pairs of shoes, 3 balaclavas, 3 pairs of fireproof underpants, 4 Marlboro-Cerruti T-shirts, 4 Marlboro-Cerruti polo shirts, 1 rain-proof racesuit, 1 Marlboro winter jacket, 1 Marlboro summer jacket, 5 hats and 3 pairs of earphones.

The Williams might have their noses in front at this stage, but the passion was very definitely red...

CHAPTER NINE

Europe

'In terms of a general feeling for aerodynamics, Rory [Byrne] is much better than John [Barnard], but in terms of neatness and cleanliness of design John is much better than Rory.'

Giorgio Ascanelli
Ferrari Chief Engineer

Over a typical race weekend the pace and the tension gradually quickens, until the tempo, like the engines is at screaming pitch. On race day, there is no room for mistakes – during warm-up everything is checked and re-checked, nothing is left to chance. Nigel Stepney was already noticing the difference in having Ross Brawn and Rory Byrne in place. 'It will take time for it to work fully, but it is a change for the better. Having our own technical people in Maranello makes life easier. We don't have to keep communicating back to England. It was the next step, we couldn't get to the top operating as we were before they arrived. Ross is very good, he's very calm and very English. He has a serious side, but he has a light side as well and both sides work well together.'

The biggest challenge was bringing in modifications for the car while also building up the technical and design office. 'The reliability is better, the car is a bit better, but the biggest difference is that the team is doing a better job in all aspects. It's the fourth year we've had a stabilised team which has a big effect, not only at the races, but also at the factory. People wanted John Barnard but the distance between us wasn't helpful. Now we are all under one roof and it is better for Jean Todt as he is here in Maranello more and doesn't have to go running off to see what's going on.'

At the track, Brawn takes overall command of Schumacher's car, whilst Giorgio Ascanelli spends more time with Irvine. However, these roles aren't cast in stone and if Brawn wanted to get involved with Irvine's set-up he will, and by the same token, Ascanelli was free to wander over and give the benefit of his experience to Brawn. For the team it was the best solution, a perfect combination of Brawn's steadiness and Ascanelli's ingenuity. As Brawn says, 'What I'm trying to bring to Ferrari is the fact that it's easy to make changes that go backwards as well as forwards. Ferrari is under more pressure than any other team, you can't understand what it is until you experience it. It's unique, there's a constant demand to succeed and consequently a pressure to make changes. If you're not succeeding then the logical thing is to make changes and I feel in the past there may have been occasions when people were forced into changes which were not necessarily for the better. They were made because the team wanted to be seen to be doing things. It's very easy to do a lot of work and not go forward. I guess it's the sort of syndrome of keeping your head down and keeping busy, and not putting your head above the parapet. I think that was something Ferrari may have suffered from in the past. If people were to make a criticism of me, it's that perhaps I'm too far the other way and I won't agree to any changes to the car unless I'm certain it's an improvement.'

Schumacher wants to win and he brings pressure on the team to make the modifications to win. That is normal but last year there was no Brawn to keep the boat steady and changes were made for changes sake, and to appease Schumacher. As Brawn says, 'Michael is pretty ambitious. He pushes hard to make improvements. His responsibilities are not to judge what should and shouldn't go on the car, but to drive the car as quickly as he can and, quite fairly, put pressure on us to progress. Michael doesn't say "you should put that front wing on the car." He says, "I want to go faster, what are you doing about it?" Last year Michael was putting pressure on the team to improve and they definitely made progress, but you need to go forward in a methodical way and ensure that each change is an overall improvement and not just a one-off for a particular track.'

The new modus operandi works well, but Giorgio Ascanelli would need time to get used to taking things at a slower pace, even if it now meant he could have more opportunities with his family. He and Nigel Stepney were rather like an old married couple, as Ascanelli pointed out last year, and this year was pretty much the same. A lot of the time they were in each other's shadow, including race day.

• • •

Leading the Pack
Michael Schumacher leads a group of cars at Imola in the 1997 San Marino Grand Prix.

After qualifying for Imola Schumacher was third on the grid and Irvine ninth, but things were looking up. In the race proper, Schumacher finished second and Irvine finished third. Both Ferrari drivers on the podium was good for the World Championship but even better for the Constructors' Championship. As usual the pit stops were critical. Schumacher was pleased with his second place, although after the race he admitted, 'I think that maybe the decisive moment was when by a hair's breath, Frentzen came out in front of me after the first pit stop.'

Ascanelli was pleased with the second and third finishes achieved by his drivers at Imola, but insists Schumacher could have won. 'Frentzen went out ahead of us by one second in the last pit stop. That's not to say our pit stop was wrong; if it had have been there would have been a ten second difference, but it shows how close it is between winning and coming second.'

Regarding his role change at Ferrari, Ascanelli feels that things are better with Brawn and Byrne. He is searingly honest about other people and about his own defects. 'We can now walk three steps to Ross' office, say we've got a problem, agree a solution and get it fixed. The reaction time is much better. Ross is a sensible person, he doesn't decide anything on the basis of feelings or emotions. Everything we do now is based on fact. I have to say that I find it extremely pleasant that [long pause] I have a reference point. It wasn't the case last year.

Nigel Stepney's Race Day at Imola

6.30 am: 'We're at the track (three hours before warm-up). We push two of the cars down to scrutineering and check out the weight and dimensions of the car to make sure it is within the regulations after we've worked on it Saturday night. The T-car is done on Saturday night, we have our own controls for that. On Sunday morning the T-car is put into place for pit stop practice. We practice re-fuelling, tyre changes and nose changes.'

7.30 am: The team uses a rota system for breakfast. After that he says, 'I wander back to the pits, and check on progress.'

8.00 am: The cars are back from scrutineering. 'We have to prepare to start-up the engines. We heat the water in the engines, which allows the block and all the components to reach about 50 degrees Centigrade, before we start the engine. We have to allow the components to expand so nothing cracks or seizes. We put fuel in for the morning warm-up.'

8.30–9.30 am: 'The hour before warm-up was busy at Imola as it was a wet warm-up, so we had to change the settings and tyres etc. We put more fuel in for the wet changes and we had to do a bit of work on the tyres and make sure the wet tyres were in the warm-up blankets. We put more wing on the T-car, and Schumacher left his race car the same on dry settings. We swapped around two or three times.'

Stepney was surprised that they looked good in the warm up as he thought they'd be struggling against Bridgestone. The tyre wars were hotting up between Goodyear and newcomers Bridgestone. Cal Lint of Goodyear was confident that his tyres would prove reliable and he was right. 'We try to be the best, but we don't push the product at the expense of safety. There is a very steep learning curve in this business, you have to be very precise. We work closely with the race engineers. The air pressure in Formula One is very critical, the difference in ½ a pound can be the difference between winning and losing a race.'

Irvine confirms this when he says 'There's more time in tyres than anywhere else. You can go ½ second quicker with the right tyres, but to find an extra ½ second in the engine is practically impossible.'

10.00 am: Warm-up is over at Imola and there have been no major problems.

A critical moment during the pit stop as the Ferrari crew change tyres and refuel – ideally, in less than nine seconds.

Stepney says, 'We check the engines by looking down a boroscope. We check compression, check there are no oil leaks by removing the undertray. Shell provide an analysis service and we check the engine and gearbox oils with them, to make sure there are no particles in the oil that shouldn't be there. We then put the race brakes on. We always put new brakes on for Imola as it is hard on brakes. We don't like to put too many new things on for the race, as we prefer to test them in warm up. We put the car back together and the track started to dry out.'

12.30 pm: 'We started to put dry settings on the car – the wings, springs and bars went back to dry set up. We then put on our fireproof overalls. If it's a hot race we end up like a wet sponge.

1.30 pm: 'The pit lane opens and the cars leave for two or three laps of warm-up and then onto the grid. They go out on wet tyres, then come back through the pit lane to change to slicks and go to the grid on slicks. We had the choice of options or prime in dry tyres, and it is a choice that has to be made before qualifying on the Saturday. Schumacher used the softer options compound.

1.40-1.45 pm: 'We set up the area for refuelling and tyre changes. We are ready in case it rains again on the formation lap. We could have changed the tyres and waited at the bottom of the pit lane.'

2.00 pm: 'We return to the pits as the race starts. Schumacher makes a good start and moves up to second. We have a good race and gain three seconds in total over Frentzen (the eventual winner). A good pit stop is a combination of things

Nigel Stepney, Eddie Irvine and John Barnard keep things ticking over in practice.

including the driver. The driver has to stay on the speed limit for the maximum time as he comes into the pit. It's very satisfying when you get it right as it's 20 people working together in the space of 7-8 seconds. We always practice 30 or 40 times during a race weekend. We also practice during the shakedown before each race. During the race we're on the radio. The engine guys tell us the fuel consumption and the temperatures and tell us how much fuel to put in the car for the next pit stop. There are two engine engineers with two chassis engineers. Concerning strategy, we can be a bit flexible. If our cars are in traffic we will call them in one or two laps earlier to get them out of the traffic.

4.00 pm: 'The race has finished, Schumacher and Irvine are second and third respectively, a great result, but we have to go into panic mode and get all the

equipment into the garage. It's a bit like facing a herd of stampeding elephants as the fans rush down the pit lane. The cars go in for scrutineering and the FIA can check whatever they want to check. We start packing the material away which took a little longer at Imola as we couldn't move for people! All members of the team have certain roles. There is a post-race debrief with the drivers and the mechanics do their post-race checks of the engine, brakes, fuel consumption. Then everyone helps pack up the equipment. It takes us about four hours to pack away everything.

8.00 pm: 'We're hungry! We're only an hour away from home at Imola so we go to eat and let the traffic ease before driving home.'

Double Success

Michael Schumacher and Eddie Irvine finished second and third at Imola in 1997, behind the Williams of Heinz-Harald Frentzen.

'As for Rory I enjoyed working with him for a couple of years at Benetton. I like him a lot. He hasn't got a personality full of tantrums like mine! We work together well. He reminds me of a Walt Disney character, I can't remember its name, but it looks like an extra terrestrial and it goes round naked except for a grass skirt and has big feet. Anyway, the whole point of this is that it is always producing helicopters, houses and so forth from under its grass skirt. It's like Rory in that it has a lot of ideas and solutions. Every time you're lost he pulls something out of the bag.'

But what about talent? 'I believe that Rory is a logical person with a fantastic feel for aerodynamics. He has got the characteristics a designer should have in racing, in that he does the job himself, he's not scared of having a drawing board in his office and drawing lines. Also, when you have a problem he jumps on it and fixes it. He's not a manager and so he's always available. I think that in terms of a general feeling for aerodynamics, Rory is much better than John [Barnard], but I believe in terms of neatness and cleanliness of design John is much better than Rory.'

• • •

For Irvine Imola saw his second podium appearance, making it 10 points in only two races. It was just the tonic he needed after last year's fiasco. 'I was able to start well and carry on through the field to bring another four points to Ferrari, which is a great satisfaction.' The only dark point on the horizon was the problems caused when the Irish tricolour was raised behind Irvine after the Argentinian race, which caused difficulties for his parents, Edmund and Kathleen who live in Northern Ireland. At Imola the British Union Flag was raised. Irvine very deliberately keeps away from politics and does not offer any views on the political tinderbox that is Northern Ireland.

The race was also a satisfaction for Goodyear, who had been criticised by Ferrari Chairman Luca di Montezemolo before the race. He had declared, 'I think it has fallen asleep and needs to be shaken up. But I have no doubt that we shall be able to recuperate.' This was a dig at Goodyear after Bridgestone had demonstrated their skills with wet tyres. Goodyear replied with all three podium places going to drivers on Goodyear tyres.

After the Imola race I hitched a lift to Maranello with two of the Ferrari security guards, Mario and Stefano. They also feel part of the mystique that is Ferrari. 'Some kids dream of Ferrari and some of them run away to find their dream. Sometimes the *carabinieri* (military police) phone us to say that a child has been reported missing and has left a note to say he's gone to Ferrari. This happened once and an 11-year-old child turned up all the way from Caserta (near Naples, which is about a nine or ten hour car journey).'

Back at Maranello the day after the race, fans predominantly German poured into the souvenir shops and meandered round the town as though on some kind of religious pilgrimage. Paolo Bortolai, who is in charge of La Galleria, the Ferrari museum and shop, has never seen anything like it. He reckons that there are about 30 or 40% more people this year than last year. 'Our record number of visitors in one day is 1,267; 70% of our visitors are foreign. We are also part of the school visits programme; lots of schools bring their kids to see Maranello and Ferrari. It's almost part of the curriculum.'

The Galleria is a new project which has only just fully opened, but it is proving so popular that Paolo Bortolai has no time for lunch and is regularly in his office for 12 hours. Even on the official day off, Monday, he has to catch up on administration. The museum is just being completed. The shop exudes style and elegance. From the smallest red leather key-rings and yellow cardboard tub of matches, to the tan leather briefcases and racing hats, Italian style and panache is in evidence.

As I was strolling down the streets of Maranello towards the Formula One factory, I was stopped by an Italian family asking if I knew the way to La Galleria. I explained it was closed (it was Monday), but they still wanted to go, just to be near to Ferrari. At this point I said 'follow me' as I was going right past it on my way to the factory. When I explained this there was a reverent hush as they whispered to each other 'She's going to Ferrari.'

Part of the reason for the resurgence in hope at Ferrari is Eddie Irvine's improved form. At Imola he was on the podium for the second time in four races. Last year Schumacher managed three wins, but Irvine's season was more or less a disaster – a third, two fifths, and a fourth.

One of the things in his favour, as has already been pointed out, is that unlike most of Schumacher's previous team-mates, Irvine did not whinge during his awful 1996 season, he just got on with things and refused to lay the blame on other people. Everyone knew he wasn't getting the testing or the new parts, but he didn't underline the fact every five minutes. There is a lot more to Irvine than his 'Irish lad having a good time' reputation suggests, or maybe that is just a convenient cover. He knows where it's at in racing terms and he's also very bright with a good grasp of financial know how in relation to stocks and shares. In addition to this, he also does a good job for the team's sponsors, which is important as his team-mate Schumacher, since the birth of his daughter, has cut back on his off track commitments. However, the one thing Irvine has no time for is people who are unprofessional in their dealings with him. In the case of the media this means journalists who ask what he considers to be stupid or ill prepared questions.

It turned out that one of his main problems last year had been his seat. For most of the time it wasn't just uncomfortable, but sheer agony. 'I was getting out of the car in real pain. I was driving round having to move my legs as I was in such pain. We tried to understand what the problem was and the first time we sorted it out was in Argentina this year. Although, we haven't fixed it completely, it's not an issue anymore. I'm not driving around thinking "Jesus, my back's killing me!"

He was also enjoying a better relationship with his Race Engineer, Luca Baldisserri. Luca is a quiet, bespectacled, serious individual, who like most race engineers, is fiercely loyal to his driver. 'It's important to have a good rapport with the driver. It's important to be friends, as if you are too professional you lose something, you have to understand what he is saying, by also understanding what he isn't saying. We had a difficult year, but we talked things over in the winter and decided to give it another go. We were helped by Ross [Brawn] who sat us both down and sorted it out. One of Eddie's main problems last year was lack of testing. He needs more stability in the corners, he hates oversteer. The car tended to be unstable in the entry of the corner and so his times would go up. The car went very well in Argentina this year, that was the best moment.'

The worst race was undoubtedly Monaco last year. 'There was lack of understanding between us. He came into the pits pointing downwards. We'd changed the nose before we realised he wanted us to do up his seat belts, as he'd stopped but managed to get started again. Not our best moment!'

Technical Chat

Ignazio Lunetta and Ross Brawn discuss the fine tuning of Michael Schumacher's car.

Baldisserri also pays tribute to Ross Brawn's arrival. 'He has brought tranquillity and organisation, especially on the technical side. He is much more methodical, now everything is planned. We do not arrive at the last moment with bits that haven't been tried.'

Like Luca, Ignazio Lunetta, Schumacher's Race Engineer, was a happier man. He and Schumacher were enjoying a close and mutually respectful relationship. Schumacher says of him, 'He's a fantastic guy. I like him very, very much. He's a good human being and a good engineer. When he's under stress he gets a bit wound up but he is the right man to have by my side.'

Lunetta was also finding Schumacher easier to handle. 'He's a bit more relaxed and trusts us more, which is nice. I enjoy working with him, working with the best is always very satisfying, and it keeps you on your toes.'

The 1997 season is turning out to be an easier year. 'It's a better car, faster and easier to work with. We need more performance from it and more grip, but progress is good.'

Lunetta also appreciates Brawn. 'He's brought tranquillity and method to the team. We are less impulsive.' They also live more ordered lives. 'Ross protects us from the outside. We don't see the Chairman of Ferrari around the factory as much as we used to do. Although it's always a pleasure to see the Chairman, at our level we shouldn't have direct contact.'

Just as the two race engineers were getting down to discussing the finer points of racing, Rory Byrne popped his head round the door. Born in Pretoria, South Africa, he has been in England in the motor racing industry since 1973. In 1994 and 1995 he won the World Championship with Michael Schumacher. At the end of 1996 he decided to leave Benetton and retire to open a scuba diving school in Thailand, where he lived with his Thai girlfriend. But after a few months of sailing the blue waters and living in the sunshine he was back in Europe. He says 'I was attracted to the challenge. Ferrari is the most famous team and attempting to win the championship after nearly twenty years was too good to turn down.' As no doubt was the money. Still, Byrne has a very positive approach to his time in Italy. He is learning the language and has rented an apartment which is near the golf course. He is a hard taskmaster especially on himself. 'I can speak reasonable Italian outside work, but I'm not advancing as far as I want to.' He's only been with the company three months.

He has started the 1998 car and always enjoys working on the initial concept and in the wind tunnel. He is a man known for his brilliance at aerodynamics so it will be a relief when the new wind tunnel is open at the end of August. Until then the true form of the 1998 car will not take shape. But he understands what Schumacher likes and should produce a car to his liking.

There was an atmosphere of quiet satisfaction throughout the team that things were getting better. And just to prove that, the next stop was Monte Carlo.

Eddie's Man
Eddie Irvine's race engineer, Luca Baldisserri concentrates on getting it right for his driver.

The Mechanics

During race weekend the mechanics are like red ants charging in and out of the garage and performing a kind of high tech dance to the rhythm of a carefully orchestrated routine. But they are also real people. Each driver has his race engineer, and each car has an engine engineer, a mechanic in charge of the gearbox and another for the chassis;, there is a mechanic in charge of electronics, others involved with telemetry and tyres and general mechanics. Thirty-four mechanics travel with the team excluding the two race engineers. It's not a job for the faint hearted. It is rare to arrive at the circuit after seven in the morning and leave before eight or nine at night at the earliest. A problem in practice can keep them there until the early hours of the morning or one night can run into the next day with no sleep taken. Combine that with the constant travel and changing climates and you have a job that needs 100% commitment. As I walk into the garage on the Thursday afternoon, the boys are buzzing around unpacking,

checking, assembling and getting ready for another busy weekend.

MAURIZIO RAVAZZINI looks after Eddie Irvine's engine. He checks the oil level and liaises with Shell in the analysis of the oil. At 32 he is in the job of his dreams. 'I like everything about the job, the environment, the travel and the work. I don't have a girlfriend, or at least I do, she's called Ferrari! There are a lot of sacrifices but it is worth it to be part of the most famous team in Formula One. From the time I was a small child I had a passion for cars. My father was a mechanic and it was my dream to get a job at Ferrari. My ambition is the World Championship, but my dream is to have a family of my own. For me Italy is like America. The best place to live in the world.'

DAVIDE IANNOTTI is the gearbox man on the T-car. 'We decide whether to change the gearbox after practice, depending on the conditions of the track and the gearbox. I enjoy working for Ferrari as you

are not anonymous, we are a small number of people but everyone is important to the success of the team.'

MASSIMO RONCHETTI has been with Ferrari seven years and is Schumacher's gearbox man. That was not a happy position last year, when the gearbox was causing problems. But Massimo takes it in his stride. 'There is a lot of pressure but that is part of the job and you have to keep cool and think clearly. This year the gearbox is much more reliable.'

LUCA FERRARI is a mechanic on the T-car. He puts it all together, assembling the gearbox, engine and making sure the chassis is perfect. Like his colleagues working for Ferrari is a dream. He declares, 'I'd never work for any other team. I'd love to win here [Imola]. I've never won here.'

IVAN PRETI is another man who had a lot of problems last year. In charge of Eddie Irvine's gearbox, he felt the pressure when it started to go wrong. 'There were a

An efficient pit stop strategy is one of the major factors behind a successful Formula One team. Two of the key elements are refuelling (left) and changing tyres (right).

lot of problems, it was a difficult time. It all came suddenly and it was an intense period of evaluation. But once we discovered the problem it was resolved very quickly. We found that one or two teeth were breaking. I like everything about the job, there is never a dull moment.' He also thinks that the presence of the double World Champion has lifted the team. 'Schumacher's presence gives something else to the team. He's the best. I dream of the World Championship and will do so until I die.'

CLAUDIO BISI works on the T-car and like everyone has the job of his dreams. 'I like everything. Schumacher is number one, simply brilliant. His presence is good for all of us.'

The last of the boys to drop by for a chat is CLAUDIO BERSINI who works on Schumacher's chassis. He is dedicated to the job but has an ambition to live in Australia. 'It's a lovely place, so much space and also clean beaches and clear water.'

Working in the garage, which is as clean as an operating theatre to make sure the cars are as free as possible from dust and dirt.

CHAPTER TEN

Winning Ways

'When you looked up at the
slopes overlooking the circuit,
there was just a sea of red flags
and red caps, even in the
appalling weather conditions.'

Ross Brawn
Ferrari Technical Director 1997

Prince Albert of Monaco was in his private rooms overlooking the harbour at the Palace. Refreshingly normal with no airs or graces, Albert is the same as any motor racing fan, except he is a Prince and therefore has access that most of us can only dream about.

Born in 1958, the first race he can remember was in 1965, when he was seven. 'I remember being close to the track and feeling the noise and noticing the smells that are a part of motor racing. Graham Hill won and I'll never forget the distinctive, piercing sound of the engine.' The Ferrari pit was in front of him and having watched the comings and goings of the pit lane, he was entranced. 'In 1967 I was fascinated by the Sharknose, it was the neatest thing I'd ever seen.' The other great thing about Ferrari was the food. 'We always managed to get invited to eat at Ferrari, it had the best pasta I'd ever tasted.'

There were many occasions for Prince Albert to get better acquainted with his new love. The John Frankenheimer film *Grand Prix* was filmed partly in Monaco and Albert was able to mix with the stars and their cars. He also made friends with the drivers like Clay Regazzoni, Michele Alboreto, who had to take the pressure of being an Italian driver driving for Ferrari, and Gilles Villeneuve, who was one of Prince Albert's favourites and a driver who 'represented motor racing through his spirit, guts and style of driving.'

Of the modern drivers Prince Albert says, 'I like Nigel Mansell who I got to know and admire. Michael Schumacher is a driver I respect for his skill and determination, although he is rather cold blooded. He has the German ability to focus.'

Even for Royal princes, Ferrari has an enigmatic, almost mystical appeal, as does its founder Enzo Ferrari. 'There is something magical about Ferrari, it is a big part of motor racing. I remember Enzo Ferrari as an intimidating, almost god-like figure. He was an incredible man, an imposing figure with a big personality.'

Back down amongst the mortals, the next stop was the Hotel de Paris where David and Chris Mills were hosting their annual exhibition of motor racing art by painter Alan Fearnley. It was the 10th anniversary of the show and the best so far. Alan is a romantic as well as being a stickler for detail and the combination produces some beautiful, colourful paintings that capture the spirit of motor racing, from the 1950s to the modern era.

Next on the agenda was the Asprey Party at The Hotel Riviera in St Jean Cap-Ferrat. Edward Asprey was, as usual, a great host and most of the in-crowd were present. Court Painter

Party Time Again
Michael and Corinna join Nino Cerruti, Prince Albert and Jean Todt for the launch of the latest Cerruti collection.

Andrew Vicari, who is famous for his larger than life paintings of people like General de Gaulle and Princess Caroline, was among the guests as was rising Hollywood star Mark Thomas. For Asprey, the Grands Prix are a way of entertaining guests, never less than 25 and up to 60 at Monaco. These privileged few are flown out to the venues, put up in the best hotels and taken to the track, where they are entertained in the Paddock Club in high style, and treated to pit tours to observe the team and get a little closer to the action. It's Asprey's way of saying 'thank you' to good clients. In 1997 over 400 Asprey guests will visit the Grands Prix. They are always impressed with what they see, particularly the pits. As Edward Asprey says, 'Doctors liken the pits to an operating table and engineers are impressed by seeing the finest skills, quality, expertise and telemetry in action.'

It hasn't been too long since Edward had his first taste behind the wheel of a Ferrari. 'I had lunch with Nicholas Lancaster, the Chairman and Managing Director of H R Owen and he offered me a car to drive, so I took him up on the offer when my wife Christina and I were going away for the weekend. The car was a 355 GTS and if it was mine my licence would last a week! The performance is outstanding and what was surprising was how easy it is to drive from a technical point of view. I've driven high performance sport cars and they can be very difficult, but the Ferrari was easy. You can put it in sixth gear at 2,000 revs, put your foot down and glide away. Sheer magic.'

● ● ●

Meanwhile in Monaco, the weather was changeable. Black clouds kept rolling off the mountains that surround Monaco and rain looked likely. Ferrari's in-house weatherman Pino Gozzo, accompanied by his English wife Carole Ann, spent the entire weekend looking at the sky with a worried look on his face. As Williams were about to demonstrate, you can make complete idiots of yourselves if you take the wrong decision. The other reason Pino looked so worried was because he'd already had a similar experience in the past. 'It was here at Monaco. I'd just finished giving a weather update in the briefing meeting a few minutes before the pit lane opened. It was not raining and it was not expected to rain, and just as I finished telling them that, the heaven's opened and the worst storm for years hit us! Surprisingly enough, I am still the weather expert.'

Schumacher missed pole position by nineteen-thousandths of a second, to Frentzen in the Williams. 'I was a bit surprised at the time I did. I thought I could go faster after the morning session, but not by that much. I thought the others would also be a lot faster. It leaves me pretty confident for a podium finish tomorrow.'

Asprey

Edward Asprey is the man who runs the sponsorship side of Asprey. A handsome, debonair man he has, like most successful businessmen, relentless energy and a capacity to exist on very little sleep. He and his second wife, Christina live near Newbury, with their daughters Louise and Julia. He also has a son George and daughter Mariana from his first marriage.

Asprey may be the shop that has held a royal warrant since the reign of Queen Victoria, but Edward never loses sight of the fact he is a shopkeeper. 'I spend a lot of time with clients. We advise and plan special commissions taking into consideration their lifestyles. If a client has a private aircraft he has different luggage needs to someone travelling commercially. In that case, we have to be more practical and provide canvas covers for the fine leather so it doesn't get damaged.'

Having downed a coffee in the morning, Edward heads up to the workshops. It is here that the usual and unusual are created by the craftsmen. David Birch, the foreman of the silver workshop has been with Asprey since he was a 16-year-old apprentice. Andrew Harrison, now in his thirties, has also risen up from being an apprentice. Many special pieces have been made including a model Concorde and a 4 ft long silver QE2. Often the craftsmen will visit the client when a special commission is made to get a feel for the finished product.

A stunning result of the marriage between Asprey and Ferrari is the Ferrari collection of products ranging from the

Ferrari chronograph watches to cufflinks and keyrings, each one taking a theme from a car. A pair of gold cufflinks take their inspiration from the distinctive grill of the F512M. A pillbox, cufflinks and key chain has the distinctive Cavallino motif on them. In addition, there are the model cars. A silver model of the F310 racing car, the F50, and two of the F355 models are all sold. They are becoming collectors items. Asprey have also commissioned from Ferrari two F355s, one F355 spider in metallic purple, and a grey F355 Berlinetta.

Meetings and paperwork take up the remainder of the morning before Edward moves off to the elegant dining room for a business lunch. Recent visitors have included the Argentinian Ambassador

Cerruti clothes and Asprey jewels. The famous Asprey starfish sits well with the stunning simple elegance of Cerruti.

Rogelio Pfirter. Days can finish at 5 pm or 10 pm, depending on whether there are evening functions to host. Lord Marchwood was a recent guest at a joint dinner held by Asprey and Moet & Chandon.

Asprey cufflinks reflect the perfect marriage between the royal jewellers and the most glamorous and stylish racing team in Formula One.

At precisely 2 pm, half an hour before the race was due to start, the sky darkened and the rain started. Williams Renault had information that it would clear up and then be showery, so they appeared in the pouring rain on slicks. As Harvey Postlethwaite of Tyrrell said, 'We have a simple policy here, if it is raining we put on wet tyres.'

Schumacher, meanwhile, was seen studying two cars, his own and the T-car, and then selecting the T-car to race in. Ross Brawn takes up the story: 'Michael had two different set-ups on two different cars, one was specifically set-up for the wet and one for dry conditions. Before the race Michael went out and had a look at the track to see if it was wet enough to utilise the car that was set-up for the wet (the T-car). It was him and him only who made that decision and I think that is correct as he was the only one who would know what the track was like.'

Schumacher was on intermediate tyres which considering the downpour was amazing. Most of the other cars were slipping and sliding all over the place. He completed his opening lap six and a half seconds ahead of anyone else, after ten laps he was in the lead by nearly half a minute and it increased until he settled into a nice, seventy second lead with which to end the race. There was simply no one else who was even close. His incredible performance in the rain at Spain last year was magic to watch, and if anyone had thought it was a one-off, Schumacher proved once again that he is simply the best. Give him a half decent, reliable car and he'll beat anyone, give him a half decent, reliable car in the wet and he'll make the rest look like amateurs.

However, although he was having a great race, the shadow of his faux pas during the first lap of last year's race was never far away. Every time he passed the barrier where he'd gone off he admitted, 'I kept thinking "Shit, I'll have to be extra careful after last year."

There was one heart-stopping moment when Schumacher ran off the track into the escape road at Ste Devote. Some people said he probably nodded off. His reason was more down to earth. 'I locked the front wheel. Maybe I could have made it round the corner, but I decided not to take the risk and to do a detour round the escape road.'

For the team it was their fourth win with Schumacher. For Ross Brawn it was his first. 'It was pretty special, even though it's not my car, it's John's [Barnard's] car. We've managed to consolidate and improve it, but it will feel better when it is actually my car that wins. Having said that, it still an incredible experience. It reinforces the fact that Ferrari is the biggest team in Formula One. When you looked up at the slopes overlooking the circuit, there was just a sea of red flags and red caps, even in the appalling weather conditions.'

For the first time since 1989, Ferrari led the World Drivers' Championship as well as the Constructors' Championship. However, both Schumacher and Team Principle Jean Todt remained cautious. Schumacher said, 'There are still twelve races to go. We have been fairly lucky so far because Williams has had certain problems which have made us jump in front of them.'

Work and Play

Michael Schumacher and his second sport, football, which he plays with as much passion and commitment as he drives a racing car.

Todt was equally pragmatic. 'We have been trying to achieve the position to fight for the Championship for four years and we have to be very careful to keep our heads clear and know where we are.'

It was a great win for Schumacher but it was also an exceptional third place for his team-mate Eddie Irvine, who had moved up the field from fifteenth. The race strategy of one pit stop worked to perfection. Irvine might have been able to go the whole race without stopping as the rain meant the race was stopped at the maximum 2 hour mark, 16 laps early, but having realised it would be difficult to clinch second, it was decided to consolidate his third place by changing the tyres and putting in a little fuel. It was a good day for teamwork and tangible evidence that progress was being made. It is easy to put it all down to Ross Brawn, but the team has been built up over four years, a time when stability and consistency have been sought and now, at Monaco, achieved.

However, the celebrations in the Ferrari motorhome were muted compared to the wild happiness at the Stewart motorhome after their driver Rubens Barrichello came second. For a new team it was the ecstasy of the first taste of near victory. For the grand dame of Formula One, it was a more laid back affair, although things hotted up after the race when the team hit the celebrated night spot, Jimmy's, staying until dawn the next day. Ross Brawn, shattered by the emotion and sheer hard work, left the others at 1 am. Nigel Stepney led the partying until breakfast time when they all dragged themselves back to the hotel.

There wasn't time to breathe before testing at Barcelona and getting ready for the Spanish Grand Prix. The Ferrari 310B is not suited to Barcelona's Circuit de Catalunya, where the long curves cause problems for the car. Schumacher doesn't understand exactly why this should be so but he tries to explain the effects. 'One guess is the long corners. You build up a lot of tyre temperature and that hurts us. It's also a balance problem. In these type of long corners, you need good balance from the beginning to the end, and we're not that good there.'

Some of the main chit chat away from the track centred on Schumacher's debut in a Swiss Third Division football match. He played for Aubonne FC before the Grand Prix, but his debut wasn't a huge success. He admitted, 'It proved to me that I should stay where I am and not go in other directions. I was in the wrong position for me (centre forward), but I was not playing well – I missed a goal.' There were mumblings about contracts forbidding dangerous sports but when you're Michael Schumacher you can do pretty well what you like.

After the first day's practice in Barcelona, tyre wear was already posing a problem not just for Ferrari but all the Goodyear runners. Irvine thought he might pick up a point or two, but in qualifying both Ferraris were off the pace with Schumacher qualifying seventh after a massive engine blow-up and Irvine in eleventh position.

Rain threatened on race morning and for one glorious moment it looked like it could be a re-run of last year. No such luck and the Ferraris had a difficult race due to tyre blistering. Schumacher had to stop on lap 12 to change his tyres, and after that the race strategy was changed from two to three stops, with additional stops on laps 30 and 46. Irvine was also originally on a two-stop strategy that was extended to three; he came in on lap 19, made an early second stop on lap 28, and then a final visit to the pits on lap 49.

Schumacher's two points for finishing fifth kept Ferrari in the lead in the Constructor's Championship by one point. After his three good races in Argentina, Imola and Monaco, Irvine had a less than remarkable race. Not only did he finish a lowly twelfth but he was also given a 10 second stop-go penalty for blocking second place Panis, who was chasing eventual race winner Villeneuve. Irvine wasn't happy about this as he felt it was unfair. He claimed that he couldn't see a thing due to the debris coming out of Damon Hill's car, and he thought the flag was for Trulli who was holding up both him and Verstappen.

•   •   •

Former Ferrari Personnel Manager Stefano Domenicali, now Team Manager, is under constant pressure to ensure the team are where they should be with everything they should have. 'In May, June and July we have an incredibly heavy test programme,' says Domenicali. 'After Imola, Schumacher and Irvine tested at Fiorano, on the Friday Schumacher had an extra test day, then

A Famous Victory
Schumacher's wet set-up proved unbeatable at Monaco where his reading of the conditions was perfect. Taking the chequered flag and lifting the trophy were special moments in what was turning out to be a highly successful 1997 season for the German.

on Saturday there was the shakedown (when the set-up for the race is checked and it is verified there are no major failures or problems) for the cars that were going to Monaco. Immediately after Monaco we have a three-day test at Barcelona, on the Monday after that the shakedown for Spain. After Spain a three-day test at Silverstone, followed by the celebrations and exhibitions in Rome, Modena and Maranello for Ferrari's 50th Anniversary. Immediately after that we all leave for Canada. The Monday after Canada there is another test session at Magny Cours for three days. On the Monday after that the shakedown for Magny Cours. Immediately after Magny Cours there is a three-day test at Silverstone. After Silverstone a three-day test at Monza, following three days at Fiorano, and so on...' A wide grin appears on Domenicali's face.

Gigi Mazzola, who leads the Ferrari test team, is also a man happy with his lot. This year

Into the Future
The weight of responsibility weighs heavily on the shoulders of the volatile but brilliant Giorgio Ascanelli.

he's already noticed a change at Ferrari with Brawn's presence. 'There's more organisation and a more detailed programme, so when we are testing we know exactly what we have to do during the day. Michael [Schumacher] fits in very well with this philosophy as he's a very organised guy. He sticks to the plan and we work through all the items we have to test. Everything has improved because of Ross. Michael's contribution is better as it's more logical.'

It's not the case that Ferrari understand Schumacher better this year than last. As Mazzola points out, 'You have to enter into the driver's mentality very quickly. You might get more feeling for him after three or four years, but you will not know him better than after two months.'

Irvine has more input this year as there are two test cars and of course, the car is more reliable. 'The situation is easier for Eddie as he has the opportunity to test. I think he did a pretty good job during winter testing. I think he's stronger physically and fitter. As soon as the driver can test, he can try out different options on the car, the handling, the setting-up of the engine or brakes. That means that when he goes into the race weekend he already knows what he has to do.'

The test at Silverstone after the Spanish GP was the first time Ferrari have tested at the British track for many years. Up until this year each team had to keep to its designated track, in Ferrari's case Monza. Now that FOCA have organised general testing which gives the less well-off teams the chance to compete with the big boys, the circuit advantage has evened out.

Test days are inevitably peppered with pauses as crashed cars are removed from the track. Schumacher went off on the Wednesday of testing when his rear suspension broke as he was

Out of the Dirt
Finally, in 1997 the Ferrari team
are heading in the right direction.

taking a corner at 200 km/h. But in tests these things happen. As Mazzola explains, 'In a test you develop new things, try new technology, make something lighter or make something different, or you want to see how long those parts will stay together. If you want to see how long the suspension lasts you keep running the car and checking all the time, until it wears out. In either case you can have failure, either because the part is new or because it is at the end of its life. These things have to happen during the test, not at the race.'

At Silverstone the Ferrari test team were trying to solve the problem of mechanical grip. 'Basically we need more mechanical grip. The car is missing mechanical grip in the slow part of the corner. A long corner is difficult, a short corner all right. It depends on the circuit: it's all right at Imola, difficult at Monaco. Spain is difficult for corners and tyres.'

Like the race team, there is more optimism this year. The car still needs some modifications but they are picking up points and this means the team is working well and of course, there is that invaluable 'x' factor – the Schumacher factor. Having the best driver makes a lot of difference, both in terms of actual results and the more intangible feeling of morale. Both were on the way up at Ferrari.

The next race on the calendar was Canada but before that were the celebrations for Ferrari's 50th Anniversary. Starting in Rome and ending in Modena and Maranello it was going to be one hell of a party.

CHAPTER ELEVEN

Fifty Golden Years

'Williams have a technical

advantage. We have one

advantage over them – his

name is Michael Schumacher.'

Giorgio Ascanelli
Ferrari Chief Engineer

Ferrari began their 50th anniversary celebrations in Rome to coincide with their first victory at the Caracalla circuit on the 25 May 1947. This venue was chosen despite the fact that Enzo Ferrari never had much to do with Rome, having visited the city only once in 1935 for a minor race. Coming from the North he regarded the Italian capital as full of bureaucrats, with a tendency for disorganisation. Having said this, he remained fascinated with the city and was always happy to hear tales and gossip from the friends and associates who came to visit him from Rome.

Fifty years later, almost to the day, the great and the good gathered to see an exhibition of Ferrari cars, old and modern, including the F310B of Michael Schumacher and Eddie Irvine. Some 270 Ferraris owned by collectors throughout the world were gathered at the Marble Stadium, which is near the Olympic stadium and better known for being the host of the Italian Open Tennis Championship.

Roman Rejoicing
A celebration of Ferrari's fifty golden years held at the Caracalla circuit.

The President of Italy, Oscar Luigi Scalfaro, Vice President Walter Veltroni, The Mayor of Rome Francesco Rutelli, Fiat patron Gianni Agnelli and Ferrari Chairman Luca di Montezemolo, amongst others, attended the opening ceremony to start the celebrations that would only end the following weekend with a spectacular fireworks show and concert at Modena.

An emotional Montezemolo, who himself would be 50 on 31 August, thanked everyone for participating and admitted that for the first time in his life he'd 'asked the drivers to drive slowly to the Caracalla, across the city of Rome. 'I'll never make this request again!' he joked.

After the official speeches were made, the President and Vice President of Italy, followed by the Mayor, Agnelli and Montezemolo, all hurried over to look at the cars first hand, and live out their boyhood dreams. Included in the line up was the only Ferrari police car, which was in service in the 1960s, complete with blue lamp, a huge radio and a still working siren! While the President of Italy was with the police car, the Vice President was gazing at Gilles Villeneuve's old Formula One car and wondering how anyone could fit inside it. Then, like a kid in a toy shop, his attention was diverted by the sight of the very first Ferrari, the Auto Avio, which was a prototype car produced in the 1940s.

Slowly the drivers came forward to once more pay homage to their cars. The Argentinian driver Froilan Gonzalez, the 'Pampas Bull', bent down to kiss the bonnet of his car, while Phil Hill admired his, which was the first Ferrari single-seater with a rear-mounted engine, and with which he won the Formula One World Championship in 1961, the first American to do so. Then the ex-Ferrari drivers, along with the current two, Schumacher and Irvine, got together to pose for the family album – but the real stars of the show were the cars.

Bearing in mind this was essentially a weekend for the Ferrari owners and collectors, thousands of people braved the weather (which went from baking hot to pouring rain) to catch the merest glance of a car that represents the best of Italy. But the poor weather failed to dampen spirits and Montezemolo laughed declaring, 'I'd have preferred to have the rain in Spain.'

For the men of Maranello it was an experience that took them out of the narrow world of Formula One and showed them the intense emotions that the name Ferrari arouses in ordinary people. As Ignazio Lunetta says, 'It was a wonderful, party atmosphere in Rome. I love the city and to take Ferrari to Rome was a dream. There were so many people, that in moments like these you realise just how much Ferrari means to them and how important it is. We don't have much contact with the general public, it is only when you come to somewhere like Rome for the 50th Anniversary, that you realise the intensity of the passion for Ferrari. They were all there just for a quick glimpse of a Ferrari and then in years to come they will say to their children and grandchildren, "I was there too."

Michael Schumacher was in deep conversation with Jody Scheckter, the previous Ferrari driver to win the World Championship. Scheckter admitted that when he drove for the team he didn't understand what it meant to be a Ferrari driver and represent not only a name but also the whole of Italy, but as time passes and he is constantly remembered as the last Ferrari driver before Schumacher to win the World Championship, he understands what it means. With

The Real Stars
Ferrari drivers past and present gather for the official anniversary photograph.

generosity he commented 'I'll be delighted when Michael has taken over this role.'

Schumacher was also experiencing what Ferrari means to Italy and the fact that nothing, not Williams nor a Benetton nor any other car can excite and tantalise like a Ferrari. 'I am enjoying being part of such a great organisation as Ferrari. It really is great being a Ferrari driver as 50% of the fans support Ferrari and the other 50% are divided between the various other teams. I'll give 100% to taking over from Scheckter as soon as possible.'

The spirit of Enzo Ferrari was very definitely present. Strong, determined and obstinate, he was known to manage his staff and the people he came across in a manner that would produce the best results for the company. John Surtees remembers his most exciting moments when he won two Grands Prix with a six-cylinder engine and Enzo Ferrari said, 'I won't pay you a lot, as being a Ferrari driver means you'll be able to get discounts everywhere.' Like Frank Williams he never made the driver more important than the car.

The 270 cars drove round the Coliseum and the Circo Massimo to create scenes which will never be repeated. The general public was enchanted, but the excitement reached a crescendo when Schumacher and Irvine climbed into their cars to drive round the Caracalla track. Instead of driving in a sedate fashion, they put on a show, overtaking and screaming round the track to the delight of the crowds, and then rounded it off with a pit stop to change tyres before they finished with a wave to the fans for whom the occasion might have been their only chance to glimpse a Formula One car.

After Rome the Ferrari cortege travelled to Fiorano. The cars followed the same road as the famous Mille Miglia (1000 mile) race with pit stops in Siena and Florence. Once in the North there were more celebrations. The streets of Modena were decorated with large graphics that reproduced the old Ferrari headquarters in viale Trento and Trieste, Enzo Ferrari's house and Largo Garibaldi where the times of the Mille Miglia were posted. Under the guidance of Antonio Ghini, Claudio Berro and Stefano Domenicali had organised most of the event, a responsibility that along with their normal jobs involved many long days and short nights. At the end of the week they were both exhausted, and with barely time to pause before the Grand Prix circus called them to Canada.

But for a short time, Ferrari once more dominated the cities which formed the character of her creator, Enzo Ferrari. In Maranello the people joined in with the celebrations as though they were all shareholders, or personal friends. Council offices, banks, schools, cafes, green grocers and supermarkets were all covered in photos of old races; even the taxi drivers drove around with the prancing horse displayed in their windows.

On Saturday 7 June the Ferrari party culminated in an evening show that eclipsed all others. Edward Asprey was knocked out by the sheer scale of the entertainment. 'There were fireworks on a scale that I've never seen before, it was as I imagine the 21st Century celebrations will be. It was absolutely fantastic, the show, and the music. It was the tangible evidence of the absolute power of Ferrari to entice and seduce anyone who comes into contact with the cars and the history. It was a special honour to be part of the Ferrari family and experience history in the making. I don't think I'll be around for the 100 year celebrations so I'm glad I was here for the 50 year ones!'

The collectors, friends and fans all mingled with one another, drinking in the rare atmosphere of shared hopes and dreams. Montezemolo was feted as the hero who slowly but

The Car's the Star
Thousands of Ferrari fans gathered in Rome to catch a glimpse of their favourite cars.

surely is bringing the Prancing Horse back to full health. Although he tries to play down the chances of Schumacher winning the World Championship this year, it is the only question on many people's lips. No longer if or maybe, but when. If Schumacher could win the Championship in the 50th year of the Prancing Horse after a drought of eighteen years he would be given the freedom of the country, never mind the city. There have been many crushed dreams during these last barren years, now the people want victory. As if part of the master plan, their faith in the future was about to be given a massive injection of hope in Canada, which was host to the second Schumacher victory of the year.

• • •

The 1997 Canadian Grand Prix was a strange affair. Schumacher ended up winning but it was a hollow victory as the race was stopped early due to Olivier Panis' accident when his Prost car crashed heavily into the barriers, breaking the Frenchman's legs. Apart from that, Schumacher owed his victory to David Coulthard's clutch problems which delayed the McLaren in the pits when he had been leading the race.

Longing Looks
Every Ferrari fan has his or her favourite car – and at Maranello there was plenty of choice!

Whilst Coulthard was in the pits the race had to be stopped after Panis's crash. When the Frenchman remained motionless in the car after it had smashed into the barriers, it brought back some heart-stopping memories for the men in Formula One, memories of the tragic day on 1 May 1994 when the great Ayrton Senna perished in a collision with a barrier wall. Giorgio Ascanelli was Senna's race engineer at McLaren and although he declares that Panis's crash did not bring back memories of Senna, the accident, indeed any accident, triggers powerful emotions in Ferrari's Chief Engineer.

'The victory in Canada was not happy. It was clouded by the Panis issue. When they stop a race you always think the worse. From what we could see from the television monitors, it wasn't good. This is always a worry and the win suddenly didn't matter at all. The bottom line is that it's my job to ensure the safe running of the cars. When something goes wrong, your worst fears come out.

'I am never relaxed when the car is on the track. There is always something that can happen. The unpredictable can happen or the predictable when you've simply been negligent. It happens, although sometimes the consequences are small.'

This is a nightmare scenario for Ascanelli and he remembers a particular incident which highlighted his fears. 'I remember something that happened not to me, but it could have done.

Leader of the Pack
Michael Schumacher in front during the early stages of the Canadian Grand Prix.

It was the first practice session for the 1994 British Grand Prix. Hill was on the third corner when both wishbones flopped out of the chassis. They had not been fitted correctly. People do make mistakes. We are only human. Drivers can make mistakes in over estimating their ability and the car's capacity and have an accident. A mechanic who is probably working until 4 am and then starting again at 6.30 am after an hour's sleep can make mistakes. This is understandable. But if something goes wrong the first thing you ask is, what did I do wrong? It's the nature of the job and part of being the person responsible for the team at the track.'

Schumacher, after his pole position and race victory, was in subdued mood, barely lifting the trophy up to the crowds and leaving the unopened bottles of champagne at his feet. But the important thing was that his ambition was back. His race engineer Ignazio Lunetta says, 'Michael's more motivated. He's always very attentive, but when his level of attentiveness goes up even further, you know he is on the case. After Barcelona he was a bit down, but after Canada he was back on top.'

The pragmatic Nigel Stepney put the whole thing in context when he said, 'Panis's accident is not the way to win points, but ten points is ten points.' He went on, 'We expected to do well but we didn't expect pole position in qualifying. We struggled a bit with the tyres; we opted for the hardest type but they were still too soft.'

So, after Canada, Schumacher was still top of the World Championship league with a seven-point lead over Villeneuve and Ferrari still top of the Constructor's table by eight points over nearest rival Williams. The basic fact of life was that Villeneuve threw it away on his home turf by spinning out of the race on the second lap. As Stepney said dismissively, 'He tried to drive like Schumacher.'

Eddie Irvine was not having a great time either for different reasons. He was off the pace in qualifying and out of the race on the first lap due to no fault of his own. McLaren driver Mika Hakkinen had clashed with Panis's Prost and Irvine was the victim as he collided with Mika's nose cone. The Irishman wasn't happy.

'This was the worst race for me in terms of qualifying. I really felt I was going to qualify well in Canada. The car was good all week. But come qualifying it all just fell apart. I don't know whether I fell apart, but I just couldn't brake late and Canada is all about braking late. I didn't have the confidence for some reason. It was very depressing. I just don't understand it. It may be a psychological reason but it becomes physical when qualifying in the Ferrari. There is some feeling I'm getting from the car when I'm out qualifying that I don't like. I feel it's going to bite me. Maybe I'm overbraking, trying to push too hard or something like that.'

Maybe Schumacher's times have some bearing. Irvine says, 'Maybe he [Michael] does have a negative effect on you when you see these amazing times and you think "I must push harder," when in effect you don't have to or you just try too hard and it becomes less natural.'

Irvine gives a good performance as a laid back, 'nothing bothers me' type character. The truth is, like anyone who is competing at the top level in their chosen sport, he's ambitious, focused and craves the sweet taste of victory, so the race was a big disappointment. 'I thought I'd have a good race. I didn't have a tyre blistering problem in Canada. I was going round the outside of everyone and it was the right thing to do as everyone was bunched up on the inside. I was on the outside thinking "Fantastic." The next thing I knew a piece of someone's car came flying out of nowhere and just went underneath the rear wheel, flicked me round and cut the engine. That was it. The end of my race. I was on a one-stop race strategy. I had no problems with blistering. I was sure of the podium. I was really very confident and it all went wrong.'

After three podium appearances in a row, Irvine declared he wanted another six. Now after two bad races in Spain and Canada I asked him if he still felt the same way. 'After two bad races, I'd be happy with the original plan of six.' Then he hesitated. 'Another four would be nice.'

• • •

After Canada the team went to test at Magny-Cours, home to the next race, and gave the new grooved tyres which will be used from 1998 their first outing. The new regulations for 1998 are wide ranging and aim to reduce speeds. There are fierce discussions about them with drivers like Jacques Villeneuve believing that they are unnecessary and speed and danger are part of the thrills of Formula One, and FIA boss Max Mosley defends the decision to reduce speed by saying, 'If you continue to go 250 km/h through a corner, there is more risk of an accident as experience shows this is the moment of greatest danger. Common sense dictates that these speeds must be reduced. There are sixteen corners which have been identified as dangerous in Formula One; if we can reduce speeds by three seconds a lap this will be cut by half to eight. If we don't do this there will be a big accident. Only in this way can we preserve great corners like Eau Rouge at Spa. My job is to make sure that the Grand Prix drivers survive past their retirement age, and the best way of doing this is with grooved tyres.'

In the Groove
The rain starts to fall during the French Grand Prix, giving Michael Schumacher the chance to prove his supremacy in the wet.

Schumacher had his own views on grooved tyres. 'The speed of entry into the corners is the same, it is the mid and exit points that are slower. As expected there is less grip as the relationship of grip to power is different. With the current car they reduce the speed by about five seconds a lap. With next year's car it will be different and we'll have to see.' Schumacher's greatest desire was to see an increase in overtaking possibilities which would not only be more interesting for the drivers but also offer more entertainment for the crowds. 'You can't overtake, they haven't found the rules to get racing back to what it was in the 70s and 80s, and we should at least be able to overtake somehow. I would like a genuine opportunity to race and overtake. That's why I do winter karting as I get satisfaction that I don't get through the year.'

Ross Brawn was taking the new regulation changes in his stride. 'We have to accept that we can't keep making the cars go faster and faster. The gain in times comes from braking and cornering. As there is little progress in engine power, we're braking harder and going through the corners faster. This means that the velocity of the car in the corners is higher so if it does leave the track it will travel further. I think something was necessary and I think grooved tyres was one solution. The drivers don't like the fact that they don't have as much grip as they used to with the old tyres. Whether you can reduce the grip in a way that makes the car driver friendly is debatable. I think it is one solution that is in place and we have to work with it. Some drivers have a different view and as they drive the cars, they know better than me. Villeneuve says it reduces the skill level but I don't understand that. If you use wet conditions as an example, the driver skill comes to the fore and technology takes a back seat. I think it will put more emphasis on driver skill. Time will tell.'

An Exceptional Team
Ross Brawn and Giorgio Ascanelli discuss strategy and tactics.

Giorgio Ascanelli reflects Enzo Ferrari's philosophy. 'Enzo Ferrari said that to go fast you need more power, less drag, more downforce, less weight and better brakes. There is no other secret. The new grooved tyres will affect brakes by limiting the braking ability of the car; you will have less powerful, smaller brakes. Brakes are a big part of the basics of a Formula One car. It is one of the reasons we went better in Imola than in other places. We have, I believe, a brake advantage and Imola is heavy on brakes.'

Ross Brawn had now been working six months with Ferrari and it seemed a good moment to ask him about the main differences between Benetton and Ferrari and discuss some of the new modifications that are coming on line and how these will affect the car. The main difference between Benetton and Ferrari? 'Language,' laughs Brawn before going on to say, 'Benetton have Flavio Briatore who is Team Principal and plays a much more entrepreneurial role than Jean Todt does here. Jean is much more of a hands-on manager, and much more involved in the everyday working of the company. This is a good thing as long as it's someone who knows what they are

Triple Delight

A third victory of 1997 for
Schumacher at Magny-Cours
in France.

doing, and Jean does. For Flavio to get involved with the everyday running of the company would have been a mistake, that's not his strength. I think I can work quite well within each system. With Flavio you have complete freedom as he didn't get involved with the technical side. His real involvement was assessing the results and discussing the funding. Jean has much more involvement with the general running of the company, but he gives more support. When things are difficult Jean is there to support you and help fix it. I had Flavio's support but in a different way – it was more a no-interference support.'

Regarding strengths and weaknesses, according to Brawn the design side of Ferrari is still not up to strength, although it is coming up to speed and Brawn expects it to be as good as, if not better than Benetton. 'We have some very good people, we need to consolidate a little more, get the design team established and then take on the world!'

When John Barnard delivered the new car in January 1997, there were various modifications planned including a new gearbox, which has now been put on hold. As Brawn says, 'We have rolled the new gearbox into next year's programme. I didn't think it was worth it in terms of performance gain. Every team is limited from a resources point of view as to what they can and can't do. In addition to this we have a new engine next year which is different enough to require another gearbox. That would have meant three different gearboxes in the space of a year, which is not something you'd do without considerable thought.'

Shell are also in the process of looking at different gearbox oils in order to improve the efficiency of the gearbox and hopefully lower its running temperature. The gearbox has important potential in the fight to get more power for the car to go faster. It is one of the chief absorbers of power in the mechanical system. A 90% efficient gearbox will still be absorbing 70+hp from a modern F1 car. Much of this is dissipated as heat, noise and wear etc. If you could increase that to even 92%, it would release approximately 15 hp and make it available to drive the car faster. The oil may have a valuable role in this and Ferrari is the ideal team to carry out this development as it is unique in having a total engine-car team.

Ross also has a programme of modifications to the suspension which will improve the handling of the car. 'I'd like to see some feel come back into the steering. I think that the sensitivity of the steering is not very good, which is something that may be hindering Eddie more than Michael. I want to have the steering more direct than it is now. We are working on suspension goemetry part of which is to do with the steering. At the moment the entry to a corner is very critical. We can't do anything about the middle of the corner as the entry becomes even more critical, so you're balancing. We can stop understeer in the middle by having a lot of oversteer on entry which is not necessarily the best solution, so what we have at the moment is the best compromise between the two. We have a power steering system, which because of its design takes a bit of feel away from the driver. I want to try and bring that back. It's a pretty major package, involving a complete redesign of the front suspension. What we're looking for is a bit more stability on entry, and a bit more consistency between entry and middle.'

To achieve this Ross plans to do a complete scan of the suspension geometry to see what they've got and what they need. What you can be certain of is that unless it gives tangible evidence of improved performance it won't be used. 'We've got a differential programme going on at the moment that we've been working on for six months, but I won't let it go on the car as we haven't finally quantified the advantage of it.

A Dynamic Engine
The Shell cover housing hides the V10 engine from view at Magny-Cours in France.

We've had it on the car many times and it's progressing the whole time, but when we put it on the car against the differential we have, the gain is either very small or not apparent at all. Obviously, people have put a lot of work and effort into it and they want to see it on the car, but I feel if we put it on the car now we might be taking a backward step.'

As Brawn points out when talking about hasty changes made in the name of progress, 'You saw it with McLaren one or two years ago. They were making enormous changes and not getting anywhere. However, if you look at the best example of cautiousness, Williams, you see their changes are very slow and methodical. They do, of course, have the advantage of being the quickest and that always makes life easier.'

However, there were still new things for France and others being planned for Silverstone. 'We've got a new front wing here (France) which is very new. We still have to decide whether to race with it or not.'

• • •

For the French Grand Prix, Ferrari did race with the new front wing and it was credited with making an important difference to the handling of the car. After Michael Schumacher expressed his doubts as to whether the Ferrari would do well at the Magny-Cours circuit, against all odds he snatched pole position, while team-mate Eddie Irvine was fifth on the starting grid. It turned out to be a great race for the stable of the prancing horse, as Schumacher went on to obtain his sixth victory for Ferrari, whilst Irvine was also on the podium in third place.

Ross Brawn explained the advantages of the new wing in more depth. 'It's more efficient, creating more downforce with less drag. Wings, particularly front wings, are very dynamic. They can affect the cars' feel and its behaviour.' Irvine agreed that the car was now easier to drive and to set up.

The new 046/2 engine was also given the go ahead at Magny-Cours and was used in the race for the first time. It had been beset by problems, which were solved by Ferrari and Shell. As Brawn says, 'We had a problem with some parts of the 046/2 engine. Paolo Martinelli identified the trouble and we looked at options to resolve it. Shell developed another lubricant which virtually eliminated the problem.'

It's Party Time
Michael Schumacher and Eddie Irvine celebrate 1st and 3rd place on the podium after the French Grand Prix.

Indeed, the Shell analysis system that is in place at the track has contributed to allaying the fears of the team, when they think mechanical failure may be about to occur or that some mistake may have caused damage. The machine can measure the amount and composition of metallic abrasion 'dust' suspended in the oil. This warns of wear, although there have been remarkably low wear rates. The machine has been used to diagnose problems, such as once when it was thought that engine oil from the tank was leaking into the adjacent gearbox. Analysis of the possibly contaminated gearbox oil showed no trace of engine oil. On another occasion there was doubt as to whether an errant gear change had caused damage to the engine. The analyser was used to assist the engineer's assessment of the problem. In addition, there were a few smaller changes to the car in France, such as the re-designed anti-roll bar at the front which made the steering a bit more positive.

Ross Brawn is not only a technical man but also an excellent 'manager of people'. His open minded approach to refusing to place people in boxes is one of the reasons for his success. 'There is a lot of pressure on people who work in Formula One, as well as a high level of skill and talent required. When you put these things together you probably have a situation where people in motor racing are not entirely "normal". We're not too worried about people's attitudes as long as they're reasonably positive. We are concerned about their ability and whether they are ultimately making the car go faster. Within reason, if someone has a lot of personality problems, it doesn't matter, as long as it's not upsetting the team. What you have to do wherever you go is learn to adapt to the people around you. I think it is a mistake to go to a team and bring people with you. There may well be more capable people at

the new team than you had working with you before. It takes a little time to adjust to everyone's
needs at your new team. It took me a few months to understand what people actually meant
when they said something.

'However, in terms of the personnel at Ferrari, they're as good as anyone in Formula One.
Giorgio [Ascanelli] is an exceptional engineer. Jean [Todt] is an exceptional Team Principal. I
look at them and they look at me, and I'm sure I do things differently to what they're used to.
However, if we can combine all those things without too much conflict we can be successful.
Jean takes away a lot of the pressure, he absorbs a lot, but there is only so much he can hold
back. The rest you have to take yourself.

'One thing that has changed is that the responsibility is now Maranello's, and nobody
else's. We have to solve problems ourselves, whereas in the past when FDD [John Barnard's
Ferrari Design and Development] in England had a different point of view, we could not find a
joint solution. Now we have the designer, the chief engineer and the technical director at
Maranello. If there's a problem, we have to solve it; there's no bouncing it about like a
ping-pong ball.'

This confirms John Barnard's view that in 1996 a lot of the problems were caused by each
side, FDD and Maranello, blaming the other, and is a good indicator that the right technical
director can bring order and prevent a damaging civil war from breaking out.

The new set up at Maranello should also help people like Giorgio Ascanelli who can now
concentrate on engineering. But, strangely enough, he was out of sorts and struggling to
come to terms with the meaning of it all at Magny-Cours. I made the mistake of calling Nigel
Stepney Team Coordinator rather than Chief Mechanic, although Stepney, up to this point, had
always been referred to as Team Coordinator. Ascanelli put me right. 'He's Chief Mechanic.' But

isn't he more than that, doesn't he pull it all together? 'My dear friend, what has he got to coordinate? Mechanics. What do you call the coordinator of mechanics? Chief Mechanic. He's Chief Mechanic, full stop.'

In 1996 Ascanelli likened his relationship with Nigel Stepney to a marriage, with each partner learning to work together through talent and compromise. It seemed that the marriage of convenience was a bit frayed around the edges, although it is also obvious that there is a great deal of mutual respect between the two. Ascanelli, it appeared, was going through a kind of early mid-life crisis. He has a creative mind which comes up with brilliant ideas, but like most creative people he needs space to breathe and a not too controlling master. Eddie Irvine says, 'Giorgio is very emotional, very volatile, but he has some great ideas. He's a very clever guy. Sometimes, you've got to listen to him because he's right, other times you just let him have his say and then do what you think is right. Ross is very methodical and will control things. He's less inspired but more organised.'

Smooth Operator

After two bad races, Eddie Irvine was pleased to be back on the podium in France.

According to Ascanelli, 'Nigel and I had one kind of relationship in the first two years that we worked together, when I was his only input. At this very minute, I think my role has slightly changed. Now Ross is here so I have a lot less input on design. In Italian I am the *responsabile operativo*, which means that any kind of engineering or mechanical operation comes under my control. Nigel is still strictly responsible to me.'

Reading between the lines, it seemed that Ascanelli was feeling slightly threatened by the changes, although in reality he was still much valued for his creativity and talent. He has more time to spend with his family, wife Stefania and daughter Camilla, but even in that he is controlled. 'In reality we do activities that are good for Stefania and Camilla, because I feel that I cause them so much stress that it's important they enjoy what they do with me, rather than me enjoy what I do with them.'

Time to himself is rare. 'I used to be a decent piano player, I used to read books, now the only time I read is during the race weekend or at tests, as this is the only time I'm alone. When I'm at home there is always something to do. I don't have the luxury of being alone. I used to be a good amateur photographer and before I broke my leg skiing, I was an awful skier, but a good tennis player and a good volleyball player.'

He wants to retire soon but has no specific dream. 'My father used to tell me, live every day of your life as though it was the first or last. I'm trying to do that and be respected. The way you feel and the satisfaction you get depends on what you are and what you bring inside yourself, not what you can do.'

Expanding into the area of philosophy and the meaning of life, he went into Zen mode and declared, 'The secret of being a good archer is not to aim at the target, but to be the target, the archer and the arrow.'

He adds 'I'm probably a bit disillusioned. I've been successful and I'm happy. On the other hand, I believe that if I was to have a much tougher life in a foundry I'd be happier.'

Disillusioned or not, Ferrari were leading both the World Championship and the Constructor's Championship, and Ascanelli had contributed to the success, even if he wasn't doing quite what he wanted to do. However, he expressed his doubts as to whether Ferrari would hang onto their lead in the Constructor's Championship. 'I believe Williams have a technical advantage. We have one advantage over them and he's called Michael Schumacher.'

Next year sees some major technical changes. Maybe the dice will roll the other way. 'The new regulations will take away the advantage of those who have it, although we don't know by how much. When you start reshuffling the cars, it's like playing blackjack, you don't know.'

Meanwhile, Eddie Irvine was still chewing over his qualifying problems and hoping he would overcome them. 'In practice [French Grand Prix Friday session] in the wet, there was nothing between us [him and Schumacher]. In fact, I was even a little bit faster, but there is still this qualifying issue to sort out which I don't understand. I used to get out of the Jordan and feel there was nothing left. It wasn't even a good car then, but every other race I would think I'd taken the Jordan to its limit. I was in the top six. The only time I ever did that with the Ferrari was in Australia [his first race in 1996]. Since then never, well, maybe Estoril was close.'

Irvine's Race Engineer, Luca Baldisserri has his own theories on the Irishman's qualifying problems. 'There is often only a 100th of a second difference between places in qualifying and I think this makes him nervous. This makes him brake more with his head and less instinctively. When he really tries to go fast, he is slower. It is better when he just does it and it is much more fluid. The other aspect that puts pressure on a driver is that it is simpler to overtake when you are higher up the grid. This can also affect your race strategy as you can have a more aggressive strategy if you are ahead – for example, you could have two stops – whereas if you're further down the grid you will try and make one pit stop only.'

• • •

Meanwhile at the French Grand Prix at Magny-Cours, Ferrari were celebrating the appearance of both their drivers on the podium. The Italian press were delirious, with one headline reading, 'Ferrari, don't dream, you are World Class.' At last, a win had been achieved that was not dependent on the mistakes of others. Luca di Montezemolo was pleased. 'We were in front from beginning to

The Jet Set

Eddie Irvine's fifth place on the grid for the French Grand Prix was an indication that maybe he is getting the 'Schumacher Factor' licked. He says 'Panis is a classic example of the 'other driver' factor. [Martin] Brundle is not a bad driver, a good solid professional, yet in 1996 [when he was Panis's team-mate] he destroyed Panis. This year [1997], by contrast, Panis is looking very good as he has a tosser of a team-mate, so he can concentrate on what he's doing and not be distracted by what his team-mate is doing.'

Irvine keeps his fitness levels high, even if he isn't in the same obsessional category as Schumacher. He runs, goes to the gym, and is supervised by sister Sonia, who is also extremely fit. The only problem he had last year was with his neck. 'This year I've been testing more so it's not such an issue. Last year was a problem because I never drove the car except at races, so I had to do work on my neck, although there's nothing to substitute driving the car.'

The pressure of racing and other commitments was taking its toll on Irvine. His life was one long stop travel circus and it was beginning to get out of hand. 'I tested before Canada and had things to do with sponsors. I flew from Italy to Dublin and stayed one day in Dublin. I then got on a plane and flew to New York. From New York I went to Montreal and the race. After the race on the Sunday night I went back to New York and onto Dublin. I was in bed four hours, before

Steady, Eddie!

I got the police round as someone had smashed all the windows in my garage! I flew to France that night, picked up a car I'd bought from Jean Todt [a Lancia Delta Integrale], drove to Magny-Cours, tested for three days, then drove to London that night. I arrived at 2 am. I got up the next day and drove to Oxford and left the car. The next morning I flew to Goodwood. That night I left there and flew to Italy. I spent all the next day with a sponsor, Valle Verde. Then I went back to London and met up with Prince Hakeem of Brunei. I got back to Dublin that night and on Tuesday and Wednesday I just mucked about the house. I was up at 6 am on Thursday to get to Magny-Cours for a 4 pm meeting and then it was the race weekend.'

The strain was showing on the Friday before the race. There was a 9.30 am meeting and at 9.20 am, the team started to ask sister Sonia where her

Eddie Irvine talks to close friend and sponsor Maurizio Arrivabene of Philip Morris.

brother was. She thought he would be on his way as he is known for cutting things a bit fine; but 9.30 am came and went with no sign of him. When Sonia called Eddie at his hotel, he was still sound asleep! Something had to be changed and this frenetic pace should slow down now that Irvine has just bought a plane, a second-hand Falcon 10. Many people think a private airplane is the ultimate luxury but to Irvine it's a necessity, and not even an expensive one. He actually made money on his helicopter as he's been offered $100,000 more than he actually paid for it. The same should happen with the plane, or at least he should break even.

At least Irvine was pleased that his Hong Kong & Shanghai Bank shares were making him money. A canny investor, the Irishman relaxes on plane journeys by reading the *Financial Times* and *The Economist* and the business sections of other newspapers. At home he'll watch the shares on Ceefax and play the guitar. 'I'm at a similar stage to EJ (Eddie Jordan) in that my guitar would have to be unplugged for anyone to enjoy listening to it, like his drum kit is unplugged. I like nothing better than sitting at home by myself looking at the stocks and shares and trying to figure out 'Sunday, Bloody Sunday' on the guitar.'

end, in the dry and in the wet. I don't want to exaggerate, but I think we dominated.'

Schumacher was expressing his surprise at the win. 'My predictions for this race were wrong and this was a convincing win. I hope that at Silverstone we can continue to make good progress as we did here. The race here, which marks the halfway point of the season, will be very important for the Championship.'

Eddie Irvine, having overtaken a couple of cars at the start, finished a highly credible third. 'After two bad races I am glad to be back on the podium. Villeneuve braked early so I was able to pass him at the first corner. Towards the end of the race, Villeneuve was closing in on me.'

For Jean Todt it was another confirmation that the team are on the right track. 'We did not expect to have such an advantage in this race, even in wet conditions. We must thank Goodyear for giving us such good tyres. Today was the first time we raced with the 046/2 engine and the decision to use it was not an easy one. The team operated a perfect strategy in a situation that was difficult to judge.'

The cool and calm Schumacher even managed to slow down on the last lap to allow his brother Ralf in the Jordan to go through and complete another lap. Because David Coulthard's McLaren retired on that lap, it allowed Ralf to pick up one point and a great birthday present from his big brother. The Schumacher brothers are very close; when they are both at the same test they are constantly together, usually it is Ralf visiting Michael, but sometimes during race weekend Michael will take refuge in the Jordan motorhome to escape the pressure of people round Ferrari, and have a chat with his little brother. There is no doubt that the elder Schumacher has enormous respect and affection for his younger brother. 'You have to think a long way back to find comparisons with someone who came into Formula One so young and so good without making major mistakes.'

One thing that is certain about motor racing is its unpredictable nature and, sure enough, after the euphoria of the Italian press and the happiness of the team in France, Ferrari were in for a cold shower at Silverstone.

The Two Schumachers
The Schumacher brothers salute the crowd together in Hungary.

CHAPTER TWELVE

A Cold Shower

'He [Todt] has absolute

integrity and also absolute

power when necessary'

Claudio Berro
Ferrari Chief Press Officer

The Ferrari team touched down at Luton at 9.30 am on the Thursday before the British Grand Prix. Before mid-day they were bustling about the garage unpacking and dressing it in the sponsors' colours. The celebratory Spice Girls tape and the Italian music cassettes that had been played after the win in France, were put to one side. In their place was a heavy beat disco-type sound that reflected their unpacking, or 'getting in the mood' as one mechanic put it. Occasionally, Jean Todt appeared like an irritated parent and complained about the noise, before taking refuge in the team motorhome and immersing himself in work.

However, mid-way through the 1997 season, Jean Todt was looking much more relaxed and at peace with himself than at this time last year, when the team were in the midst of coping with

Mr Professional
Jean Todt feels the disappointment of Silverstone. Behind him Claudio Berro prepares to meet the press.

disaster after disaster. His personal success with the team was not only surviving but managing to build the team in the way he wanted to. The external and internal pressures of achieving this have been great. It has only been Todt's determination, hard work and vision of the way the team needed to go, that kept things moving in a forward direction. The panic factor, when everything is turned upside down in the face of severe problems has been eradicated, and Todt's calm influence can take most of the credit for that.

'Last year at this same point, it was a nightmare, a disaster. I could not feel happy,' says Todt. However, this did not involve sleepless nights over his professional life. 'Most of the time I sleep well, which is probably why I'm still here. I don't panic. Business is business. It's a part of life, but it's not vital, you don't have your family involved. You have to be pragmatic. If you are affected by something close to you then you are not pragmatic – you are just reacting with your heart. In business you must react with your head.'

Reacting with his head, means that he is separated from his family for a lot of the time. 'I work in Italy and most of the time I'm alone. It's part of the deal and I have to accept it. Anyway, the Italian people who you meet in restaurants and so on are very nice. It's too difficult for someone to be with me while I'm working sixteen hours a day in the middle of nowhere. When I go home to Paris for the weekend I go to my other life, but I can never be completely unplugged from business. I couldn't go two days without knowing what is happening.'

So how does he switch off? 'I just walk around. I don't really switch off completely until I go on holiday and then I can relax on the beach and swim.'

After four tough years things were finally coming together. 'From an organisational point of view, we [Ferrari] have almost achieved what we wanted to achieve. It's taken four years to bring things together, find the right people and put them in the right places. Out of 100 people (including engine, chassis, production, composite, foundry, and administration staff, etc) we still need a software expert, two chassis designers and a composite designer. Once we've found them, then there will be the normal turnover of staff, so we will always be looking for new people.'

At this point Ross Brawn appeared in Todt's office and it is clear that there is mutual respect and admiration between the two. It has also given Jean Todt a partner. 'Ross is a great guy, very professional and very level-headed. He's achieving what he was brought in to do.'

Todt is not a person to celebrate wildly when Ferrari win a race. He is always aware of the consequences that such an action could bring. 'I'm not the kind of person to jump on the table and show how happy I am, because first and foremost I am always concerned about the next race. I just think we must have a silent and [a pause as he searches for the right word] humble approach, otherwise the boomerang comes and lands on the back of your head very quickly. I am always scared it will come back.'

Silverstone was the right place to be cautious. 'When we say we're reliable, it's difficult to get the words out as I think that maybe tomorrow we won't be reliable.' Quite.

The first indication that things wouldn't go quite to plan at Silverstone was when Eddie Irvine collided with a hare in qualifying and needed a new nose cone and turning vane. The incident scared the hell out of him, although he pulled himself together and qualified seventh, three places behind Schumacher, who said, 'I hope I can make it onto the podium on race day.'

Unfortunately for Schumacher, it wasn't to be. The German took control of the race when Jacques Villeneuve had a very slow 33 second pit stop after a wheel nut jammed, and quickly built up a big lead before the left rear wheel bearing failed on his car which put him out of the race with twenty laps to go. Ten minutes later, Eddie Irvine experienced the second mechanical failure when his right half shaft failed, as he was pulling away from his pit stop. Nil points for Ferrari at Silverstone.

Despite the disappointment, Schumacher was trying to be positive about the situation. 'It would have been better if I could have finished the race, but these things happen. We had confirmation of another important aspect, the fact that we are

Slippery when Wet
A change of fortune at Silverstone saw Schumacher retiring from the race with a damaged wheel bearing.

The Menu at Silverstone

The menu for the Ferrari team at Silverstone wouldn't be out of place in a top Italian restaurant.

FRIDAY
Lunch

Penne with a spicy tomato sauce
Grilled turkey
Duck with rosemary
A selection of vegetables including broccoli, mushrooms, grilled onions, grilled aubergines, Brussels sprouts, grilled peppers, carrots and runner beans

Dinner

Rice with parmesan cheese
Breast of chicken in an asparagus sauce
Proscuitto and melon
A selection of vegetables

SATURDAY
Lunch

Penne with tomato and basil sauce
A special proscuitto from Modena
Grilled meats

Dinner

Gramiglia with courgettes
Runner beans, carrots, tomatoes with mozzarella and salad

SUNDAY
Lunch

Pasta with mushroom sauce
Bread rolls
(most of the team don't have time to eat on race day)

now competitive during the race. When I retired from the race, I was leading it by a good margin. We have to improve our qualifying performance, but I'm sure we will resolve our problems before the next Grand Prix in Germany.'

However, behind the scenes a much worse disaster, at least in the eyes of the paddock gourmets, had occurred – the team cook, Claudio Degli Espositi, had been taken ill with a fever and had to stay in bed on the Saturday. He struggled out of bed on race day, but was still pale and under the weather. In Italy everything revolves around the kitchen and Salvatore from the Philip Morris motorhome was drafted in to help Bruno Romani keep the team fed and happy.

Back to the race, it was sad to see Ignazio Lunetta walking back disconsolately into the garage from the pit wall clutching his laptop computer, but the atmosphere was not too depressed. Schumacher still lead the World Driver's Championship by four points and Ferrari were top of the Constructor's Championship with a three-point lead over Williams. But as Nigel Stepney said about the Ferrari team, 'We just have to get ourselves together.'

● ● ●

Meanwhile, the desire to be anonymous was reaching epic proportions for Eddie Irvine. But if he wants to succeed he'll have to get used to the unwanted trappings of fame. The telephone stresses him, but he keeps it on as it's his only contact for people who need to get hold of him. I suppose the answer to that is try an answerphone. Irvine is undoubtedly quite a complex character: a lad who likes the women and the nightlife, but hates people staring at him; an ambitious racing driver who wants to be number one for one of the top teams but hates the thought of the loss of privacy. 'It's very important for a racing driver to be the centre of attention. You have to feel that the whole team is behind you and relying on

Sonia Irvine's Race Day

Sonia Irvine is not only Eddie's big sister but the person who acts as a combined nanny and business adviser. She prepares all his food, ensuring he eats and drinks at the proper times, and also entertains his guests and makes sure he is with his sponsors when he is supposed to be with them. She describes her race day at Silverstone:

7.00 am **Wake up call, train in my room for half-an-hour.**

7.45 am **Leave for the circuit on the Ferrari scooter.**

8.10 am **Collect Eddie from the helicopter pad.**

8.20 am **Arrive in pit lane. Prepare Eddie's breakfast (he eats special muesli with grapes, strawberries, banana, melon and pineapple).**

8.45 am **Prepare Eddie's rehydration drinks for the day (an orange based drink designed for rapid absorption).**

9.00 am **Organise race gear, overalls, correct gloves and cap for the day. Check on any changes to the day's events.**

9.15 am **Arrange for Eddie to autograph hats, cards, photographs etc.**

9.30 am **Whilst Eddie is out for warm-up, I prepare carbohydrate drinks. He does not like eating normal forms of carbohydrate on race day, so I make special drinks in order that he has enough energy to sustain him through race distance. I eat my breakfast.**

10.00 am **Drinks taken to drivers' briefing.**

10.15 am **Eddie's guests shown** around Ferrari pit (these include friends, celebrities such as Chris de Burgh and sponsors like Apep, Valle Verde and Motorscan, who produce exhausts and gas analysers).

10.45 am **More drinks taken in to Eddie,** fan mail read and responded to (Eddie always signs the mail himself).

11.15 am **Driver escorted to PR event, in** this case an appearance at The Marlboro Experience. Drinks bottle provided. The encouragement of fluid all weekend is a very important aspect of the physiotherapy role due to the detrimental effects dehydration can cause during a race.

11.30 am **Post-race pasta sauce prepared** (Eddie likes an Italian based tomato sauce with mushrooms, bacon with the fat cut off, and onion).

12.00 noon **I go out on the scooter to** check the venue for the 12.15 PR event.

12.15 pm **Collect Eddie from technical** meeting and guide to the event, in this case a lunch with Aer Lingus, where he meets the guests and makes a speech.

12.20 pm **Prepare the physio room for** Eddie's massage, and make sure that the Marlboro umbrella is ready for use on the grid.

12.40 pm **Eddie's massage.**

1.25 pm **More drinks encouraged. He has** a carbohydrate drink with banana, yoghurt and other fruit. Last photo session organised. Hat, umbrella and drinks bottle collected and taken to the starting grid.

2.00 pm **Watch race start. Aborted start,** so I go back to the grid.

2.15 pm **Watch race start again for a few** laps. Return to the Ferrari motorhome, wash Eddie's kit and lay out his clothes.

2.20 pm **Return to the Marlboro** motorhome to treat two people during the race.

3.15 pm **Eddie drops out of race due to** mechanical failure. Drinks bottle and cap taken to driver. No massage required. Food prepared and taken to driver. Finished treatment on Marlboro personnel. Organised time for helicopter to collect Eddie.

5.00 pm **Took Eddie by scooter to** the helicopter pad and then returned to the pits.

5.30 pm **Drinks bottles collected** and washed. Physiotherapy equipment packed away. Collect all pit passes.

6.00 pm **Ate my lunch!**

6.15 pm **Departed for the Jordan party!**

Giorgio Ascanelli has a word with Eddie Irvine as sister Sonia looks on in the background.

Press Ahead
Claudio Berro makes notes as
Schumacher's PR man, Heiner
Buchinger keeps his eyes on the
monitor.

you. Michael has that. I'd like to be number one at Ferrari or any of the top teams, such as McLaren, Jordan, or Benetton. At Benetton you can see the input a driver can have – they've achieved little since Michael left – and yet they have a better car now than they've ever had before.'

Not that Irvine is unhappy with his lot. Racing has brought a lot of material benefits. 'The amount of money you make at the race track gives you a good lifestyle away from it. I've got a house bought and paid for. All my toys are paid for. I don't owe anybody anything. I don't owe the bank anything. To have that independence and control is quite nice.'

The delightful Corinna Schumacher was at Silverstone. Corinna is as unaffected, natural and friendly as she was when she and Michael first met. The thing that seems to keep both their feet on the ground is a love of the simple things in life. Neither of them are big city sophisticates, preferring the country life of dogs and children and long walks. Baby Gina Maria is five months and beginning to pull herself up to sit, while Floh, the stray dog, is becoming more of a character and entertains everyone with her antics and her almost human ability to let her owners know what she wants. Corinna keeps out of the limelight and lets husband Michael get on with his job. Unlike some of the drivers' wives and girlfriends who pirouette and preen about the paddock as though they were the stars, Corinna takes a more low profile approach. Despite this, there is a price to be paid for being the wife of a double World Champion and the television cameras and photographers are never far away. Although Michael admits, 'I find it difficult to talk about myself' it is clear he finds peace and tranquillity with his growing family in the relative peace of his country home near Lake Geneva in Switzerland.

Who's the Boss?
Michael Schumacher explains the
technicalities to Fiat legend
Gianni Agnelli.

Following Silverstone, the Italian press were keeping admirably calm instead of screaming for someone's head. This most unusual situation could be attributed in part to the fact that Ferrari was having a good season, apart from the lapse at Silverstone, and also to Claudio Berro, Ferrari's Chief Press Officer. Level-headed and with a balanced temperament, Berro is always organised and very methodical in his approach. At the races he directs the interviews with the help of Stefania Bocchi and Nigel Wollheim. Stefania, an accomplished part of the Marlboro team is a welcoming hostess and also provides first-class secretarial back-up. Nigel has been around Formula One for many years, speaks almost every known language fluently and as well as acting as official translator, he also smoothes the path for foreign press contact with the team. For the first time Ferrari is noticeably relaxed in its approach to the media, who are encouraged to drop in for coffee or lunch, with well-researched articles always noted and the writer contacted and thanked.

A workaholic who having worked with Jean Todt knows how to deal with the team and the media in a way that will keep everyone happy, Berro is always on the go. Ring him at seven in the morning and he's arriving at the office, ring him at ten at night and he's just finishing doing his round up of what the Italian media are up to.

One of the most popular Berro initiatives is the instigation of a very useful media booklet, which as well as giving pertinent information about the race track – including previous races, quotes about the circuit from Jean Todt and the drivers, dates and times of practice, qualifying, the race and the press conferences – also gives a summary of what happened in the current Championship year races, and has blank pages for recording information and writing down interviews.

Driver Power
Michael Schumacher checks the set-up on his car.

During the week leading up to the race weekend the media pressure builds up. The usual 25 to 30 pages of the press cuttings turns into 60 or 70 on the Wednesday and Thursday before a race, 120 on the Friday and Saturday and 150 on race day. The day after race day it peaks at 200.

Each day Claudio Berro receives anything up to a dozen faxes requesting interviews from all over the world, including the old Eastern block countries, who having eschewed communism are now heavily into consumerism. In addition, the television stations want access to Fiorano on test days and have to be monitored and given help. At the races the planned interviews have to be monitored and organised. The drivers and team personnel involved in the FIA official press conferences have to be escorted to the venue of the press conference and escorted back through the melee (in Schumacher's case) of journalists, radio and television reporters. Race Day is almost peaceful in comparison, according to Berro.

'It's quite calm after the run around of the weekend. I receive the press cuttings between 7.15 and 7.30 in the morning. One set comes to me, one set to Jean Todt, and two sets for the journalists. While reading my copy, I eat a ham sandwich and some fruit. Then we have warm-up. I'm always in the garage to make notes of everything, the cars used, the tyres used and the time the drivers leave and return to the garage. If a journalist asks me for the information and it's not secret, I can then tell him. If, on the other hand, a journalist makes a mistake I have the information to correct him. When warm-up is over Stefania accompanies Schumacher and records his interviews with the media, Nigel is with Eddie and I go to Jean Todt.'

Berro is Todt's security blanket. Like most clever men, Todt feels the cold blast of insecurity and likes backup. 'You have to know him to appreciate him. He can appear to be hard and rigid if you don't know him. But when he shakes his hand and gives his word, it is the same as a written contract. He has absolute integrity and also absolute power when necessary.'

Formula One is like a battle and Todt effectively goes into battle at every race. Berro adds, 'Everyone responds to his orders. When he has time he will listen to everyone, but when the moment arrives to take a decision he always takes it.'

Before the race Berro walks around observing other teams. It is, as he puts it, 'the calm before the storm.' Another factor is his technical ability. In the past when other teams saw the Ferrari press officer strolling around the cars they didn't take much notice – that was until they discovered that Berro had studied for an engineering degree. Now when Williams, for example, see him approaching them on the starting grid they form a human barrier round the car!

During the race Berro is in the garage with the team to observe the pit stops of both Ferraris and the other teams. After the race there is a flurry of activity. The press release has to be written and printed and Berro also assists Todt and/or the drivers in their interviews after the race. Then faxes are sent to the sponsors, a document of information on the Grand Prix prepared and an internal press release written which contains more information and is highly confidential to team members only.

Hero Worship
Life-sized Michael Schumacher cutouts keep the crowd happy at the German Grand Prix.

Like most of his colleagues Berro believes the team is more together this year. 'We are more of a team. It's more complete now that we have a technical director who works at Maranello. The exchange of information is more immediate. All the meetings are at Maranello and the car is built in one place, so no one can blame anyone else.'

Next stop for the millionaire boys with their flash toys was Hockenheim – and a home race for Michael Schumacher. Now we would see if Ferrari's challenge for the World Championship was serious or just a flash in the pan.

CHAPTER THIRTEEN

The Fightback to Victory

'I've been involved in the sport too long not to know that until you pass the chequered flag anything can happen.'

Jean Todt
Ferrari Team Principal

Although Ferrari and Williams were the only teams with a serious chance of winning the World Championship, the German Grand Prix was all about Benetton and the comeback of old-timer, Gerhard Berger. The Austrian driver had been absent for the previous three races, and had suffered the devastating loss of his father in a plane crash. Alexander Wurtz had proved he was a worthy replacement. So at Hockenheim, Berger had everything to prove and he did it in style: pole position and race winner. It was Benetton's first victory since 1995. Michael Schumacher was the first to congratulate the experienced Austrian. 'He drove a great race,' said the Ferrari No 1.

Berger pulled away from the chasing pack right at the start of the race, and by lap 5 he was extending his lead by half a lap. Giancarlo Fisichella was lying second with seven laps remaining when he had to retire due to a tyre puncture, and Schumacher took advantage of this to move up from third. However, five laps from the end of the race the Ferrari team had to call the German into the pits for an unprogrammed 'splash and dash' fuel top up. Fortunately, Schumacher rejoined the race still ahead of third-placed Hakkinen, and managed to pull away from the Finn to finish second.

It turned out that the Ferrari team's planned one-stop strategy had to be altered for their No 1 driver when insufficient fuel was put into the tank. This wasn't the only problem. The gears had been playing up during the last thirty laps, with the result that Schumacher couldn't engage fifth, while trouble with the rear wing meant

V for Victory
Engines Manager at the track, Pino D'Agostino, shows off the Ferrari V10.

that the Ferrari was losing a certain amount of grip. Ross Brawn explains: 'When fifth gear became reluctant to engage we were losing out slightly on straight-line speed. In addition a small flap on the rear wing disappeared, so Michael started to get oversteer. He thought it was the tyres, but when we lost the flap he gained one or two kilometres in a straight line. We could see what was happening on the telemetry from about lap sixteen.'

But in the end, second place for Schumacher meant six points, keeping him ahead of rival Jacques Villeneuve by ten points. The Canadian didn't finish the race, having gone off under pressure from Jarno Trulli. As usual Schumacher was calmness personified. 'There's work to do and we'll get down to it immediately, even if we're still leading the Championship.'

This wasn't the first time in the season that a Ferrari had done a 'splash and dash' to take on more fuel. In Melbourne a similar thing happened. Pino D'Agostino, the Ferrari man in charge of the engine at the track and also the man in charge of fuel explains: 'All the teams occasionally experience this problem. It occurs because the fuel tank is divided into several cells, to make sure the weight distribution of the car is even. This can lead to regurgitation of the fuel into the hose when one cell is full. By monitoring the amount of fuel that has gone into the cells we

Hockenheim Hero
The Ferrari team and the *tifosi* congratulate Michael Schumacher on his hard-earned second place in Germany.

should know when some has been left out.' At Hockenheim 10 kg by weight was left out, enough to mean that Schumacher didn't have sufficient fuel in his tank to make it to the end of the race.

Schumacher declared after Hockenheim: 'I will try and win the World Championship, but I don't want to succeed because an adversary [presumably Villeneuve] goes off the track. I like to battle and beat my rivals during the race.'

Team-mate Eddie Irvine, on the other hand, did not have a happy race. Still beset by qualifying problems, he nevertheless managed to move from tenth place, where he had qualified, to fifth place at the start of the race, only to be struck from behind by Villeneuve's Williams team-mate, Heinz-Harald Frentzen and so the Irishman's race ended before it had properly begun. His race engineer, the faithful Luca Baldisserri had his own ideas on why it had gone wrong in qualifying. 'Before Hockenheim all the other drivers tested at Monza, which is a similar low downforce circuit. Eddie tested at Fiorano and so we arrived in Germany with a disadvantage. Eddie is improving on qualifying, but he still finds it difficult to unblock himself and give the maximum on a qualifying lap.'

Giorgio Ascanelli, who now has overall control of Eddie's car, sees things in a similar light. 'Eddie overdrives the car. These cars are extremely sensitive; you can't "hassle" them. They're light, they act strangely when you overdrive and as a result you feel as if you're going to slide all the time. Eddie is much quicker when he thinks he hasn't tried. Michael is smooth because he lets the car have its head. Eddie is much better in the race when he's alone in the car and not listening to anyone on the radio. He can get distracted – and as a driver you must have one hundred per cent concentration. Having said this, I have to say that for anyone to be compared to Michael Schumacher is very difficult. Eddie is without doubt as good as any of the other drivers after Michael.'

Ascanelli regarded Hockenheim as an opportunity missed although he admitted, 'Having said it was a lost chance, Williams had a dreadful race and again that helped us. We made mistakes, but Williams made bigger mistakes.'

Out of the Blue
Despite huge support for Michael Schumacher at Hockenheim, the Ferrari No 1 had to accept second-best to the Austrian Gerhard Berger who returned from injury to clinch a memorable victory for Benetton.

A Test of Tyres

The Ferrari crew ensure that the correct tyres are provided for the cars at the start of the race.

After the Hungarian Grand Prix, Ross Brawn commented: 'We run higher tyre temperatures than other teams, about 10 to 15 degrees centigrade more, particularly in the rear tyres. We've taken steps to reduce that from an engineering point of view, and we are in constant discussion with Goodyear who are giving us considerable help.

The problem this year is that there is no warning when the tyre is going to blister. Before, the tyre would feel good, then the car would start to slide a bit, then blister – you could feel the onset of blistering. Now the tyre feels good, and then, bang!, the tyre's blistered and it's finished. It literally happens within two or three corners' distance. Not all blistering is negative. Some teams feel that if they have one or two blisters at the end of the race, they have got the most out of the tyres. Goodyear have responded well in terms of competition

from Bridgestone, but sometimes we go too far and have too soft a tyre. It gives a good qualifying performance but it's the race that counts, and you end up tip-toeing round when you need to drive hard and get the maximum from the tyre. The softer, faster tyre that you are scared to push in the race ends up being slower than the more durable tyre that enables the driver to race the car to the limit without any worries. That's what we have to have.'

Goodyear are fully committed to motor racing and have a slick trackside operation to ensure maximum benefit for all their teams. Perry Bell is the new Operations Manager. He explains the ins and outs of racing tyres. 'Each team can use nine sets of slicks, either the harder Prime or the softer Optional, and up to seven sets of wet tyres. We assign an engineer to each team. John Taube is the engineer who works with Ferrari. During

the weekend we evaluate the car setups to optimise performance.

'Decisions about which tyre to use have to be made during the free practice before the qualifying session on Saturday. We bring over two thousand tyres with us for the race weekend. We have seven teams and fourteen cars and we bring twenty-five people to each race meeting.

'We returned to Ferrari in 1982 and since then development has continued. Obviously development accelerates with competition from the likes of Bridgestone. There is constant pressure to outperform and come up with new things. I think we have done well this year. People said we would have problems competing with Bridgestone in the wet, but we have surpassed that test with victories in the wet. Both Williams and Ferrari are Goodyear teams, and they are competing for the Constructor's Championship.'

Next season will be different and Perry Bell has a few reservations about how the grooves in the grooved tyres will actually be controlled. 'We have already started testing with the grooved tyres (three grooves on the front tyres, four on the back), and it is not easy to check the rubber wear. If the driver is off line, he will tend to pick up rubber and when the tyre is cool this can appear like a smooth tyre, and so confuse the actual situation when he comes to be tested to make sure his grooves are up to standard.'

It had been a tense week for Eddie, whose contract ran out on the 31 July. For some time, there had been speculation in the press that either one of the Finns, Salo or Hakkinen, would be chosen for the Ferrari No 2 hot seat. But it all ended happily for Eddie when he was reconfirmed as Schumacher's team-mate for 1998.

• • •

For the next Grand Prix a fortnight later at the tight and twisty Hungaroring, Ferrari was looking forward to putting more distance between themselves and Williams in the Constructor's Championship. On their part, Williams was desperate to close the gap on their rivals and put the misfortunes of Hockenheim behind them.

Things began brightly for the Scuderia as Schumacher qualified brilliantly on pole and Irvine was fifth. However, during the race day warm up, despite a reconfigured F310B, equipped with a Step 1 V10 engine instead of the Step 2, Michael Schumacher crashed the lighter chassis car, and was forced to drive the spare car. This resulted in bad tyre wear and three pit stops rather than the planned two.

Having led on the first lap, Schumacher soon discovered that the team had chosen the wrong tyres and he had to stop on lap 14 and then stop twice more during the race. In one of the best races of the year so far, the Arrows of Damon Hill was leading before clutch problems forced Hill to slow down, allowing Villeneuve to overtake the hapless 1996 World Champion on the last lap. Meanwhile, Schumacher was staggering round on tyres that were almost wearing out before his very eyes. He was helped by his brother Ralf (which went down like a lead balloon in the Jordan camp) and by team-mate Irvine, who protected the Championship leader by forming a barrier behind him, which enabled Schumacher to cross the line in fourth place. Eddie Irvine, meanwhile, was having a torrid time, having been shunted out of the race by Shinji Nakano when in sixth place with only one lap to go. With his exit, one valuable point for his team disappeared into thin air.

So Ferrari left the Hungaroring with Schumacher still leading the Driver's Championship by three points and with the team leading the Constructor's Championship by two points. Jean Todt was resigned to the results of the race. 'I've been involved in the sport too long not to know that until you pass the chequered flag anything can happen.'

Giorgio Ascanelli felt that Hungary was one race where perhaps Williams had outfoxed the rest. 'I don't think Hungary was down to luck. I think Villeneuve was clever. We knew the tyres were going to blister as soon as we started pushing. It's a difficult circuit to overtake on, so I felt

'We Will Continue to Improve'
Team Principal Jean Todt monitors closely the performance of his drivers during practice at the Hungaroring.

that we should have taken it easy. Damon [Hill] was pushing, but he wasn't in contention for the World Driver's Championship so maybe we should have let him go and saved our tyres. We knew the first six laps would be critical and Michael did his best time on the first lap. I'm not saying the drivers are stupid, I'm saying the team wasn't strong enough in taking into account the tyres. We briefed the drivers on tyres, but maybe we weren't as decisive as we should have been.'

Schumacher, however, had been aware of the need to save his tyres. 'We had serious tyre problems from the first lap, just like at Barcelona. During the first few laps I tried to go slower to conserve them as much as possible, but it was useless.' According to Ignazio Lunetta, 'We seem to stress the tyres more, because of the way the drivers drive and also the characteristics of the car, compared to either Williams or Benetton.'

● ● ●

Safety First

The heavens open and the safety car is out at the start of the Belgian Grand Prix. Michael Schumacher was ready to take advantage of the conditions with his intermediate setup on the spare car.

After Hungary, Jean Todt was still in fighting mood. Known as the Napoleon of the pit lane, Todt is not one to give up easily. 'The battle will be long, we will defend ourselves by working even harder. At least for now, it's the others that have to follow us.'

Schumacher may be cautious by nature, but he is not one to give up either. 'I always look to the future with optimism and as the next race is Spa, my favourite circuit, there is a good chance of success. I am a little more worried about Monza. We didn't go very well at Monza during the last test session, but we are testing there from tomorrow so we'll try and improve the situation.'

Next stop: Spa. According to Lunetta, 'We always travel happily to Spa. It's a beautiful circuit for drivers, with the formidable Eau Rouge and Blanchimont corners. You always have to be aware of the weather, of course, as it is so unpredictable. It is a constant challenge to keep one eye on the skies and the other on the competing teams.'

In Schumacher's case, it is usually a case of the other teams keeping an eye on him. Spa 1997 turned out to be as good as Spa 1996 for the German. Before the race, Schumacher had taken the precaution of preparing two cars with different setups. Twenty minutes prior to the start, the heavens opened. The German made the crucial decision to go for the immediate setup on the spare car, while both the Williams and Benetton on the grid in front of him were on full wet. Schumacher's gamble worked perfectly, for the race began behind the safety car, expertly driven by Oliver Gavin, the former British Formula Three champion, until the start of the fourth lap. Then it was the Michael Schumacher show. The crowd watched in awe as the German roared round Spa Francorchamps on his intermediates.

Some teams complained about the presence of the safety car and said that if they'd known at the start of the race, they would have changed their set up and strategy. Lunetta is dismissive of the whingers. 'The rules are clear. If the safety car is there at the five-minute board, then it will start the race. If it's not there, then the start is regular. It's clear for all to see.'

You would have thought that people would have learnt from Schumacher's supreme performance in the rain at Monaco. As he says, 'My race car, with the lightweight chassis, was set up for the dry, and the T-car for mixed conditions, with less fuel on board, because of the possibility of having to make an early stop for slicks. When the pit lane opened, I ran one lap in the race car and then decided to go with the spare.

'Most people were on wets, but I decided to go with the intermediates. They had worked for me at Monaco, and I thought it was worth gambling on the fact that it was a heavy shower and wouldn't last long.'

As the heavens opened Ross Brawn smiled. 'I think the weather gods may be Michael Schumacher fans!'

Giorgio Ascanelli explains, 'With a bit of cunning we waited until the last minute to send the cars out on the track as we know it can rain here as it's done so many times in the last ten years. We sent the cars out in the rain to give them the feel of what the circuit was like. One driver made a choice which was conservative, and one made the aggressive choice and won.'

It took Schumacher a mere two laps of the race proper to pass Villeneuve and Alesi as though they were just incidentals to the main party, and establish a lead of six seconds. By the next lap it had increased to 17 seconds, until by the end of the race he had won by over 26 seconds. It was yet another masterpiece of skilful driving by the German.

Unfortunately for team-mate Eddie Irvine, Spa was an instantly forgettable race as he tangled with Pedro Diniz on the last lap. Luca Baldisserri explains, 'Spa was the only race this year where Eddie and his team really got it wrong. A true disaster. The car went quite well in the wet but Eddie only had two complete laps on Saturday in free practice and qualifying. We had

Fastest Men in the World
Michael Schumacher takes some speed tips from American sprinters Carl Lewis and Leroy Burrell in the Ferrari garage during the Grand Prix weekend in Belgium.

Walking on Water
Jean Alesi's Benetton is taken on the inside of La Source by Schumacher's Ferrari as the German drives to an awe-inspiring lead at Spa Francorchamps.

The Mechanics

Behind the scenes at the Ferrari garage, an army of mechanics works round the clock to prepare the cars for the big race day.

GIANNI PETTERLINI is the head mechanic on Michael Schumacher's car. At 35 years of age, he has been with Ferrari for fifteen years. As he says, 'First it was work and then it became a passion.' Unmarried he is, he insists, 'married to Ferrari.'

WALTER CAROLI is the man in charge of Schumacher's engine. He has been with Ferrari for over 25 years and still feels the same passion and excitement for the job. He has lived through the Enzo Ferrari reign and now works under the modern rule of Luca di Montezemolo. Working with the best driver in the world is a stimulus to work even harder. 'Michael Schumacher is the best driver. Having the No 1 is a great incentive to work to your maximum.'

ALESSANDRO FERRI is Schumacher's mechanic and has been with Ferrari for ten years. He explains, 'We have worked together as a group for three or four years now, and so we have a good understanding of each other and can work together better. It would be very special to win the World Championship.'

GIOVANNI CASU works on the bodywork of Schumacher's car. He has been with Ferrari for nine years and is married and has a son. Like the other mechanics, work is more of a passion than a routine. 'There is always something new and I like the different routine and demands that the job entails.'

FRANCESCO UGUZZONI is 35 years old and works on the bodywork of Eddie Irvine's car. He is the man who has to try and make Irvine's seat as comfortable as possible, which was difficult in 1996. But like the others, he loves his job. 'We all work very well as a team and I think stability has brought us success.'

FABRIZIO GRANDI is 31 years old and works on the T-car. He says, 'The best moment of 1996 was winning at Monza. The emotion and the excitement of the fans is something I'll never forget.'

The mechanics, and an Eddie Irvine lookalike, take a well-earned break from testing at Monza.

only one complete lap in qualifying due to a series of problems. In the race we chose the wrong tyres. It was wet, but we could have chosen intermediates.'

But if Michael Schumacher, the grand rainmaster, chose intermediates, then why didn't Eddie follow his example? 'We were further down the grid,' Baldisserri explained. What about the radio? 'We try not to discuss strategic decisions on the radio as the other teams can hear us.'

• • •

Schumacher left Spa twelve points ahead of Jacques Villeneuve in the Driver's Championship while Ferrari were eight points ahead in the Constructor's Championship. Next race was Monza, where the *tifosi* would be baying for a repeat of the consecutive Spa-Monza victories of 1996.

However, before the race there was testing. The pressure was building as the hugely powerful Gianni Agnelli graced the test session with his presence on the Wednesday of the test session. Accompanying him was Ferrari Chairman Luca di Montezemolo. Both men were relaxed and optimistic. Sitting at the top of the Driver's Championship and the Constructor's Championship is a good vantage point from which to view the world. As Ross Brawn says, 'If the fans look back to where we were in January and February, I think they would have snapped your hand off if you'd asked them "Do you want four victories by September?"

Meanwhile Michael Schumacher and Eddie Irvine were hard at work. One of the most pressing problems was getting the aerodynamic setup on the car just right for the fast Monza circuit. They still had ten days but it would be tight. For Ferrari, Monza is the circuit where there is the most pressure. The eyes of the world are on the Scuderia, including Fiat, the media, the *tifosi,* and the celebrities and VIP guests of the sponsors. It's four days of constant chaos. Montezemolo would be watching the race at home, as he always does. 'I'm very nervous when I watch Monza. I want to be on my own. I don't want to feel under any obligation. I want to be free to express my reactions, either positive or negative. I don't want anyone to distract me by asking questions.'

Except, that is, Agnelli who admits, 'I often call Luca during the races to get information that he has at his fingertips. I always find him very nervous and agitated...and, in truth, I have to say that I have my heart in my mouth during the races.'

For good reason, the way things turned out in Italy.

'We're *this* far from the Championship'
Back to the basics for Chairman Luca di Montezemolo and Luca Baldisserri during testing at Monza.

A Wet Kiss
Jean Todt expresses his delight to Schumacher after his strategic triumph at Spa Francorchamps.

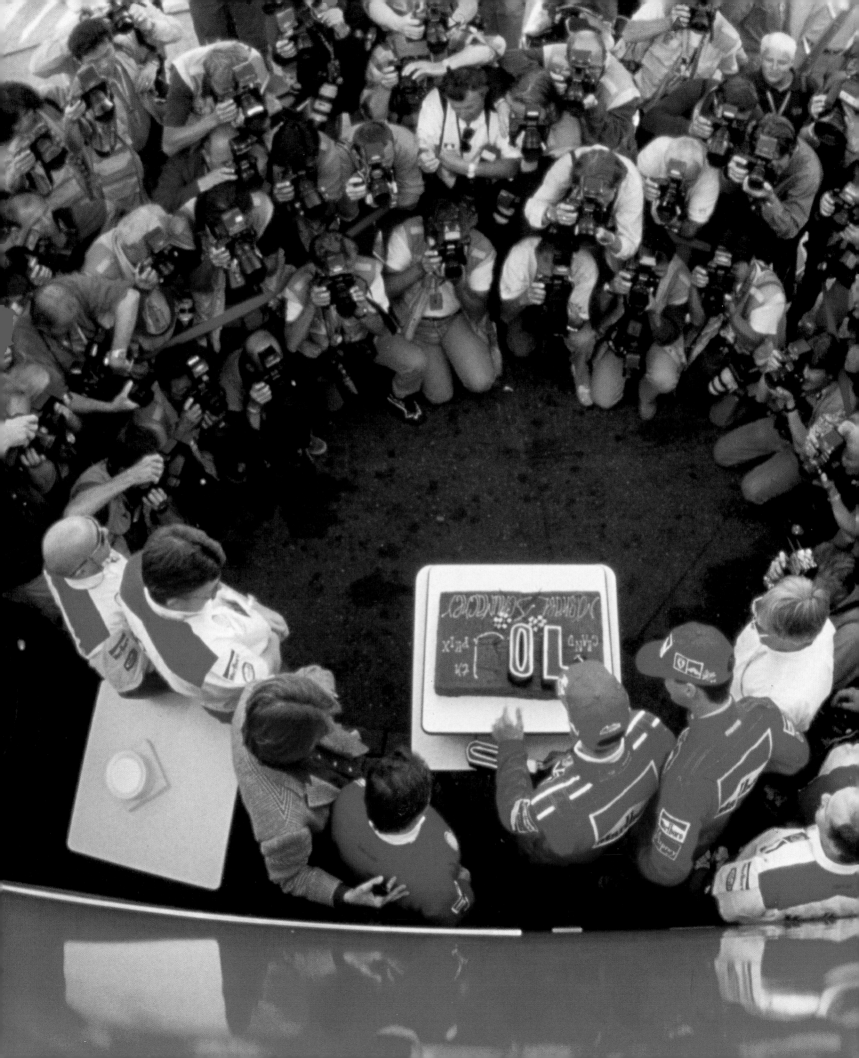

CHAPTER FOURTEEN

September Doldrums

'The challenge of designing

a car for Ferrari was enough

to persuade me to come

out of retirement.'

Rory Byrne
Ferrari Chief Designer 1997

All the attention was now focused on Monza and the Italian Grand Prix. On the Friday during the free practice the Ferrari team had been working hard in preparation for race day. As Jean Todt says, 'On Friday it was difficult to get a clear picture of our car's performance as some of the cars' times had been set on new tyres and, furthermore, we did not know how much fuel the other cars had in their tanks.'

By the end of the qualifying session on Saturday, they did have a clearer picture – and it wasn't good. Michael Schumacher ended up in ninth place, his worst qualifying position of the season, while Eddie Irvine was tenth. Ross Brawn commented, 'Last year Michael was a second off pole position and third on the grid. This year he is six-tenths of a second off pole and he's ninth.'

The Ferrari team were convinced that there was not much more that could be done in developing the 1997 car. Brawn declares, 'We've got to the stage where there's nothing left to do on the basic car. We've had new wings, new floors, a different chassis and suspension, in fact we've done everything without re-designing the car completely.'

Much Ado about Nothing
One point was a disappointing return for Michael Schumacher at Monza in the Italian Grand Prix.

One of the principle new designs has been the lightweight chassis. Brawn says, 'I looked at ways of saving weight together with Rory Byrne (the new chief designer). The major advantage of having a lighter chassis is that we can put all the weight on the floor of the car and lower the centre of gravity. This means the car will corner faster and brake better. At the same time, we took advantage of the fact we were creating a new chassis to increase the car's fuel capacity. At Melbourne our race strategy was compromised because we couldn't put any more fuel in the car. It looked likely that Monza was going to be a race where fuel capacity would be important. In fact it was, and we were able to stay out one lap longer than Berger who was challenging Michael during the race, as a result of which we kept Michael in front of him. It was a lot of work, but it was worthwhile as it gained us a point and that might be crucial at the end of the year. It's obvious that a 600 kg car is faster than a 640 kg car. However, if you have two cars that each weigh 640 kg then the one with a lower centre of gravity, with all other things being equal, will be faster. That is basic mechanics.'

So what was the problem at Monza? Ignazio Lunetta had a few observations. 'At high speed circuits we reduce the wing and the car loses a lot of aerodynamics, and the speed doesn't increase by as much as it should do. The car is then not very efficient.'

So at the end of a disappointing Italian Grand Prix for Ferrari, Michael Schumacher finished sixth with Eddie Irvine a further two places behind. As Giorgio Ascanelli said, 'We're eight or nine kilometres an hour slower than most and you can't win Monza like this.'

The 1997 Pit Stop Team

LEFT REAR WHEEL
Wheel off: MAURIZIO RAVAZZINI
Gun: GIANNI PETTERLINI
Wheel on: FABRIZIO GRANDI

LEFT FRONT WHEEL
Wheel off: ENRICO FACCIOLI
Gun: CLAUDIO BISI
Wheel on: MAURO MADRIGALI

BRAKE BOARD
FRANCESCO UGUZZONI

FRONT JACK
CLAUDIO BERSINI

RIGHT REAR WHEEL
Wheel off: GIOVANNI CASU
Gun: GIANLUCA SOCIALI
Wheel on: WALTER CAROLI

HOSE SUPPORT
ANDREA VACCARI

REFUELLER
NIGEL STEPNEY

RIGHT FRONT WHEEL
Wheel off: ALESSANDRO FERRI
Gun: LUCA FERRARI
Wheel on: ANDREA GENONI

VISOR WIPE
IVAN PRETI

But it could have been worse for Schumacher and Ferrari. Jacques Villeneuve finished in fifth place, so he only made up one point on Schumacher, leaving the German still ten points ahead in the Driver's Championship, and Ferrari a perilous one point ahead of Williams in the Constructor's Championship. Lunetta thought Williams had acted strangely. 'If you are in Villeneuve's position, you have to attack. Michael has only to defend. Yet Williams made the first pit stop – this is a defensive move.'

DASHBOARD

E   Extinguisher

R   Reverse

N   Neutral. This is for when the marshals have to move a car that is parked on or near the track.

Blue button: Menu to select information on the steering wheel

Yellow button: Indicates that the red rear (fog) lights are on for rainy conditions

STEERING WHEEL

Six display units: Provide information as programmed (fuel consumption, laps remaining, split time, warning messages etc).

Two clutch paddles:

    Right – up-shift

    Left – down-shift.

S   Safety Button – stops engine and cuts out fuel injection.

L   Pit Lane Speed Limiter

N   Neutral

Six dial switches:

1   Brake Balance

2   Engine fuel mixture

3   Recovery – disables the clutch.

4   Engine Mapping

5   Throttle Mapping

6   Spare

Ascanelli seemed happy enough. 'I am content about the result as I wasn't expecting anything better. Frankly, Villeneuve finishing fifth and Michael sixth was a blessing. If Villeneuve had won the race and Michael had come second with a final sprint, everyone would have said "Fantastic, the performance is there" and so on. But we would have lost four points to Villeneuve instead of just one.'

Monza, of course, is all about the *tifosi* and they were out in force in their painted faces, waving their Ferrari flags and banners and hoping for a repeat of 1996. They were to be disappointed. However, with a World Championship still possible all was not lost. The fans have waited eighteen years for a champion driver, and they're not going to give up until the end.

• • •

After Monza there was still an air of optimism around the Ferrari factory at Fiorano. According to Ross Brawn, 'Michael's in a pretty good frame of mind. He's had a hard period. He had five days testing at Monza to try and find a better solution with the car, which we didn't really achieve. Then there was the three days of the race itself. If you include the previous race at Spa, he's done a lot of driving. It was frustrating for him at Monza as it was the first race in quite a while that he knew would be difficult to win. At this stage we can't afford an off weekend with Michael.'

Brawn is clearly settling in as technical director and taking control, and this was having an effect on Giorgio Ascanelli. Whereas Ascanelli was stressed in France, he was calm and philosophical after Monza. 'I feel that my job, as it was, is finishing. Ross is more confident, and more familiar with every aspect of the team, and he's learning Italian. A technical director who is in place and goes to the races doesn't need someone to be in charge of engineering.'

What of the future? 'I don't know what's going to happen,' says Ascanelli. 'I don't want to leave. Ross and I will have to decide what we're going to do with ourselves.'

For his part, Brawn was adamant that he wanted Ascanelli by his side. 'You need the capacity to solve problems when they occur, and that means having two or three valued opinions on what needs to be done. I value the input of Giorgio, Rory and the others even though at the end of the day I make the decisions. But it isn't a one-man show.'

Brawn was also mulling over the pressure of Schumacher being in the running for the World Driver's Championship. 'There will be an enormous amount of disappointment if Michael doesn't win the Championship this year. But this should be balanced against the fact that we've won more races than last year. We've built up a good team at Maranello. We've made a lot of

Creative Advertising

Ferrari and Shell are a potent combination: power and passion allied to technical excellence. This message is being broadcast across the world with the help of some stunning new advertising campaigns. One such advertisement, called 'The Journey', simulates the path taken by some Shell Helix oil through the engine of a Ferrari car. As the Ferrari speeds through a tunnel and the oil flows into the inner parts of the engine, the viewer gets a chance to see some of the old cars from yesteryear and a waving of Ferrari flags. In another advert, Eddie Irvine features in 'The Pit Stop'. He comes in for a change of tyres and refuelling, but instead of concentrating on the race, he wants to know if it is Shell petrol as he is collecting the Collezione Ferrari cars. Thirty million people are collecting these model cars, and the two advertisements are being seen by a billion people in more than 100 countries.

The third advert is perhaps the most ambitious. Shot in the Mojave Desert, a huge transporter plane flies in low over the Ferrari Formula One car driven by Nicola Larini. With both aircraft and car hurtling along at high speed, a refuelling line emerges from the plane to link up with the car. After filling up is complete, the plane flies off into the distance. This awe-inspiring image was not a computer simulation. Kathy Trautman, who is part of the Shell Brand and Communications team, explains, 'We had to do an aerodynamic test to see the effect a low flying plane would have on a Formula One car. We wanted to be sure it wouldn't flip over.

'We were filming on a normal road, so we could only shoot for fifteen minutes at a time, as traffic had to be allowed to pass through. We also had to work out how to avoid blowing the engine, so we put the car on a truck and hauled it along for some of the shots. The whole operation was very satisfying.'

progress with a car that looked quite difficult at the beginning of the season. I think the team should be congratulated for their achievements this year. If we should be unfortunate and fail, I don't want people to say that Ferrari threw it away. The truth of the matter is, we weren't expecting to be in this position anyway.'

The fact of the matter is that Michael Schumacher's brilliance covers up the true situation. As Brawn says, 'In some ways the barometer of the car's performance should be judged by Eddie. He's as good as any driver after Michael and you can see the car has only been competitive at three or four circuits: Argentina, San Marino, Monaco and Magny-Cours, for example. Michael can mask the situation as he's such a good driver. I think, touch wood, as I don't want to tempt providence, that when we're given half a chance Michael will take it. Spa was a case in point, whereas Silverstone was an example of where we were running strongly before we blew it through mechanical failure. Championships are won over the season, not on the results of a few races.'

After Monza, Nigel Stepney was also feeling the cold wind of failure. 'It was a disappointing result but Villeneuve was only one point ahead of us. I'm satisfied as both cars finished and the team did the best they could. Maybe we didn't go down some of the routes we should have, but it's easy to look back after the event. To be twelve seconds behind the leader in sixth place is unusual in Formula One.'

'I think we made very good progress very early on in the season and we were finishing races and coming up with good strategies when other teams weren't. But the rest have caught up since then. Monza and Hockenheim, for example, weren't strong circuits for us. I think we've lost a bit of our competitiveness.'

• • •

Nineteen ninety-seven is certainly a quieter year for Mario Almondo, the man who is head of the Production and Quality Control Department. Last year there were constant reliability problems and Almondo was under enormous pressure. This year things are much better. Almondo explains, 'The best part of the job is to construct and develop a new car every year. The Production Department is involved in everything. If we have too much to do, we have alternative suppliers to make sure reliability is high.'

Meanwhile, Ross Brawn is looking ahead to next year. 'If we can produce a car for 1998 that's competitive from day one, and performs well, then we can concentrate on developing it further, rather than having to recover the situation. I think next year will be the year we can be judged on, as it will be our own car produced at Maranello.'

The new regulations mean in theory that less competitive teams have a chance to catch up. However, Brawn feels that the best will shine through. 'A lot of the success of teams is down to the way they work. Those that know how to test, develop and design, will be successful. Sometimes, when the rules change a team comes out with a radical approach. For a year the others may be behind, but normally those who do a good job catch up. Next year Williams and McLaren will be competitive, and so will we.'

With the departure of FDD from the Ferrari equation, the design and development of the entire car has passed back to Maranello. With the loss of the wind tunnel facilities at Bristol, a new wind tunnel is being built by the factory at Fiorano. The man in charge of aerodynamics is Australian Willem Toet. A lively, dapper dresser, he has been at Maranello since December 1994.

These days aerodynamics is more a space science than a terrestrial activity and it's no different at Ferrari. There are five aeronautical engineers working with Toet, each one with his or her own area of responsibility. Toet explains his philosophy on aerodynamics. 'We look at the basic car and isolate the areas that we want to concentrate on. For example, we examines the parts that will

Inspecting the Goods
Fiat boss Cesare Romiti has a close-up look at the Ferrari team during race day with the help of Luca di Montezemelo, Jean Todt and Eddie Irvine.

Media Magnetism
Filippo Marrai, Stefania Bocchi and Nigel Wollheim provide a first-class service to the media as part of their work with Phillip Morris.

The Chief Designer

Rory Byrne knows Michael Schumacher as well as his ex-Benetton team-mate, Ross Brawn. Byrne was Chief Designer at Benetton during the 'golden era' when Schumacher won two World Championships. Fresh from a six-week retirement in Thailand where he was planning to open a scuba diving school, he decided to take on the ultimate challenge of designing a World Championship winning car for the stable of the prancing horse. It is a task that is both challenging and exciting. 'The reason I didn't renew my contract with Benetton was because I'd achieved what I set out to do. We'd won two World Championships and if my contract had ended in 1995 I would have left then. The challenge of designing a car for Ferrari, the world's most famous racing team, was enough to persuade me to come out of retirement.'

First impressions of Ferrari are positive. 'I have found it better than I thought it would be, from the point of view that when you're on the outside you hear all these rumours about the politics

within Ferrari. To be honest I haven't found any of that. Everyone is working very hard to keep us in contention for the Championship and it's excellent. The facilities are fine, there's a lot of investment, a lot of equipment and other resources - so, all in all, it's good.'

The new car for 1998 will be different from the 1997 car, not just because the regulations change but also because John Barnard and Rory Byrne have different ideas on design. Barnard was a talented perfectionist who didn't always feel the way Schumacher drives was best for the long term development of the car. Byrne has different ideas. 'I think John [Barnard] and I have a different philosophy on how we design cars. Even before I worked with Michael my design philosophy was more in line with how Michael would want to drive the car. It didn't stem from working with Michael, but from previous experience and how I think the car should be designed. Basically, my philosophy is to maximise the aerodynamic performance and that normally dictates keeping the front fairly stiff, which is how the Williams cars work. Aerodynamics is still the single most important factor governing the performance of the car. The set up of the car is different now to when I arrived and I think both drivers find it easy. I think it is wrong to say we're designing a car specifically for Michael. We are designing one which we believe will give the best performance irrespective of who drives it. Mind you, it helps having Michael driving for you as he's a superb racing driver. He's fast and

quick thinking, he makes very few mistakes and can react to changing circumstances.

Rory Byrne is not a designer who starts with a blank piece of paper, but relies on research data. 'My main role is turning the aerodynamic shapes into something we can engineer into a practical car. I see myself as an intermediary between aerodynamics and design.'

Nineteen ninety-eight sees a big change in the FIA regulations for Formula One, including grooved tyres which will slow down the cars, particularly through the corners. Byrne explains, 'The cars will look narrower, the wheels come in by 200 mm, which is about four inches each side. This makes a huge difference to the aerodynamics. We're progressing pretty well and are fairly advanced on big components like the gearbox. Most of the design was completed by September 1997. The change in the regulations doesn't affect the engine, although we can make the gearbox lighter due to a lessening of stresses. However, the biggest change is in the chassis and suspension. We will always chase maximum drivability as we don't want the car too sensitive.

'Tyres have been a difficult element this year. You always try to run the softest compound possible because as soon as you put fuel in the car, the tyres start running hot. If you overheat you start blistering, and the performance of the car drops. Making the right tyre choice is one of the challenges of Grand Prix motor racing.'

An Ideal Partnership

The lubricant for the Ferrari engine supplied by Shell also plays a vital part in the design and development of Formula One racing cars. According to Ferrari Chief Designer, Rory Byrne: 'We have made a very significant improvement on the gearbox, which is due to the development of a lubricant that runs cooler than before. If we are dissipating less heat in the gearbox, the oil cooler can be smaller. This helps with weight saving, and also with aerodynamic efficiency.'

Byrne is also excited about the potential of the new hydraulic oils being developed by Shell. 'There are new oils under development which will help the performance of all the hydraulic components, from the break balance system and the engine throttle and trumpets through to the gear shift and the power steering.'

The close relationship between Ferrari and Shell is highlighted by the one-to-one contact between Ferrari engineers and Shell personnel. For example on the fuel side Maurizio Bollini of Ferrari is in constant contact with Holgar Paesler of Shell; Christoph Mary talks to Simon Dunning on research and development; and Marco Inoretti sorts out the complex logistics with Shell's Jean King. Finally, at the track Giorgio Ascanelli has Ian Galliard as his Shell contact.

Celebrating a perfect partnership – Shell personnel (from left to right) Jackie Ireland, Simon Dunning, Raoul Pinnell, Kathy Trautman and Doug Wright.

be affected by the change in regulations or the fact that they were sensitive in last year's car. We look at how much damage has been caused by a certain aerodynamic factor.

'We design the initial car allowing for certain areas to be modified, for example the space for the driver's feet. We can still play with the length depending on the height of the driver. We have a preliminary fitting in a mock-up car, which should eliminate most problems, and then we do another final fitting. We try and make the car as aerodynamically perfect as possible, while also allowing for driver comfort.'

In 1998, however, things will change. 'Next year we will not only have a mechanical penalty but also an aerodynamic penalty. We started looking at next year's car in March 1997 and we had a 25% loss in downforce, which we believe will translate to a 10% loss once we finish the optimisation process. We would lose mechanically even if the tyres weren't grooved, as the car is narrower. I think the best teams have the most to lose.'

The new Ferrari wind tunnel is as impressive artistically as it is technically. The concept of Renzo Piano, it will form a stunning architectural masterpiece. However, the pragmatic Giorgio Ascanelli declares, 'It will be a stylish piece of work – although I would have preferred it to be

Austrian Angst
Michael Schumacher was out-qualified by Eddie Irvine amidst the stunning scenery of the A1-Ring in Austria.

less flashy and ready earlier.' When it is finished it will be one of the most modern wind tunnels in Formula One. There are three independent foundations for the building, the rolling road and the model. As Toet says, 'We will be able to simulate the vibration of the car as it bounces over the road. We'll also be able to run a 50% or full-scale model. Williams were the first to be able to investigate changes involving cornering. Now we will have the facility to measure cornering and steering capability. We will also have more accurate results as we will be able to measure the air pressure at more specific points than other wind tunnels. This will help us to maximise the aerodynamic efficiency of the car.' Willem lives in Italy with his wife Susan, who also works at Ferrari.

• • •

After the setbacks in Monza, Ferrari had great hope for the next two races, the Austrian Grand Prix at Zeltweg and the Luxembourg Grand Prix at the Nurburgring. For one of the senior personnel at Ferrari, the race in Austria meant returning to his home country. Gustav Brunner, head of research and development, was born in Graz, Austria, which is the nearest town to Zeltweg. His objective is always the same – to make the car go quicker. 'We start at the tip of the nose and work through solving problems and looking at new ways of doing things. Sometimes we work on the existing car, and sometimes the new car. We are fortunate in that we do not have pressure to produce a car. We have more time to think so we can be creative. We are the only department that has the freedom to dream.'

What about the change in regulations for next year? 'With less grip from the tyres, we are putting more effort into developing the suspension. I think this will favour Schumacher as with less grip there will be more drifting and more need for control. It will not depend on the car so much, now it will be more of a Driver's Championship than an Engineer's Championship.'

At Zeltweg Michael Schumacher qualified in ninth position, just as he did at Monza two weeks earlier. However, this time round he was having a great race, lying third with a strong possibility of finishing second behind Villeneuve, when team-mate Eddie Irvine was involved in an accident with Jean Alesi. This caused the yellow flag to be waved but Schumacher, who was

Telemetry

Ferrari work closely with sponsors Magneti Marelli on the telemetry. Giancarlo De Angelis is the Racing Department Technical Manager for Magneti Marelli, while Valentino Ferrari and Giacomo Debbia are Ferrari's men in charge of telemetry. Valentino says, 'Ten years ago we didn't have telemetry, but recently it has developed into one of our most sophisticated instruments. Whereas before we had to rely on the driver's own feedback based on his feel for the car, now we can see precisely what is happening from a technical point of view on our screens back at the garage.'

It is certainly complicated. De Angelis explains, 'There is an antenna on the car which feeds data from the car's computer to a microwave radio on the pit wall. A receiver takes information from the car while a transmitter sends information to a point just outside the team garage. From the receiver on the garage wall, the information is passed along a cable to the modem box. This box transforms up to half a million bits of data into readable form. There are up to one hundred and twenty-eight different parameters. Each parameter relates to one piece of information, for example, the speed of the car, oil pressure and fuel consumption, battery voltage, air pressure, and so on.'

Luca di Montezemelo and Jean Todt keeping an eye on other teams.

The Engine

One of the happiest Ferrari men is Paolo Martinelli, engines director. Although the car still has a way to go in terms of being on par with the Williams, the engine has performed well. 'There has been less consumption of fuel this year, which is due to the improved aerodynamic efficiency of the car. We had a good strong start to the V10 last year, and this year we have concentrated on research to improve it. Considering that we bench-tested the V10 in June 1995, and raced it in 1996 it has performed well and reliably. The V10 was born with Shell and to date we have had seven victories. I think that is indicative of the close rapport Ferrari has with Shell.'

Unlike Ford and Mercedes, who have both had problems with engine reliability, Ferrari has lived up to its reputation of producing a good engine. Vincenzo Castorino, who is Schumacher's motor engineer is passionate about the tradition of the Ferrari engine. 'It is the centre of the car, the chromosome around which everything is built. Enzo Ferrari wanted the engine to be an important part of his cars and it is.'

Mattia Binotto is also part of the race team and responsible for Eddie Irvine's engine. For him the engine is also the centre of his world. 'Working for Ferrari is a passion rather than a job. We have always put a lot into the development of the engine and changing from the V12 to V10 was an important step.'

Anselmo Menabue, who is head of the motor mechanics has been with Ferrari since he was fifteen years old. Like most of the people who work at Ferrari, it is more of a marriage than just work. Enea Spallanzani is the 31-year-old head of the engine test room. Here the engine is tested for reliability by using a simulator to reproduce the exact characteristics of the circuit. With the constant background noise of the engine changing up and down through the gears, it is the beating heart of Ferrari.

In 1997, Ferrari supplied some of their own engines to Sauber.

behind Frentzen, didn't see it and overtook the Williams driver. This resulted in a ten-second penalty, as it is illegal to overtake another car when the yellow flag is waved to indicate a dangerous situation on the track. This put him back to ninth, but all was not lost and Schumacher fought back to sixth place, overtaking Damon Hill on the very last lap to gain one point.

Eddie Irvine's crash with Jean Alesi started off a war of words after both drivers retired from the race. Alesi went storming off towards the Ferrari garage declaring, 'I'm going to hit him. I don't understand what goes through a driver's head when he does things like that. He's crazy.' Irvine was just as dismissive. 'I was overtaking him on the outside when he touched a wheel and flew into the air. He's a fruitcake and unstable.'

The sad conclusion to Austria from Ferrari's point of view was that Schumacher's lead in the Driver's Championship was reduced to just one point, while Williams took over at the head of the Constructor's table with a twelve point lead.

Nigel Stepney was thinking about the press. 'We didn't get destroyed after Monza which is unusual. I think the press have seen that we can win. Last year I didn't speak to many of them. They've learnt that if they give us hassle, we'll say less. However, a leopard never changes its spots.'

The team, however, were much more together this year than last. Stepney also feels that having all design functions in-house has greatly improved relationships. 'Having dropped FDD and with everything now at Maranello, I think the working environment is a lot better. If the people above you are calm and stable, then it makes everyone else more relaxed. The arrival of Ross Brawn has been beneficial. Michael and Eddie also help by not using the press to complain about the team.

'Everyone has a lot more respect for their colleagues. Before with FDD, we lost so much time talking and not actually doing anything. John [Barnard] didn't want to trust anyone and give anybody experience. We're now taking on all aspects of the car and we're doing all the design at Maranello and that's a big step for us. We make mistakes but we have enough experience and time to keep it all under control. Now we can find the answers and cure the problems.'

Back in the Formula One offices Luana Piccinini and Anna Maria Consani are keeping things moving as the phone and fax constantly ring, bringing information and demanding answers. Luana is Claudio Berro's PA, while Anna Maria looks after Jean Todt. Luana says, 'The number of requests from foreign journalists has increased enormously. We always try to accommodate the requests and make sure that each country gets access to us.'

Mauro Boreggio is the personnel man who has taken over from Stefano Domenicali. 'The important thing is to keep positive, without going over the top in celebrating if we win, or falling into a depression if we lose. We must keep to the general strategy.'

● ● ●

The Purple Party

Asprey crowned the 1997 season by presenting two totally unique Ferrari cars at a party at their Bond Street showrooms that has become known as 'The Purple Party'. Ferrari drivers Michael Schumacher and Eddie Irvine unveiled the Asprey F355 Berlinetta, a two-seater in metallic titanium grey and the Asprey 355 Spider, a cabriolet in metallic Asprey purple.

Over 800 guests helped celebrate the event with champagne and canapes. Edward Asprey was feeling good about the season. 'After a year's experience, our sponsorship with Ferrari has worked really well in 1997. Our guests have been entertained superbly at the Grands Prix, and have enjoyed the special pit tours organised by Ferrari. In addition, Michael Schumacher is challenging for the Driver's Championship, which puts the icing on the cake.'

Schumacher and Irvine get the party going...

The Mechanics

PAOLO SCARAMELLI is the co-ordinator of the test team, a job that brings him into direct contact with Michael Schumacher. 'Michael is always serious and well prepared for the tests. He is consistent and works well. If we succeed this year, it is thanks to Michael and the team.'

MAURO MADRIGALI is a mechanic who has been with Ferrari for seventeen years. 'It was always my wish to work for Ferrari and to be a part of the team. To participate as a member of the pit crew is a wonderful job.'

GIULIANO ZINI has spent four years working at the races and seven years with Ferrari. 'Our objective is to make sure we give the driver the car in the best possible condition to race.'

CHRISTIAN CORRADINI is one of the fuel men, working with Luca Baldisserri on Eddie Irvine's car. 'Luca decides how much fuel goes in. I also prepare the brakes for all three cars.'

ORESTE GIOVANNINI has been with Ferrari for twenty years and is in charge of the store room, i.e. spare parts, and making sure that everything that is needed goes to the race track. 'I have a passion for cars and so this is more than just a job, it is a part of my life.'

GIANLUCA SOCIALI is the head mechanic on Eddie Irvine's car. 'I organise Irvine's car when I have a list of things to do from Nigel (Stepney). We always work to a tight schedule and so we check and double check that everything has been done to the right specification.'

ANDREA GENONI also works on Irvine's car. 'It's important that we all work as a team and understand what he is needed. The fact that our group is young and has been together a few years is an important factor.'

ENRICO FACCIOLI's dream came true when he got a job at Ferrari working on Eddie Irvine's car – 'one of the best things that's ever happened to me.'

LUIGI PIETORRI works with Oreste Giovannini organising stores and supplies. 'We have to be on the ball and make sure the team has the right support at the track.'

LEONARDO POGGIPOLLINI looks after Michael Schumacher's tyres. 'If things go well, I'm happy. We always have to be prepared for changes or for rain. At Silverstone when we saw that Villeneuve was coming in for his pit stop, we quickly changed our strategy and called in Michael before Eddie. You have to be ready for this. We listen to the radio and make sure we do not make mistakes. The tyre pressures must be at at the right setting, 24 for the front and 20 for the rear. I like this type of work as we are part of a team but also independent.'

Leonardo's tyre partner is **ALESSANDRO PEDRONI**. 'I work as a member of the pit stop team on the rear jack. Pit stops are always critical and at first I was very nervous. I'm calmer now, which is important as time is absolutely vital.'

ANDREA VACCARI is also a fuel man. 'I work behind Nigel [Stepney] on re-fuelling. You need two of us to help lift the re-fuelling hose as when it's full it weighs about 60 kg(!), and it has to be at a perfect angle to make sure the petrol goes into the car.'

ANDREA GALLETTI looks after the electronics for the car. 'I liaise on the electronic programme for the chassis and gearbox for Eddie Irvine's car. We work with Luca Baldisserri on the setup by analysing the data.'

UMBERTO BENASSI is the team's reference point at Maranello. He is the man who stays behind to co-ordinate all the material and get parts to the circuit if needed. 'We are always working against time, getting parts to the races by air or truck as quickly as possible. However, Ferrari means everything to me.'

A Ferrari mechanic carries out a bit of fine-tuning on the car.

Next on the Formula One calendar was the Luxembourg Grand Prix, held at the Nurburgring. It marked the 100th Grand Prix for Michael Schumacher. How did he feel? 'Old! It always used to be my predecessors like Nigel Mansell who were celebrating 100 Grands Prix. Now it's me.'

Frank Williams, sitting next to Schumacher at a press conference, was in a devilish mood before the race. When asked about the possibilities of his man Villeneuve winning the Driver's Championship, he admitted 'the only problem on the horizon is sitting two metres to my left.' When asked about the one point difference that separated his driver from Schumacher he was quick on the draw. 'We will strengthen our suspension.' A timely reminder of the Schumacher-Hill accident in Australia, during the last race of the 1994 season.

At the Nurburgring Schumacher qualified fifth and Irvine fourteenth. Ahead of the two Ferraris, Villeneuve was second with Frentzen third. Schumacher was not happy. 'It's worrying to have the two Williams in front of me. It will be an advantage if Frentzen is in front of me and Villeneuve. Hakkinen [in pole position] could help me by winning the race.'

One thing Michael Schumacher wasn't expecting was a boot up his backside from his little brother. But that was what happened. As the race started and the cars went into the first corner, Schumacher senior pulled up alongside Giancarlo Fisichella but then found brother Ralf going faster outside the both of them. Michael wisely switched to the outside, which left Ralf to continue his charge into the corner with Fisichella. The two Jordans collided and Ralf flew across the track and landed on brother Michael's car, breaking a suspension arm on the Ferrari in the process. Michael staggered on for another two laps before retiring. He stormed into the team truck where he was joined twenty minutes later by Ralf. Both brothers admitted it was just a racing accident, but Michael was obviously devastated. 'It is a shame that the incident happened with my brother, but I don't think anyone is to blame for what happened as it was not a deliberate move. These things can happen and that is motor racing.'

Eddie Irvine's car died on him on the 22nd lap, and that was that for Ferrari. The two McLarens were leading when one by one they both had engine failures. That left Villeneuve in the lead and on his way to ten points. However, Jean Todt will not give up until the battle is well and truly over. He summed it up by saying, 'We could not have had a worse result. The other cars in the race did not help our cause. However, while it is still mathematically possible for us to win the Championship, we will try as hard as we can right to the end.'

Niki Lauda gave his usual blunt opinion. 'Ralf is completely mad. When I saw him up beside his brother I said to myself "what's he doing?" If he'd used his head he wouldn't have caused an accident like that. I've never seen anything like it.'

After Nurburgring it was time to regroup before the final two deciding races in Japan and Spain...and a nerve-wracking climax to the season for Ferrari.

Brotherly Bash
In this sequence from the Nurburgring, Ralf Schumacher is sent flying by team-mate Fisichella, much to the chagrin of brother Michael in the Ferrari who tries to take evasive action – too late!

6 TIMES
WORLD CHAMPION
1992–1997
RENAULT
RENAULT
Marlboro
RENAULT
Marlboro
Rothmans
Marlboro

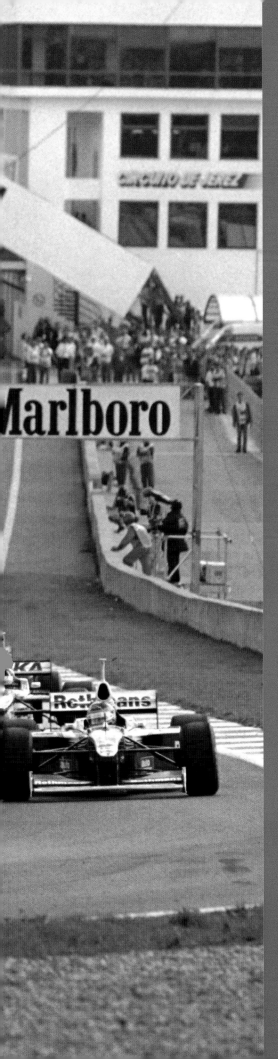

CHAPTER FIFTEEN

A Breathtaking Finale

'I told Michael before the race that

it was possible to overtake there,

but he thought it wasn't.'

Eddie Irvine
on his overtaking of Jacques Villeneuve in Japan

For Japan, strategy was always going to be vital for Ferrari after the news that Jacques Villeneuve would be racing under appeal following an incident in the Saturday morning practice session when he ignored a yellow flag. The spectre of being stripped of any points he would gain in the race was sure to influence his and therefore Ferrari's race tactics.

The hero of the weekend was Eddie Irvine. Finally shaking off his paranoid fear of qualifying, he came good at the right moment to take third place on the grid. 'I think testing has helped,' said Irvine. 'The team understands now what I need from the car. I cannot tolerate mid-corner understeer. As I turn in, I'm more progressive on the throttle. Also I've just realised that I needed more front wing to make handling better.' Schumacher himself qualified on the front row. For Villeneuve on pole position, having one Ferrari by his side and the other behind him was not a comforting experience, and so it proved.

At the start of the race, the Canadian made an aggressive move across the track and blocked Schumacher from overtaking him into the first corner. Once in the lead, it became clear that Villeneuve was on a go-slow strategy. As one Ferrari manager said, 'He [Villeneuve] was driving as though he expected to lose any points gained from this race, so his idea was to hold us up. It was very silly as when Eddie got past him, he had Michael right up behind him and no time advantage when coming into the pits. When the Williams team messed up his second pit stop and he lost five seconds, it just put him further into trouble.'

The Ferrari plan was to have Irvine behind Villeneuve, so that if the Canadian tried anything untoward then he would take out the Irishman, leaving Schumacher's bid for the World Championship intact. So on lap two, at the start of the first turn, Schumacher backed off enough to slow down Hakkinen behind him, a manoeuvre which allowed Irvine to overtake both drivers, and then set upon the hapless Villeneuve. By the end of the third lap the Irishman had passed Villeneuve (Irvine: 'I told Michael before the race that it was possible to overtake there on the outside but he thought it wasn't – too slippery, he said') and sped away into the distance, opening up a staggering lead of 12 seconds after three more laps.

After the first pit stops, Irvine remained well ahead but with Schumacher now just in front of Villeneuve. It was then that Irvine 'received the calling' on his car radio and slowed down so that by lap 25, in exactly the same place as before, Schumacher took over in front again, a lead he was never to relinquish as Irvine closed the door on Villeneuve. For the Canadian it was downhill all the way as a disastrous second pit stop saw him drop from third to seventh place.

The performances of Villeneuve and Frentzen in Japan suggested that the Williams drivers hardly knew each other. Frentzen finally woke up halfway through the race and started to

Battle for Supremacy
Villeneuve, in pole position, closes the door on Schumacher at the start of the Japanese Grand Prix.

'The bleating after Japan was pathetic. Williams made tactical errors...they totally screwed up.'
EDDIE IRVINE

'The strategy in Japan was nothing special...for me, Monaco was better.'
JEAN TODT

'The Constructor's Championship seems to have got lost in the race for the Driver's crown.'
NIGEL STEPNEY

'Japan was typical of my luck. When things are going well and I have a chance to win, it's taken away from me.'
EDDIE IRVINE

challenge Schumacher, but it was too late, and despite Damon Hill's apparent blocking tactics (Brawn: 'It wasn't particularly fair, but he must have had his reasons.') Schumacher was first past the line to claim what he described as 'one of the most important victories of my career.'

So it was first and third for the Ferrari drivers, who were quick to congratulate each other after the race. 'I told you that you could go around the outside at turn six,' said a cheeky Irvine. Ross Brawn was delighted. 'For our pit stop strategy, we had to change things round on the second stop. Michael was going to come in first when he found himself behind traffic but then he managed to get past and so we brought in Eddie first instead. We had to act fast!'

A dejected Villeneuve finished in fifth place and saw his lead in the Driver's Championship cut to one point, pending his appeal. One small consolation for Williams was winning the Constructor's Championship. The Ferrari team were generous in their praise: 'We must be honest and say that the best constructor won.'

And so to Jerez and the final showdown between Schumacher and Villeneuve. The Williams team decided to withdraw its appeal against Villeneuve's ban the week before, which meant that Schumacher had a one-point lead in the Championship going into the last race. Suzuka hero Eddie Irvine was in no doubt about his role. 'I'm going to help Michael in Jerez. It's in my contract. If I don't, then I won't get paid, it's as simple as that!'

• • •

By the Saturday of the European Grand Prix weekend, Jacques Villeneuve was showing the strain. At the end of the morning's free practice, he rushed over to Irvine, who was sitting in his car, and accused the Irishman of blocking him for three or four corners. 'F***ing idiot!' he screamed before storming into the neighbouring Williams garage. 'I don't know what he'll do next,' said Villeneuve later. 'He doesn't like other drivers. We all know he's a clown, but there's no need to play like that.' Irvine was dismissive. 'No one can possibly think that Villeneuve deserves to win the Championship. Schumacher is the best driver.'

Qualifying was electric. Villeneuve on pole, Schumacher second and Frentzen third, all with exactly the same 1min 21.07sec qualifying time – never before in the history of Formula One had that happened. Schumacher was pleased to be on the front row. 'The start will be crucial,' he said. And the German gave himself a brilliant chance by powering ahead of Villeneuve into the first corner, with Frentzen creating a surprise by also pulling in front of his Williams team-mate. By the end of the first lap Schumacher already had a two-second lead, but on lap 7 Frentzen allowed Villeneuve through into second to put pressure on the Ferrari. Meanwhile, Eddie Irvine was in seventh and making little impression on the leading pack.

Slick Strategy
Schumacher and Irvine congratulate each other after brilliant teamwork secures a podium position for both drivers.

Last Chance Saloon
The Ferrari of Michael Schumacher roars into an early lead ahead of the Williams of Jacques Villeneuve at the start of the European Grand Prix.

It soon became clear that both Ferrari and Williams were on a two-stop strategy when Schumacher came into the pits on lap 22, followed by Villeneuve a lap later. Frentzen was now in the lead and was doing his best to hold up Schumacher after the latter emerged from the pits ahead of Villeneuve. But Frentzen was soon forced to go into the pits for refuelling, which left the two protagonists for the World Championship alone out at the front in a head-to-head

German Grief

The end of the race and the 1997 World Driver's Championship for Michael Schumacher after his collision with Jacques Villeneuve at Jerez.

dogfight. By lap 44 both drivers had made their second pit stops with Villeneuve starting to make ground on Schumacher. Four laps later, the race battle was over. Villeneuve attempted to take Schumacher on the inside of Dry Sack; the German kept to his racing line but then as Villeneuve edged ahead, he tried to shut the door. Too late. Schumacher's front right wheel hit the side pod of the Williams and the Ferrari ended up on the gravel and unable to restart. At first, the worry from the Williams garage was that their Championship had also been wrecked, but Villeneuve managed to nurse his car round for the remaining 21 laps to finish the race third behind the McLarens of Hakkinen and Coulthard – and more importantly gain a precious four Championship winning points.

For Ferrari the hopes and dreams of a Formula One World Championship lay in ruins. Two and a half hours after the race had ended, Schumacher finally spoke. 'I've had happier days in my life, but that's racing. I was always ahead of him [Villeneuve] and able to keep him behind me. He made an opportunist move which went well for him and badly for me. I braked on the maximum limit and he braked later. If he had stayed behind me he would have lost the Championship, so he had to make a move. To be honest, I would have done the same.'

Jean Todt was bitterly disappointed but not beaten. 'We didn't expect to be in contention for the Championship but with Michael Schumacher driving for us we were up at the top. I believe he will drive for Ferrari for many years.'

There were no hysterics outside the Ferrari garage, just silence. As Ross Brawn pointed out, 'Ferrari must remember how far they've come, not that they've lost a Championship they were never expected to win at the beginning of the season.' Shirts were exchanged between the teams as the Williams party got underway. A few members of the Ferrari team looked on longingly. One day... However, the Scuderia are on their way back: five Grand Prix wins this year with Schumacher, on 78 points, just three behind the newly crowned champion Villeneuve; and next year a car made completely in Maranello.

The V10 engine roared for the last time as Eddie Irvine's car was examined. The Irishman had finished fifth, but the real prize was still to come. Nigel Stepney paused for thought, then took a deep breath. 'We'll be back next year. Then watch out.'

The legend lives on.